Christiane Weidemann

Salvador Dalí

Prestel
Munich · Berlin · London · New York

Context

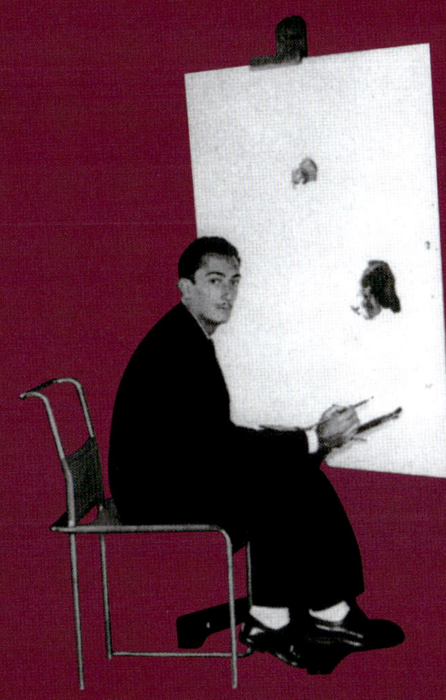

"I think you have to paint without any aesthetic doctrine of any kind, paint for painting's sake, without accepting any constraints, following the impulses of your own totally liberated sensibility."

Salvador Dalí

In the years post-1900 ...

... a rush of new styles developed in parallel that together constitute classic modernism—Expressionism, Cubism, Futurism, Surrealism, and abstract art. Technical progress, revolutionary social changes, and the bitter experience of war all contributed to modernism. In the inter-war years, Paris remained the capital of Western art, only to be supplanted by New York as the new art metropolis after World War II. A young Spaniard experienced these events at first hand—Salvador Dalí, whose artistic career got off to a flying start in Paris and soon reached a high point in America.

Sigmund Freud and Psychoanalysis

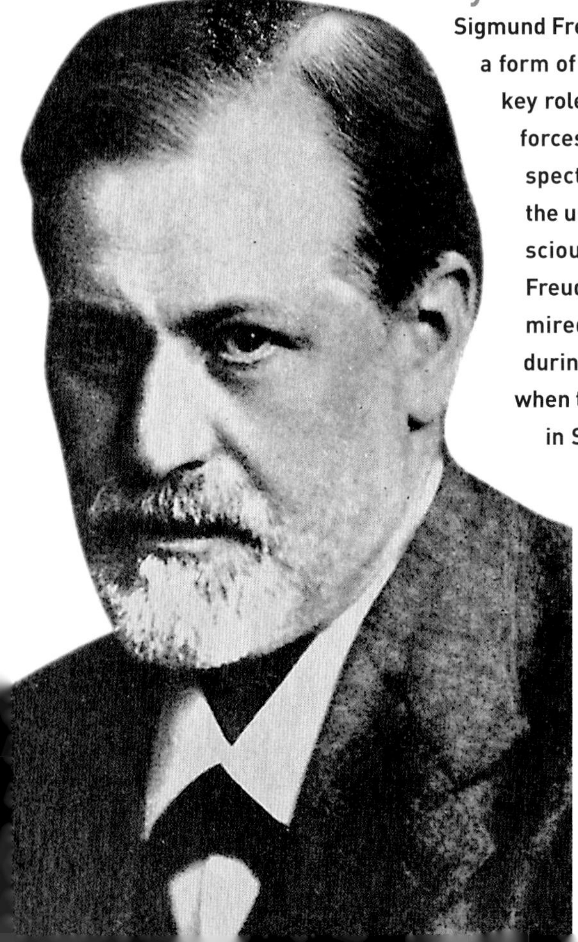

Sigmund Freud developed psychoanalysis as a form of therapy in which dreams have a key role as indicators of hidden psychic forces and processes. He achieved spectacular successes by bringing the unconscious to the surface of consciousness. Later, Dalí numbered Freud among the people he most admired. He discovered his writings during his student years in Madrid, when the first volumes were published in Spanish translation. In his memoirs, Dalí describes reading Freud's *On Dreams* as "one of the major discoveries of my life."

Surrealism

--> Along with abstract art and Expressionism, Surrealism was one of the most important stylistic developments in 20th-century painting. It demanded from its adherents an ability to turn unconscious processes, dreams, and fantasies into art without the mediation of the conscious mind. The technique of "automatism" led to highly distinctive personal styles. One of the most distinctive was that of Salvador Dalí, who created meticulously executed mental landscapes derived from his own complex psychic obsessions and imbued with obscure sexual symbolism.

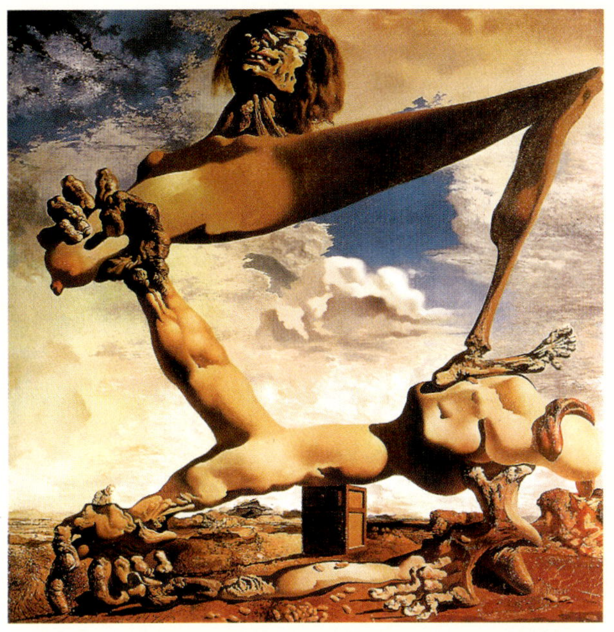

The Spanish Civil War …

… broke out on 18 July 1936 following a coup led by extreme right-winger General Franco. The Republic was overturned and replaced by a Fascist dictatorship that lasted until Franco's death in 1975. In pictures such as *Soft Construction with Boiled Beans* (later renamed *Premonition of Civil War*) and *Autumn Cannibalism*, Dalí revealed his personal vision of the bloodbath, though he was not in fact very interested in the political dimension of what was happening in his homeland. Dalí saw the Civil War as a "natural historical phenomenon." When the war broke out, he escaped to Italy.

"I believed in Surrealism as if it had set up the tablets of the law."

Salvador Dalí

"Bienvenida Salvador Dalí"

… was the headline in Barcelona periodical *Destino* when the now famous Catalan artist returned from exile in America. Unlike other internationally known Spanish artists and intellectuals, Dalí—always the pragmatic opportunist—sided with the victorious dictator, Franco, and made no bones about it publicly. Franco attempted to bring as many celebrities as possible back to Spain, including Picasso. The latter, however, was unwavering in his hostility to Fascism and could not be persuaded to return.

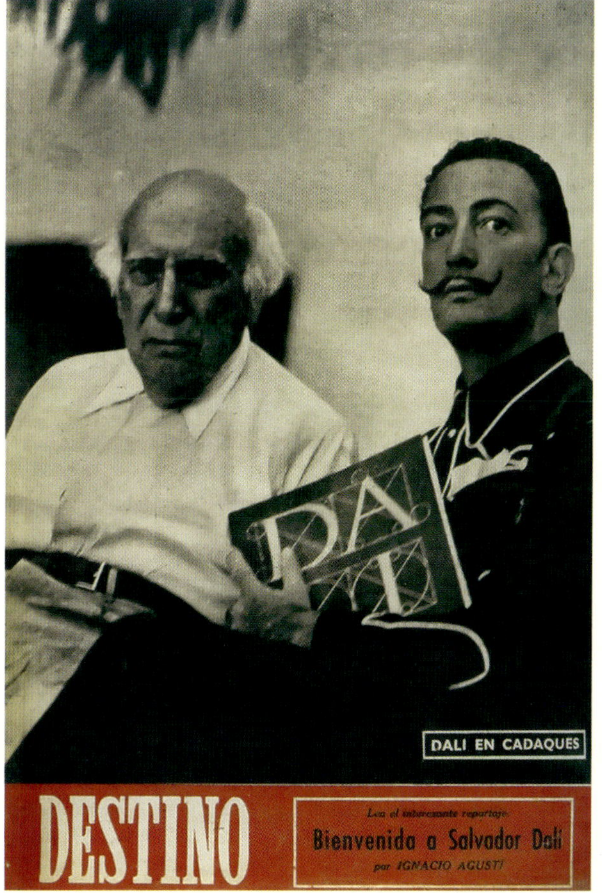

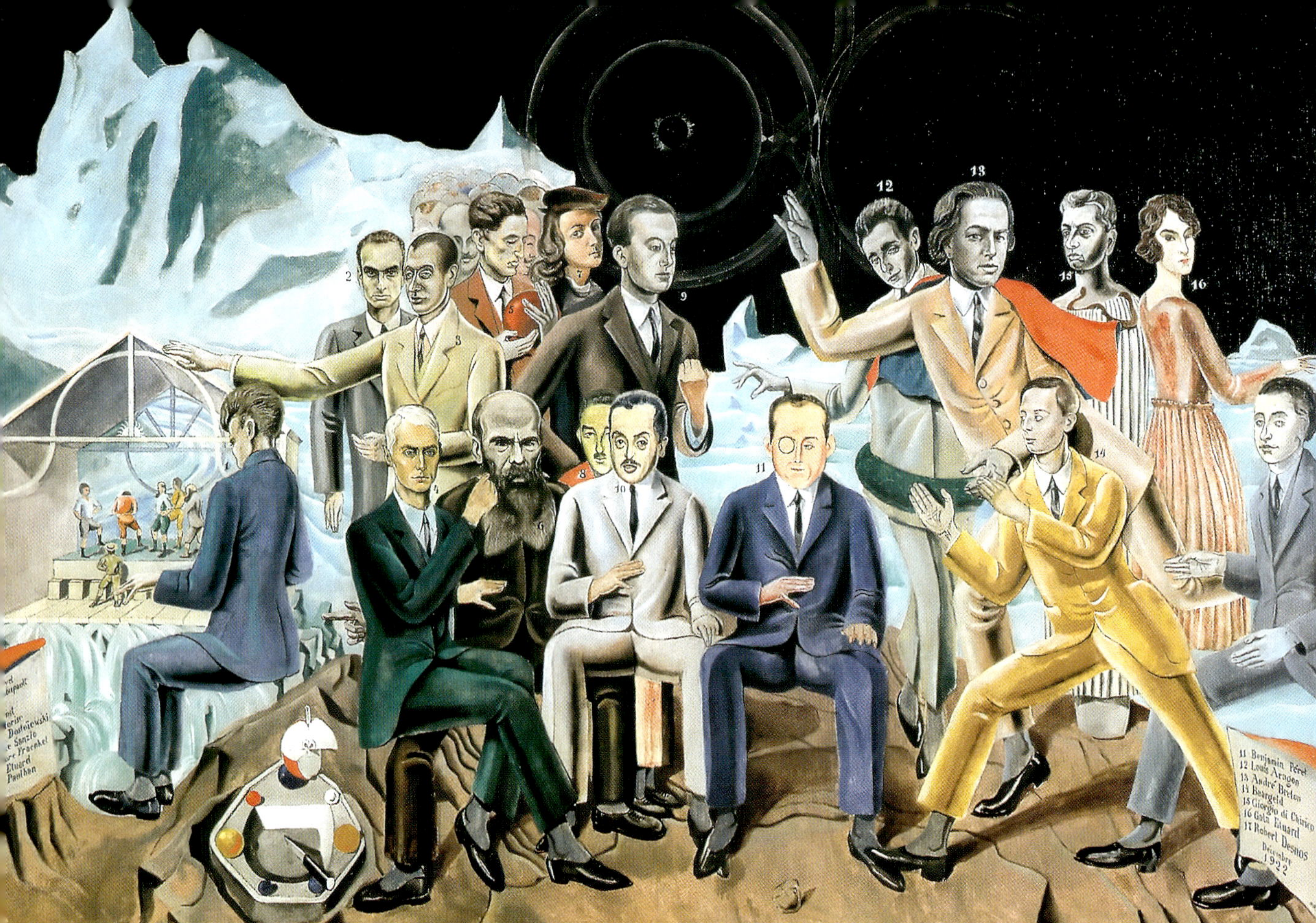

Max Ernst's *Rendezvous of Friends* features the Dadaists and later Surrealists (with Dostoyevsky and Raphael): 1) René Crevel, 2) Philippe Soupault, 3) Hans Arp, 4) Max Ernst, 5) Max Morise, 6) Dostoyevsky, 7) Raphael, 8) Théodor Fraenkel, 9) Paul Eluard, 10) Jean Paulhan, 11) Benjamin Péret, 12) Louis Aragon, 13) André Breton, 14) Johannes Bargeld, 15) Giorgio de Chirico, 16) Gala Eluard, 17) Robert Desnos.

DU 7 AU 18 JUIN

EXPOSITION SURREALISTE

PEINTURES. DESSINS. SCULPTURES. OBJETS. COLLAGES.

ARP. ANDRÉ BRETON. SALVADOR DALI. MARCEL DUCHAMP. PAUL ELUARD. MARIE-BERTHE ERNST. MAX ERNST. GIACOMETTI. ARTHUR HARFAUX. MAURICE HENRY. VALENTINE HUGO. MAGRITTE. JOAN MIRO. PICASSO. MAN RAY. YVES TANGUY. LE CADAVRE EXQUIS.

VERNISSAGE LE MERCREDI 7 JUIN

DE 3 HEURES A 7 HEURES

PIERRE COLLE

29. RUE CAMBACÉRÈS

Invitation to the Surrealism exhibition at the Galerie Pierre Colle in Paris from June 7 to 18, 1933, where Dalí also exhibited.

Surrealism's New Dawn

The search for new ways to look at the world was a feature of the period around the turn of the century, as was a readiness to break with all accepted customs and prejudices. Freud's psychoanalytical theory was among the pioneering intellectual achievements that changed attitudes and values profoundly.

Innovations in Art

> "Surrealism is based on a belief in the higher reality of certain previously neglected forms of association, the omnipotence of dreams, and the undirected operation of thought."
>
> André Breton

At the beginning of the 1920s, a group of artists for whom Freud was a mentor and patron saint came together in Paris, then still the fertile center of much of modern art. The Surrealists continued the exploration of the irrational and the subversion of art begun by the Dadaists, most of whom joined the new movement. Both movements turned against the middle classes and the traditions of religion, morality, and reason. But whereas Dada had been characterized by anarchic spontaneity, the Surrealists followed a program formulated by a leading French writer, André Breton. He set out the theoretical basis of

A poster Dalí designed for the regular meeting of the Surrealist conferences.

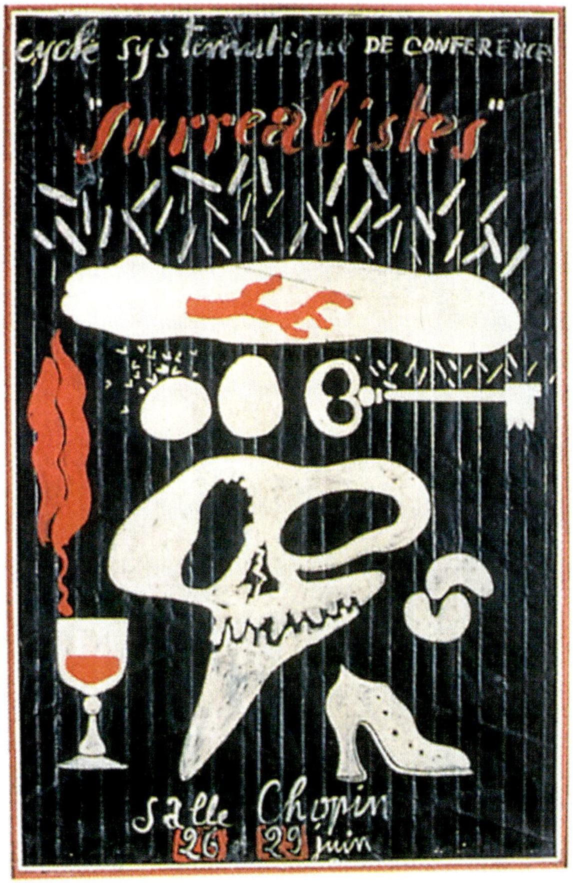

the movement in his *First Surrealist Manifesto* in 1924, where he famously defined Surrealism as "pure psychic automatism through which we seek to express the real course of thought in speech or in writing or in any other way. Thought dictation without any supervision by reason, over and beyond any aesthetic and moral consideration." The call for total liberation applied to all artists.

For the Surrealists, the subconscious represented an inexhaustible source of hitherto suppressed artistic creativity, and generated "automatically" created works of art free from the oppressive constraints of rational control. Max Ernst was one of the first to produce Freudian art successfully. Using the technique of *frottage* (rubbing) he created some eerily beautiful pictures: just as children do with coins, he took rubbings of worn floorboards or other everyday objects on paper, or pressed them on oil paintings. Then there were the mysterious pictures of Belgian artist René Magritte, the nightmarish images of Yves Tanguy, and the much more playful and sunnier color compositions of the Spaniard Joan Miró. Among the first batch of painters were also former Dadaist Hans Arp, Francis Picabia, Man Ray, and André Masson.

Dalí and the Surrealists

Meantime, a young Catalan had also been experimenting with a wide range of painting styles. Dalí soon heard that Surrealism was not just a style like Expressionism or Cubism, but a revolutionary and subversive movement that sought to change the world by liberating the forces hidden deep in the psyche. Before long, he was of the view that only Surrealism could express the sensibility of an age that had discovered the subconscious. Dalí soon supplied impressive examples of the new Surrealist thinking—works steeped in feelings of obsession,

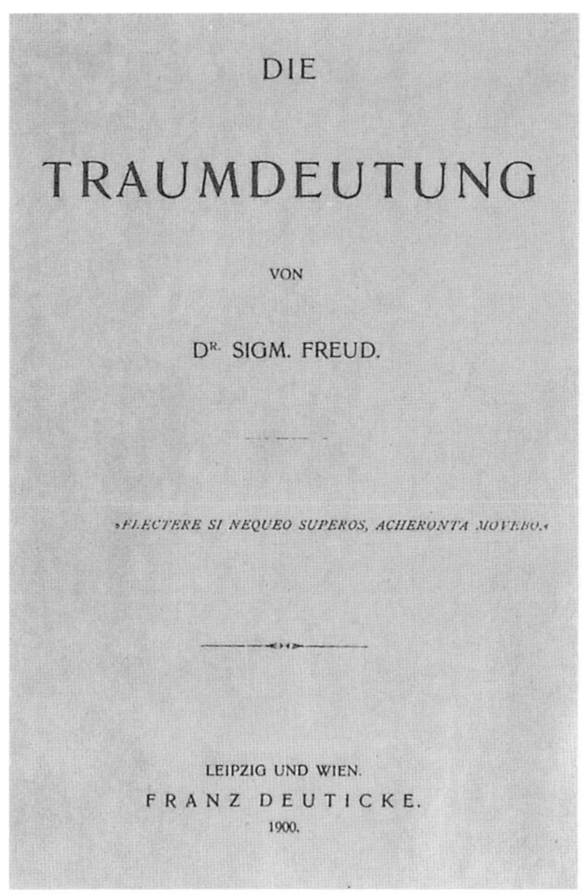
DIE

TRAUMDEUTUNG

VON

D^R. SIGM. FREUD.

»FLECTERE SI NEQUEO SUPEROS, ACHERONTA MOVEBO.«

LEIPZIG UND WIEN.
FRANZ DEUTICKE.
1900.

Die Traumdeutung (The Interpretation of Dreams), which appeared in November 1899, post-dated to 1900, was an early milestone in Freud's career as the founder of psychoanalysis.

in an intensive preoccupation with sexuality and dreams, and in a delight in provocation. Joining the Surrealist movement marked the beginning of the most significant phase of his painting, and soon the leading writers and artists of Paris saw Dalí as one of their most original representatives. "It cannot be denied that the poetic, visionary content of these pictures has an extraordinary pithiness and explosive force. At any rate, nothing ... has taken on such a 'revelatory' character since Max Ernst's works between 1923 and 1924 ... or Miró's works of 1924," was the admiring comment on Dalí's work by Surrealist spokesman André Breton.

From Paris to New York

Whereas the principal innovations in art had hitherto taken place in Paris, at the end of World War II there was a decisive shift. The migration of many intellectuals and artists from their European homelands to the United States meant that Europe gradually lost its cultural supremacy. New York became the new metropolis of art, superseding Paris. The leading European styles of art now regrouped here. In the 1930s, most exiles arrived from Nazi Germany, fleeing political and racial persecution. A second wave came from Paris after the fall of France in 1940. Among the refugees were Max Ernst, Marc Chagall, Piet Mondrian, and Dalí. Whereas many exiles landed in New York with existential worries, personal or political, Dalí saw exile as a new beginning full of potential—and his success justified his confidence. New York welcomed Salvador Dalí as the Parisian and Catalan ambassador of Surrealism.

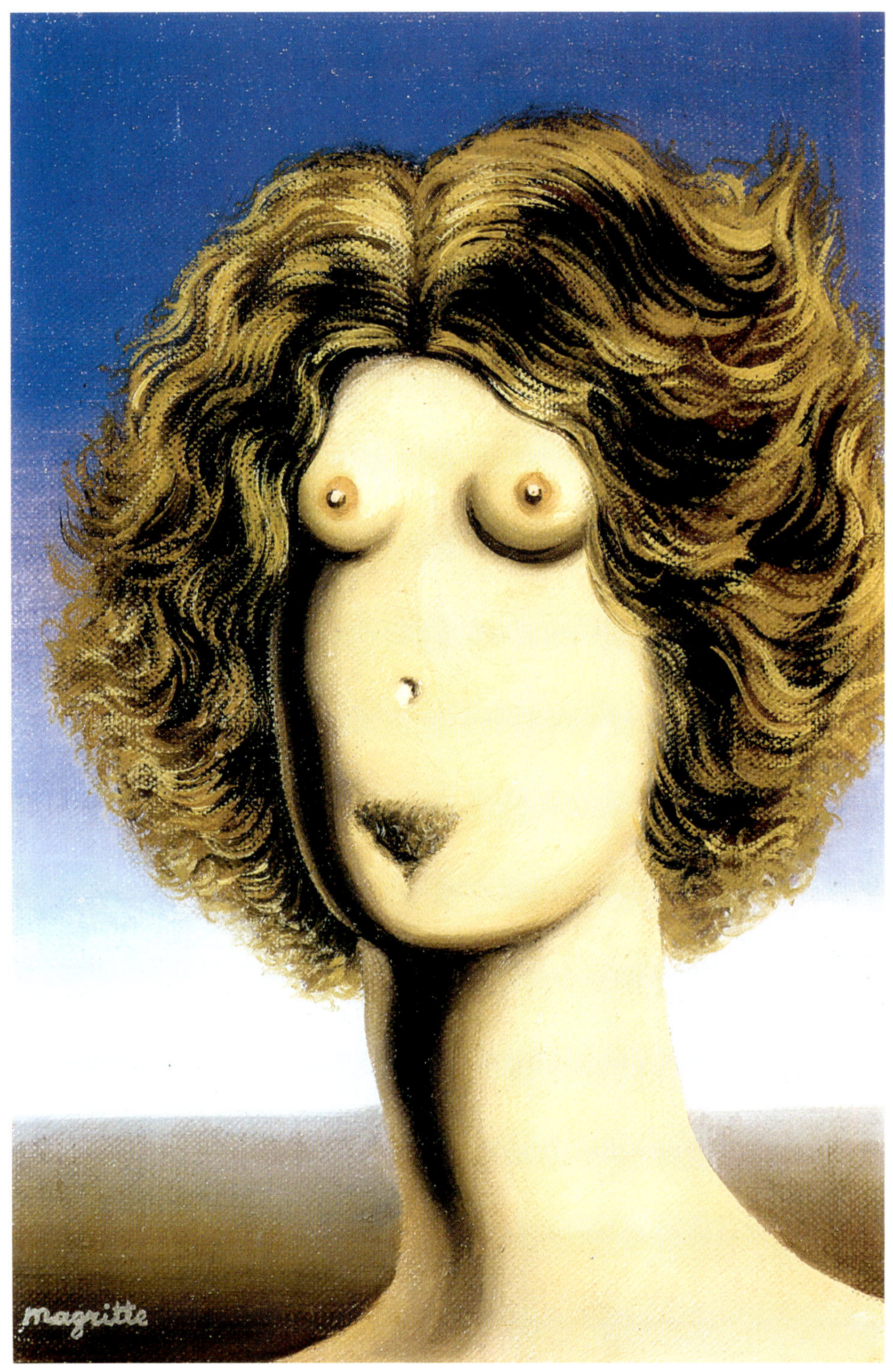

Mysterious René Magritte's fantasy realism challenges conventional notions of pictures, with Freudian symbolism particularly evident in his works. His painting *The Rape* was seen by the Surrealists as an emphatic representation of their objectives.

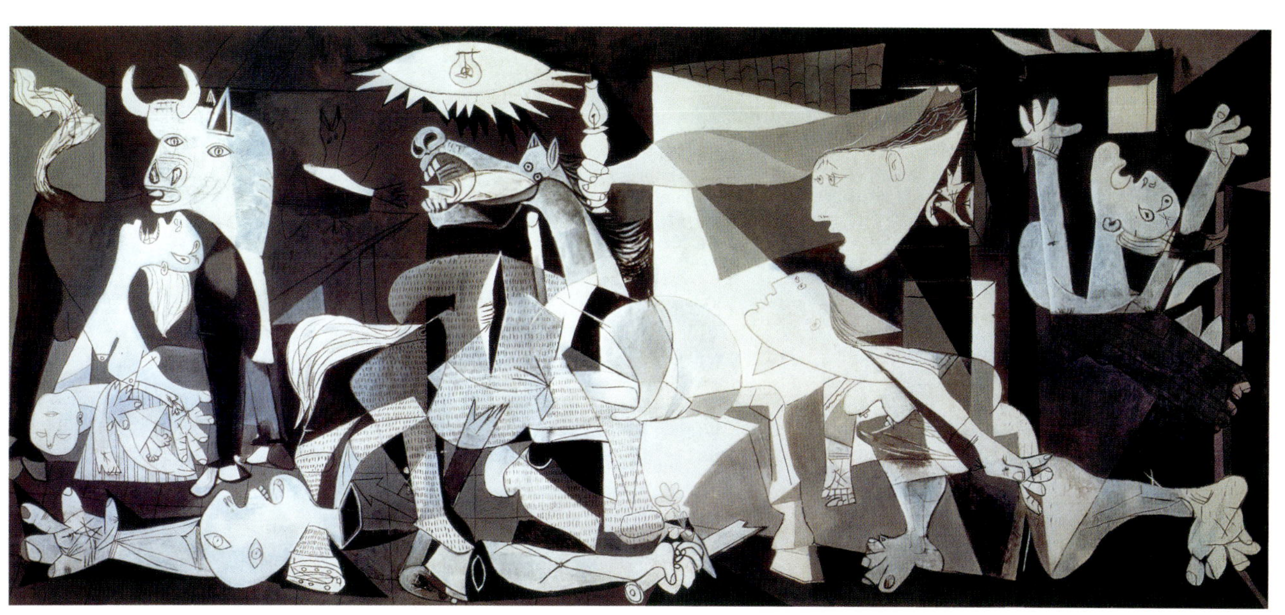

War In *Guernica* Picasso shows us with poignant mastery the horrors of the Spanish Civil War. As a key work of modernism, the painting stands for the horrors of the century, the terrors of bombing and genocide.

Fame

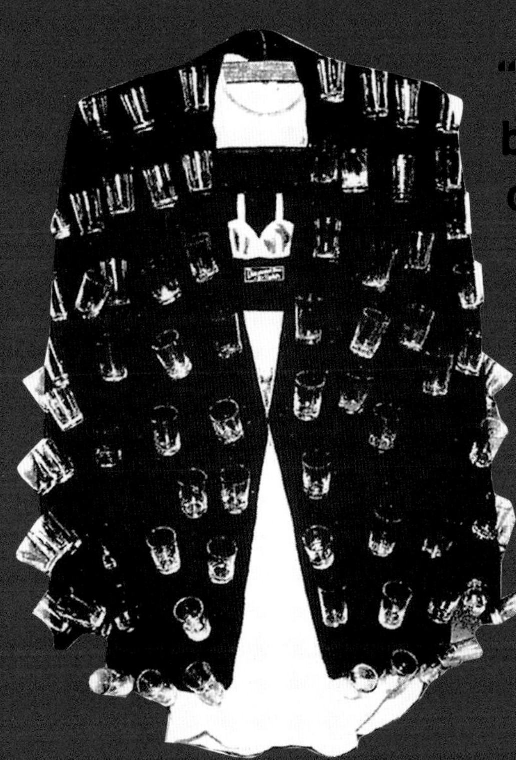

"As far as celebrity, my bank balance, and the consequence of my art and my ideas were concerned, I was a king of the world. It never stopping raining dollars."

Salvador Dalí

Ambition

The sixteen-year-old Dalí sketched out his future very precisely and with singular clarity: he wanted to "work like mad" in Madrid for three years, then continue his studies for another four years in Rome. He would then return to Spain in triumph: "I shall be a genius, a great genius, I'm sure of that." With this conviction, his artistic talent, and his remarkable capacity for hard work, it's no surprise that success was not long in coming.

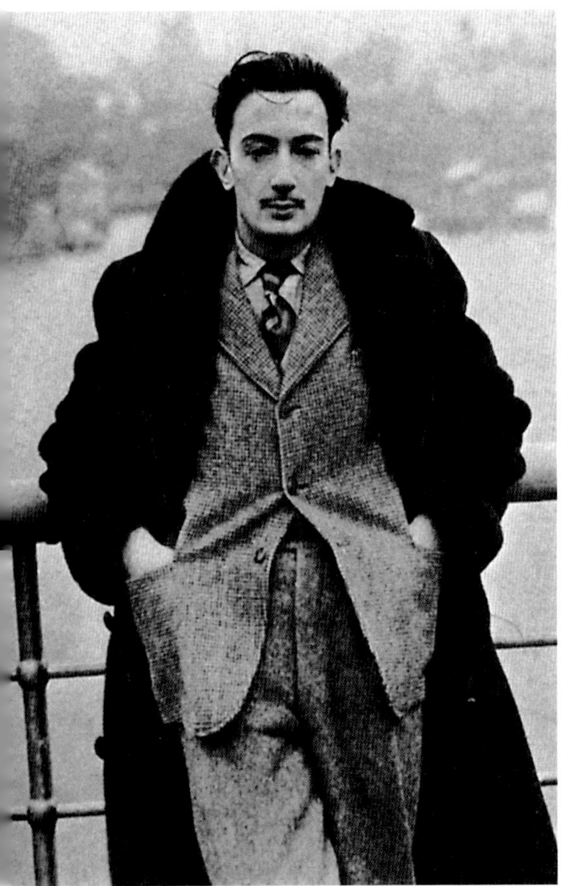

Dalí on board the *Normandie* on arrival in New York, December 1936.

"Mr Surrealism"

After his first successes in Barcelona and Paris, Dalí then made his international breakthrough in the USA, where he was celebrated as "Mr Surrealism." Americans loved *The Persistence of Memory*, perhaps the best-known Surrealist picture of all. But he was not just a painter—Dalí saw himself as a universal genius, writing and illustrating books, working in films and advertising, and designing costumes and sets for the ballet and theater.

"Avida Dollars"

--> "My best days are the ones when I ... earn $10,000 between waking up and breakfast," claimed Dalí, frankly admitting that he couldn't get too much fame and money. His passion for money soon earned him the memorable nickname "Avida Dollars"—coined by Breton as an anagram of his name. Dalí's reaction to his new name was enthusiastic: headlines of any kind increased his popularity, which was always good for business.

Awards and Rewards

Both artistically and financially, the last twenty years of Dalí's life were highly successful. From 1970 onwards, his annual net income was estimated at half a million dollars. International retrospectives such as those at the Pompidou Centre in Paris and the Tate in London enhanced his career, and in the United States his works were bought for New York's Metropolitan Museum and the Museum of Modern Art. His homeland also conferred its highest awards: the government of Catalonia awarded him their gold medal, and the Grand Cross of the Order of Charles III. And King Juan Carlos of Spain added the final touch, transforming plain Señor Dalí into the Marquès de Dalí y Púbol.

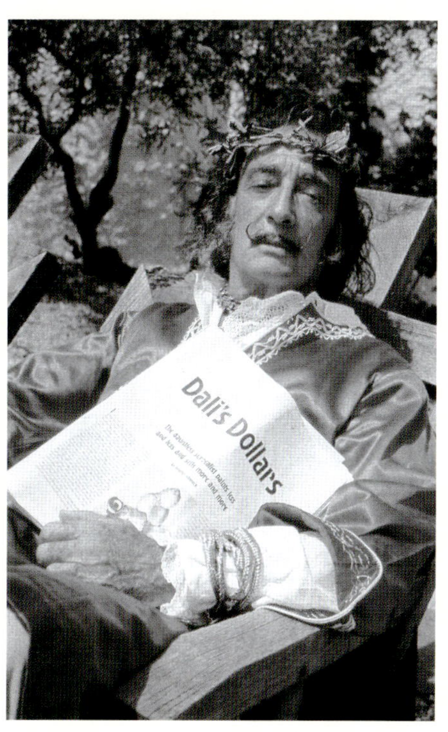

"I'm a poseur"

Dalí was not only convinced of his own genius: he was also superb at selling himself. Always the poseur, he put himself across as a highly theatrical, larger-than-life artist. He had no difficulty in turning himself into an appealingly photogenic icon with high recognition value, his very distinctive moustache—Gertrude Stein called it the finest moustache of any European—functioning as an unmistakable trademark. Above all, it was decades of collaboration with the photographer Philippe Halsman that helped to create the highly memorable images by which Dalí sought to define his public persona.

Dalí's Mustache. A Photographic Interview was published in New York in 1954. It featured photographs by Philippe Halsman focusing entirely on Dalí's moustache.

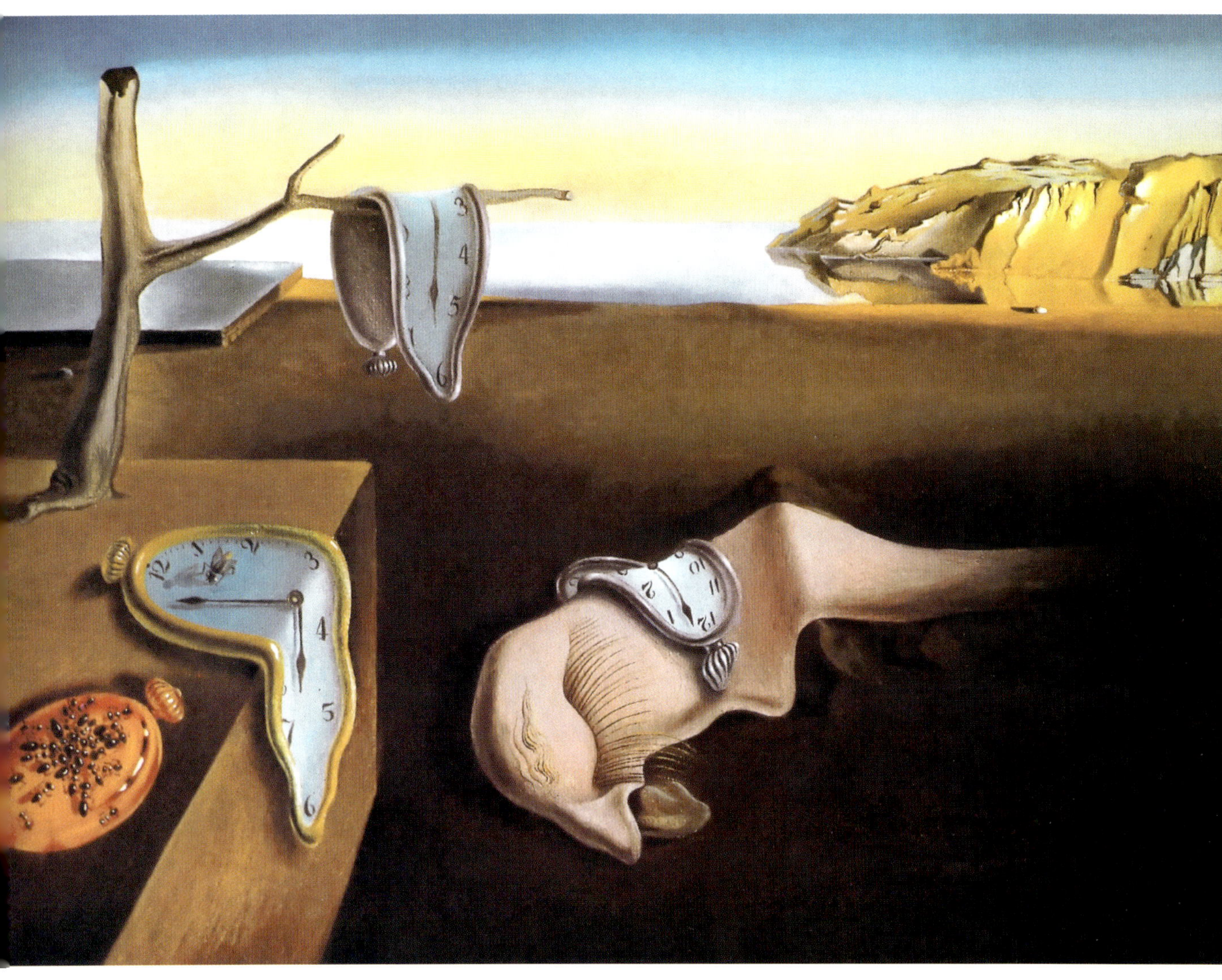

Dalí left us an account of the genesis of his most famous work. "To finish our dinner, we had a very strong Camembert, and after everyone had got up, I remained seated at the table for a long time thinking about the philosophical problems of 'super softness' that the cheese brought to mind." After this fit of brooding, he finished his painting with the soft watches, *The Persistence of Memory*.

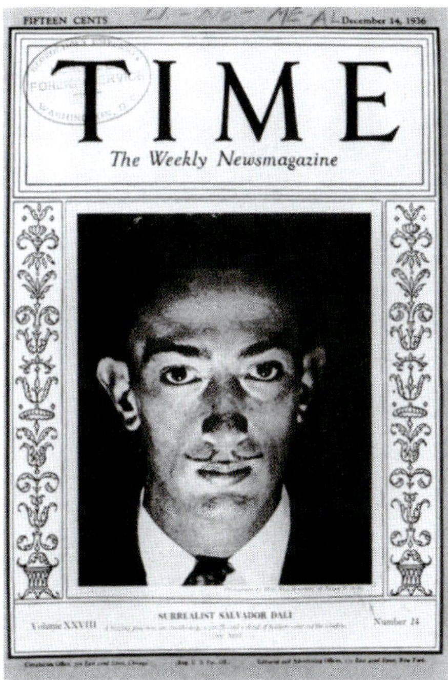

Dalí on the cover of *Time* magazine, December 14, 1936, photographed by Man Ray.

Success

Dalí managed to achieve in his lifetime a degree of celebrity that few artists attain. His fame, however, was as much attributable to his extravagant behavior as it was to his works. As an exotic eccentric, he had the doors to aristocratic society opened to him, which in turn led to useful contacts and finally brought him international fame as an artist—and considerable wealth.

The First Steps

Dalí's road to fame led from his homeland Spain—where his pictures had already caused a stir, and where he had already made a name for himself with his attacks on contemporary art—to the legendary Paris of the late 1920s. Joan Miró, a Catalan like Dalí, introduced him to the leading Surrealists there and so paved the way into the Paris art establishment. He also put him in touch with art dealers Pierre Loeb and Camille Goemans, with whom he soon signed up. Step by calculated step, he soon conquered the French capital.

"When I was six, I wanted to be a cook, when I was seven, it was Napoleon. Since then, my ambitions have only risen."

Salvador Dalí

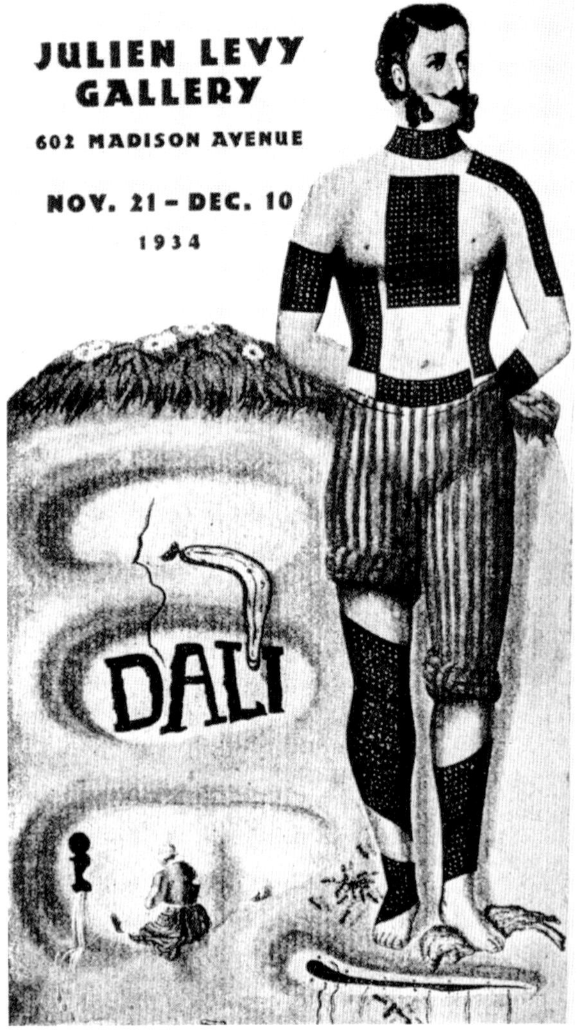

Catalogue cover for the Dalí exhibition at the Julien Levy Gallery in New York, 2 November—10 December 1934.

Scandal on Screen

Two provocative films he made in collaboration with Luis Buñuel—now classics of film history—increased his fame greatly. *Un Chien Andalou* was the shock sensation of 1929, with every image a provocation, and with no scene subordinated to any kind of logic. The opening scene is legendary: Buñuel smoking and sharpening a razor blade, which he then uses to cut a woman's eye. All the leading film critics declared the film a turning point in cinematic history. The second film, *L'Âge d'Or*, made the following year, likewise poured bitter scorn on the values of bourgeois society. Its revolutionary nature was soon recognized, and after twelve days of screenings that attracted angry attacks and demonstrations, further performances in Paris were banned by the police.

"The most incredible things happen to me here"

At an exhibition at the Galerie Pierre Colle in Paris, Dalí was discovered by young American Julien Levy, who was on the point of opening a new gallery in New York. Levy (who also championed the Mexican artist Frida Kahlo) would be the man who made the Catalan famous in America, and who first launched the Surrealists in New York, which at the time knew little of European art.

On 14 November 1934, the *New York Evening Journal* reported Dalí's arrival in New York.

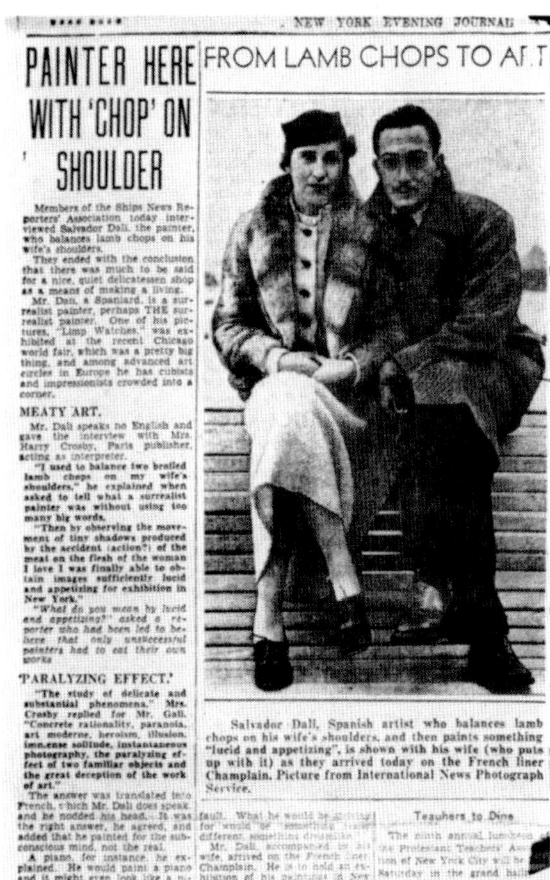

NEW YORK EVENING JOURNAL

PAINTER HERE WITH 'CHOP' ON SHOULDER

Members of the Ships News Reporters' Association today interviewed Salvador Dali, the painter, who balances lamb chops on his wife's shoulders.

They ended with the conclusion that there was much to be said for a nice, quiet delicatessen shop as a means of making a living.

Mr. Dali, a Spaniard, is a surrealist painter, perhaps THE surrealist painter. One of his pictures, "Limp Watches," was exhibited at the recent Chicago world fair, which was a pretty big thing, and among advanced art circles in Europe he has cubists and impressionists crowded into a corner.

MEATY ART.

Mr. Dali speaks no English and gave the interview with Mrs. Harry Crosby, Paris publisher, acting as interpreter.

"I used to balance two broiled lamb chops on my wife's shoulders," he explained when asked to tell what a surrealist painter was without using too many big words.

"Then by observing the movement of tiny shadows produced by the accident (action?) of the meat on the flesh of the woman I love I was finally able to obtain images sufficiently lucid and appetizing for exhibition in New York."

"What do you mean by lucid and appetizing?" asked a reporter who had been led to believe that only unsuccessful painters had to eat their own works.

'PARALYZING EFFECT.'

"The study of delicate and substantial phenomena," Mrs. Crosby replied for Mr. Gali. "Concrete rationality, paranoia, art moderne, heroism, illusion, immense solitude, instantaneous photography, the paralyzing effect of two familiar objects and the great deception of the work of art."

The answer was translated into French, which Mr. Dali does speak and he nodded his head. It was the right answer, he agreed, and added that he painted for the subconscious mind, not the real.

A piano, for instance, he explained. He would paint a piano and it might even look like a piano.

fault. What he would be ... for would be something ... different, something dreamlike.

Mr. Dali, accompanied by his wife, arrived on the French liner Champlain. He is to hold an exhibition of his paintings in New York.

FROM LAMB CHOPS TO ART

Salvador Dali, Spanish artist who balances lamb chops on his wife's shoulders, and then paints something "lucid and appetizing", is shown with his wife (who puts up with it) as they arrived today on the French liner Champlain. Picture from International News Photograph Service.

Teauhers to Dine

... the Protestant Teachers' Association of New York City will be Saturday in the grand ball of the Hotel Astor.

New Yorkers—public and critics alike—were both disturbed and fascinated by Dalí's pictures. Dalí was "one of the greats," pronounced the *New York Times*, which featured his photo on the front page on 14 December 1936: "Surrealism would never have gained the attention it currently enjoys were it not for Salvador Dalí, the handsome, 32-year-old Catalan with the soft voice and trimmed filmstar moustache."

"Fame intoxicated me like a spring morning," wrote Dalí, who had always dreamed of being famous.

The United States offered Dalí a broad stage on which to perform his sensational antics. His reputation as an eccentric artist opened the doors to all social events to him. "I was indispensable at all ultrasnobbish receptions, and my walking stick was the magic wand for all successful evenings. ... One day I appeared with a transparent mannequin with red fish swimming in it. Every appearance was an event awaited with excitement." Dalí accepted the invitations to the luxurious villas of rich international figures living in America, such as Coco Chanel and Lord Gerald Berners, and acquired prosperous patrons: initially the Noailles, leading benefactors on the French literary and artistic scene, later the wealthy Edward James, and finally the Morses, who over thirty years would assemble the world's largest private collection of Dalís.

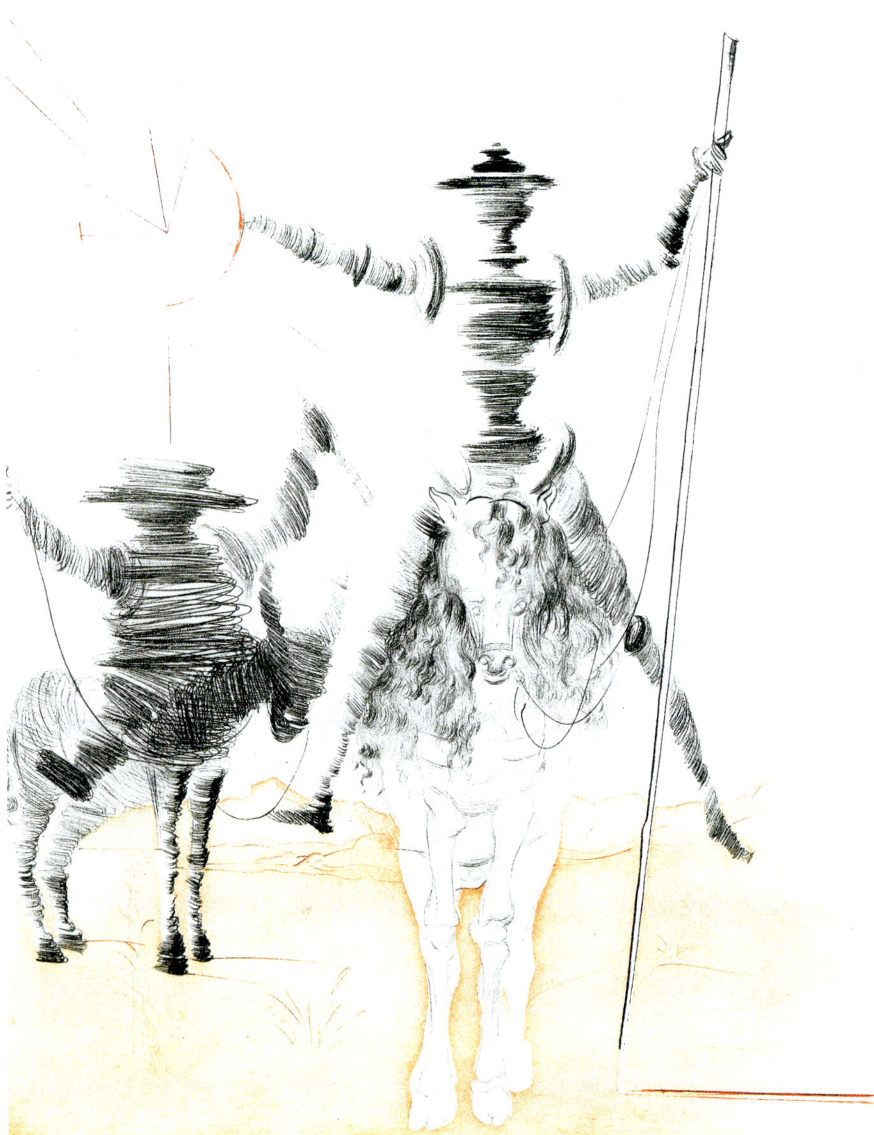

Dalí illustrated works of international literature, like this etching for *Don Quixote*.

Dalí's American Years (1940–1948)

When he and his wife Gala fled to New York after the German occupation of Paris in August 1940, Dalí had already convinced America that he alone was the greatest representative of Surrealism.

With Gala as his manager, and thanks to her shrewd business head, the long-desired financial success was not long in coming. Dalí began to earn on a grand scale—in the 1940s, the prices of his pictures steadily rose to reach an astonishing $300,000. It was mainly commissioned work that brought in the large sums: portraits of American high society such as cosmetics and beauty salon queen Helena Rubinstein, or British actor Laurence Olivier. He was also happy to provide designs for all kinds of ad, such as those for Jack Winter sportswear, Lanvin chocolate, Elsa Schiaparelli perfume and body oils, as well as designs for furniture, ties, and socks. Apart from these, Dalí also did dozens of book illustrations (notably for Shakespeare's *Macbeth* and Cervantes' *Don Quixote*); stage sets and costumes for the theater, opera, and ballet; and designs for the film industry, where he worked for Alfred Hitchcock and Walt Disney.

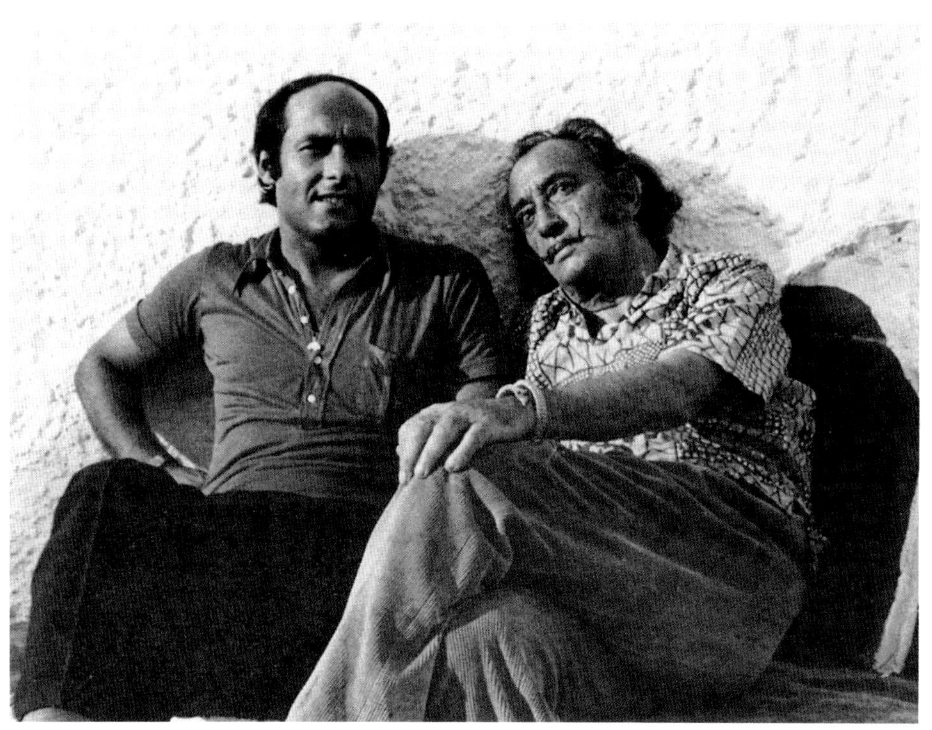

Dalí with his secretary and business manager Enrique Sabater.

Dalí now led a life that enabled him not only to work hard—he drove himself like a man possessed—but also to indulge in the world's riches. As commissions multiplied, in 1960 the Dalís appointed a business manager, who got ten percent commission on all the deals he handled. Thanks to this, John Peter Moore became a multi-millionaire. As his successor Enrique Sabater admitted: "Working for Dalí, I earned more than the president of the USA!"

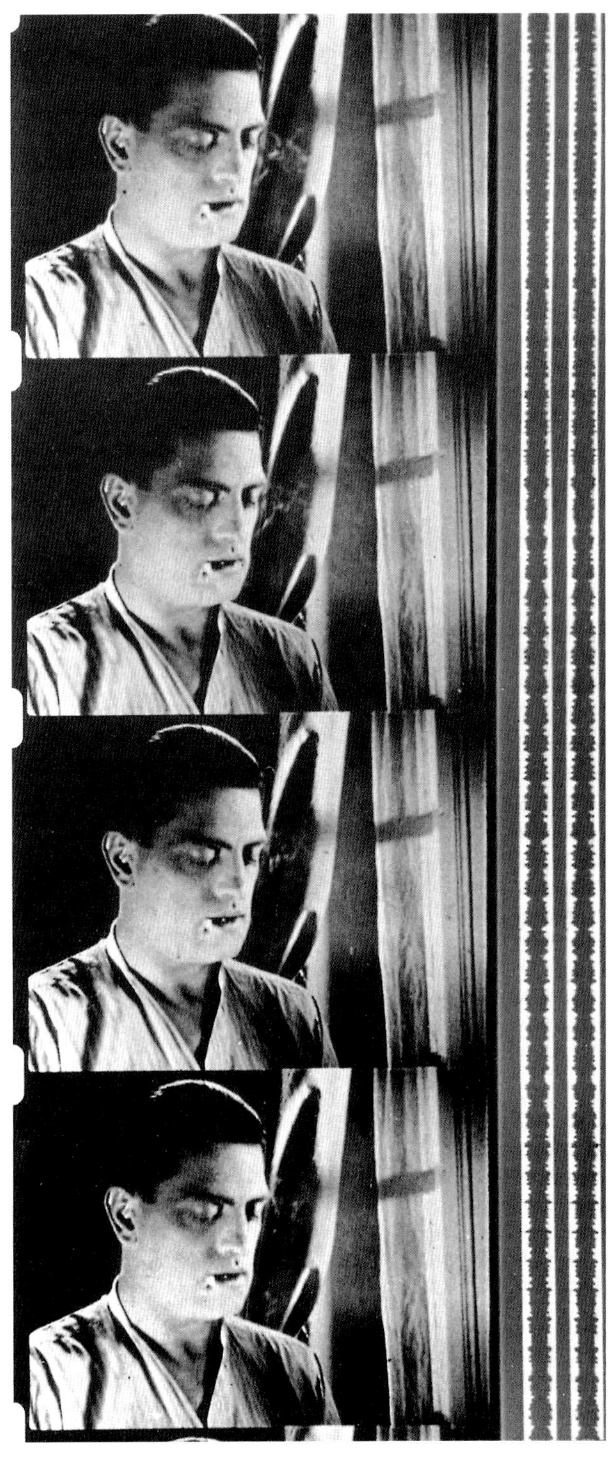

On location in Paris *"Un Chien Andalou* was a film about puberty and death in which I stabbed the heart of witty, elegant and intellectual Paris with the whole reality and sharpness of an Iberian dagger," was Dalí's comment on his legendary Surrealist experimental silent film.

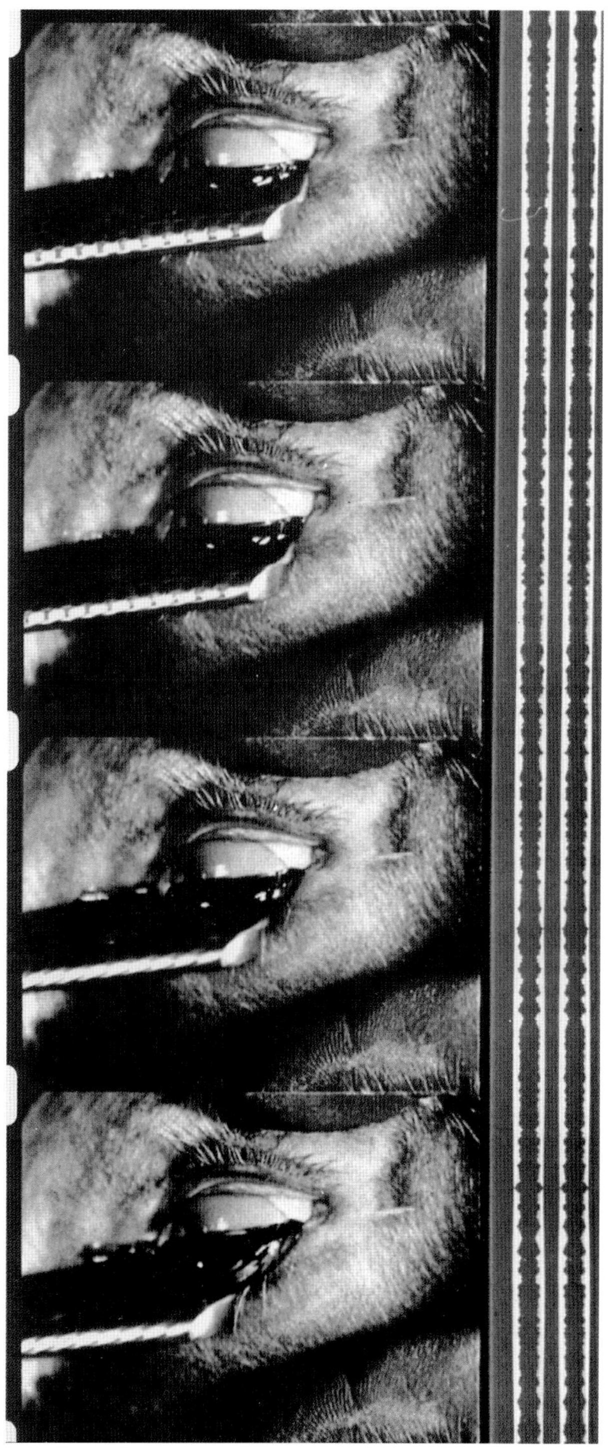

Experimental "We let 'irrational' images rise to the surface of our minds without explanation," said Buñuel, describing his collaboration with Dalí on the screenplay of *Un Chien Andalou*. On its first screening at Studio 28 in Paris, the film caused uproar. One of the most famous scenes is the scene when Buñuel (see picture on page 24) cuts through an eye with a razor blade.

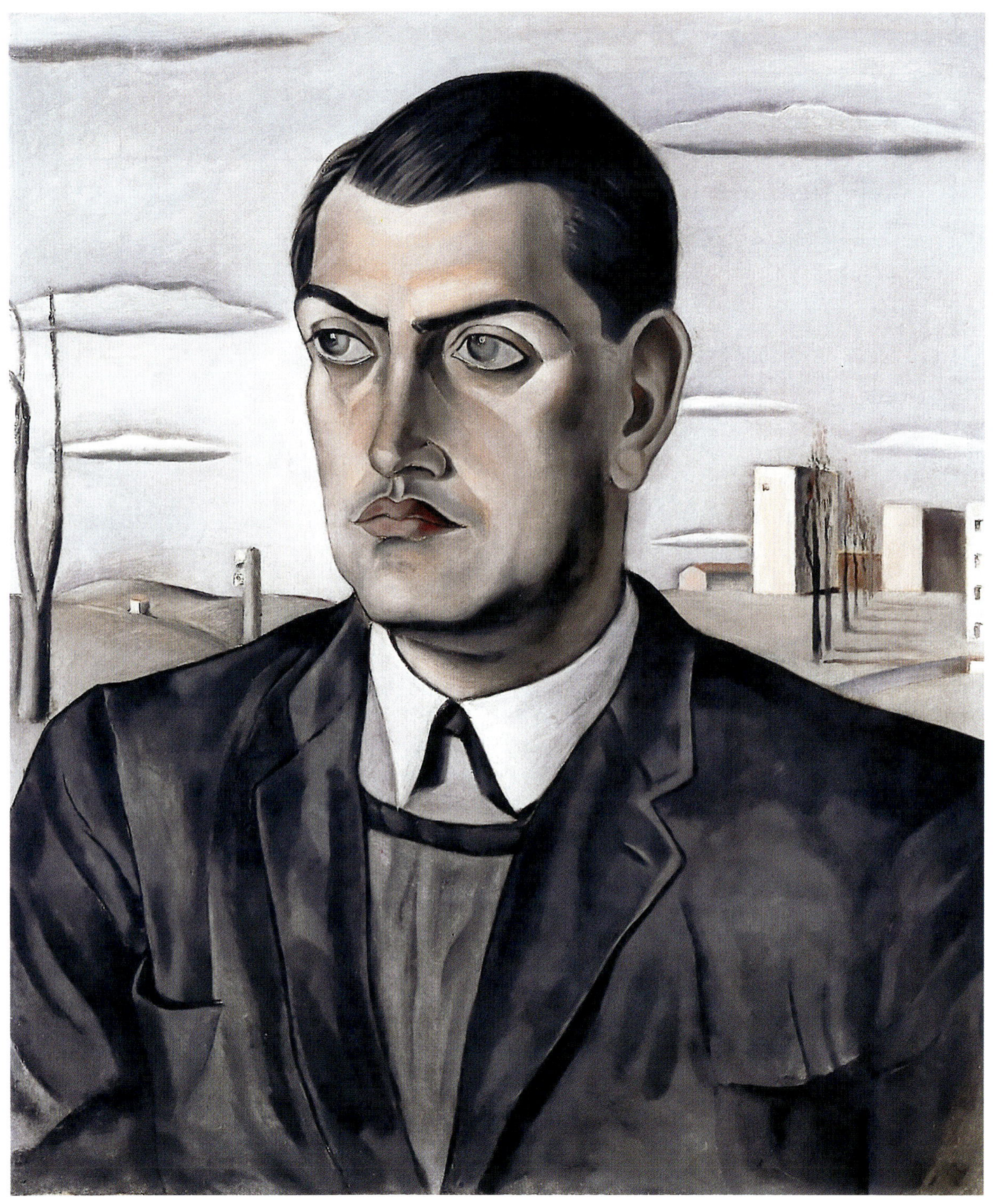

Portrait Filmmaker and later Oscar winner Luis Buñuel was among Dalí's closer friends when they both lived at the student hostel in Madrid. Dalí found that Buñuel's radical views were similar to his own quasi-anarchistic thinking, and the mordant irony of Buñuel's films—merciless exposés of bourgeois society—later proved much to his taste. The twenty-year-old Dalí painted him with a sobriety and sculptural death reminiscent of Ingres and the new Objectivity.

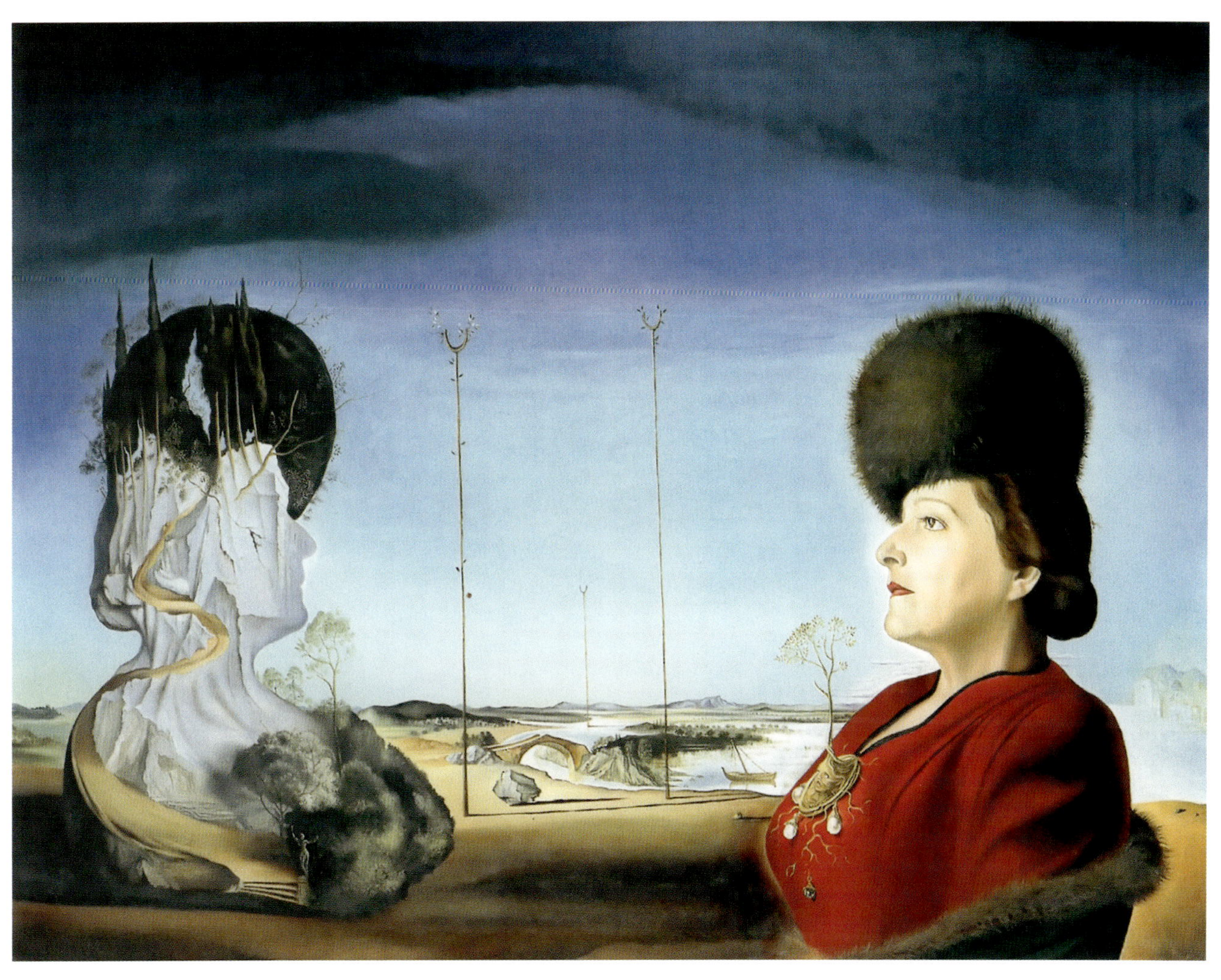

High society Commissioned work brought him money on a grand scale. The *Portrait of Mrs. Isabel Styler-Tas* in 1945 shows an American multi-millionairess. Formally, it echoes the famous double portrait of Duke Federico da Montefeltro and his wife by Renaissance painter Piero della Francesca.

Art

"I was ... the king of nonsense, the clown, the street juggler; no one grasped the pent-up force and Nietzschean willpower behind the external appearance."

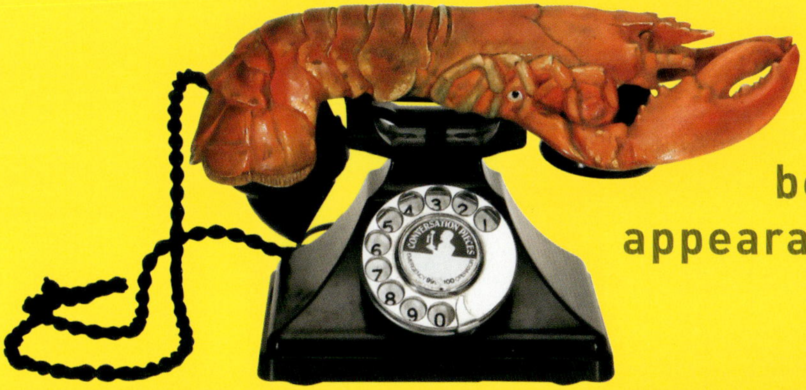

Salvador Dalí

Talent and Genius

Dalí was a virtuoso at translating his fantastical ideas and visions into a wide variety of artistic productions. The results are enigmatic works steeped in an idiosyncratic symbolism that is not easy to interpret. To decode his works, we have to take a much closer look at the man and his ideas.

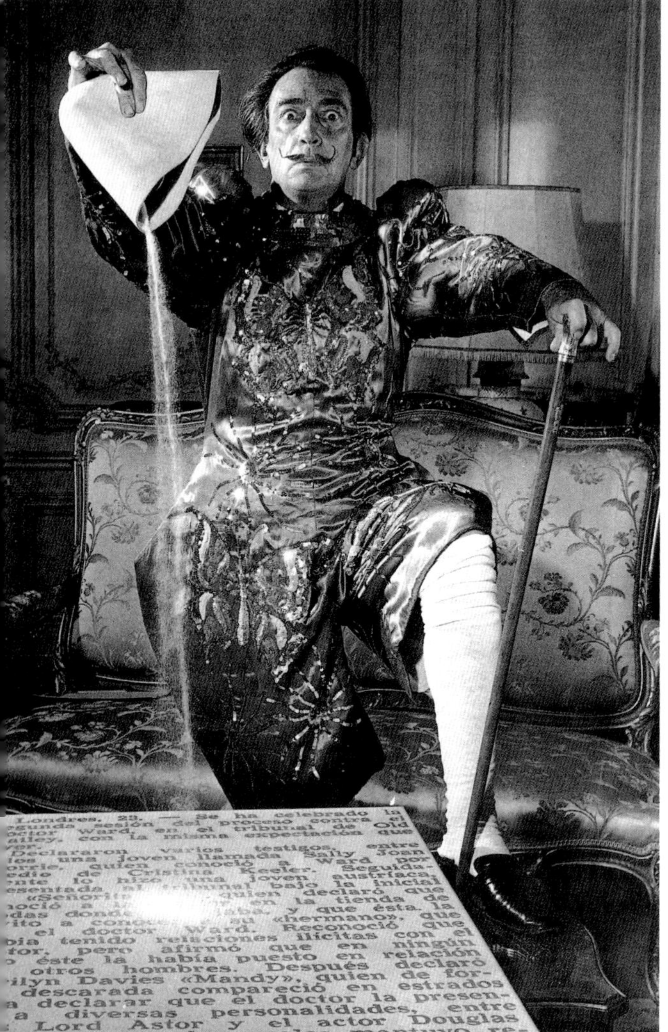

Paranoia as a Method

Dalí claims that even as a child he had the ability to discover secrets hidden behind visual phenomena. He later called this skill "critical paranoia"—an invented method he uses as a fundamental principle of his work. "My whole ambition in the field of painting consists of making the mind's images of tangible irrationality manifest with the most domineering fury of precision ... Images in the imagination that for the time being cannot be explained or traced back through systems of logical perception or rational mechanisms." With paranoiac perception as a model, Dalí made new, perplexing images of reality from his "delusional perceptions" and visions.

A multiple talent – the "magician" Dalí.

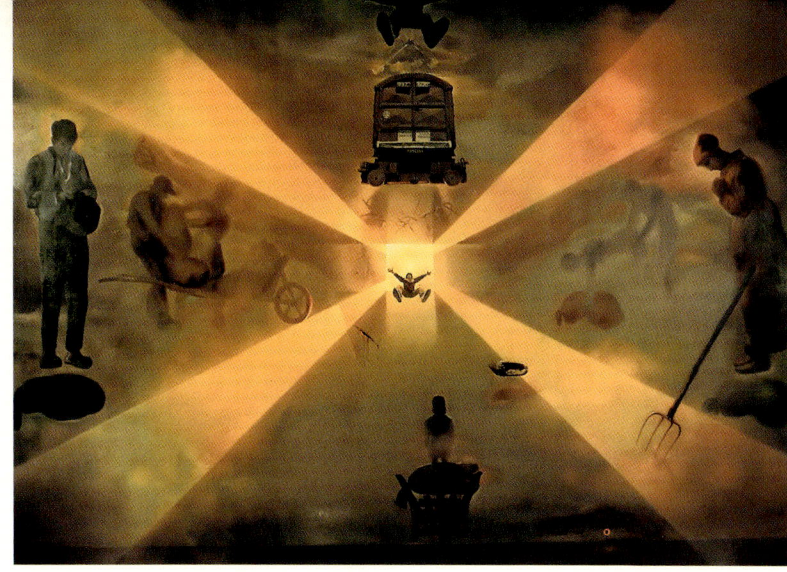

Inspired by an ecstatic vision, in 1956 Dalí painted his famous monumental painting of *The Railway Station at Perpignan*.

Dalí's "Cosmic Ecstasy"

Dalí had one of his visions at Perpignan station in southern France, which he had to pass through when traveling from Spain to Paris or France to Spain. "I could see a radiant aura around the station that formed a perfect circle ... I had an erection out of sheer joy and ecstasy—I had grasped the truth ... Everything became overwhelmingly obvious. The center of the universe lay there in front of me." This conviction demanded expression: *The Railway Station at Perpignan*, according to Dalí his best painting to date.

"I cannot feel any violent pleasure unless my mind is stretched like a fabric on which brilliant pictures are superimposed."

Salvador Dalí

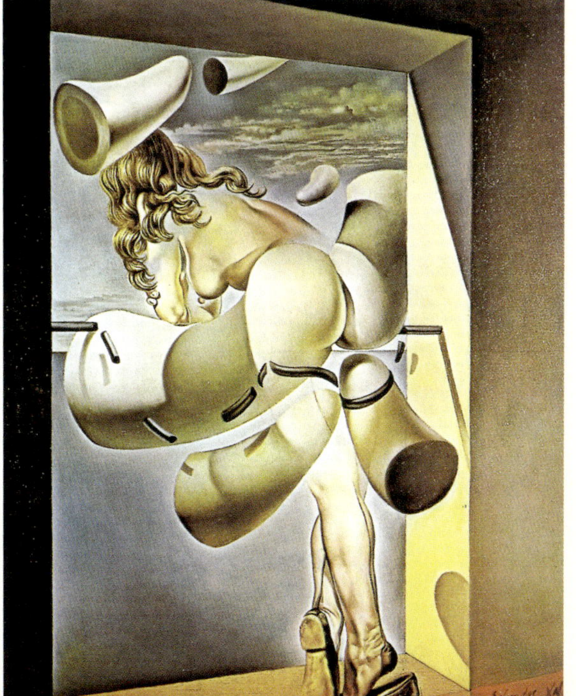

Dalí's titles are scarcely any more helpful in promoting an understanding of his works:

Medium-sized French White Loaf with Two Fried Eggs on the Plate without the Plate, on Horseback in Attempted Sodomy with a Piece of Portuguese Bread

Young Virgin Auto-Sodomised by the Horns of her Own Chastity (left).

The Coincidence of Illusion and a Frozen Moment, or Baked Eggs Offered on a Spoon

"The horn of the rhinoceros, the only unicorn, is in reality the horn of the legendary unicorn, which symbolizes chastity. This youthful virgin can support herself on it and play with it in her mind, as in the medieval Minne period," said Dalí.

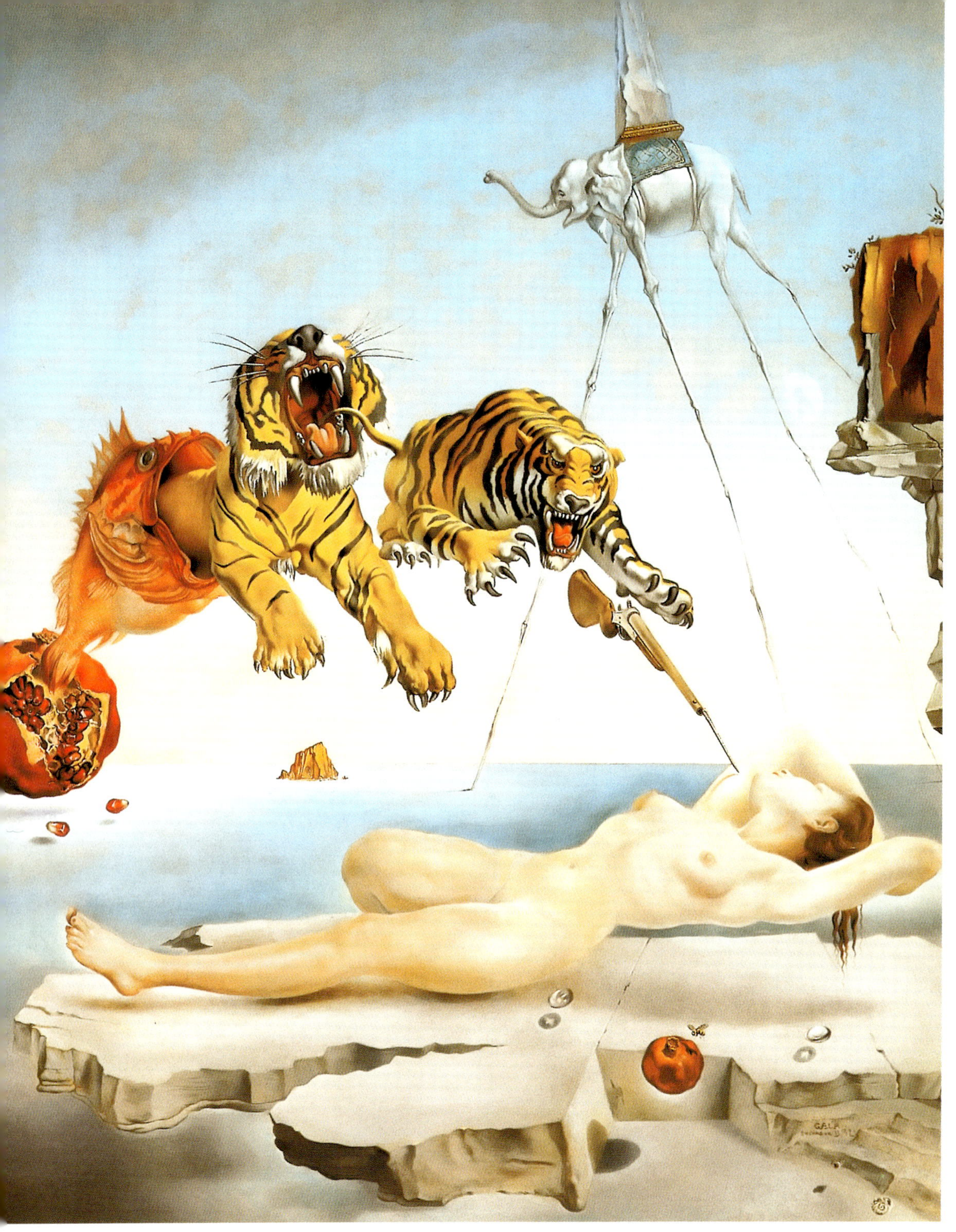

Dalí's comment on his picture *Dream Caused by the Flight of a Bee Around a Pomegranate One Second before Awakening* was: "For the first time, a painting has been made of Freud's discovery that a typical dream is a long, instructive fable, where the chance of a moment leads to awakening."

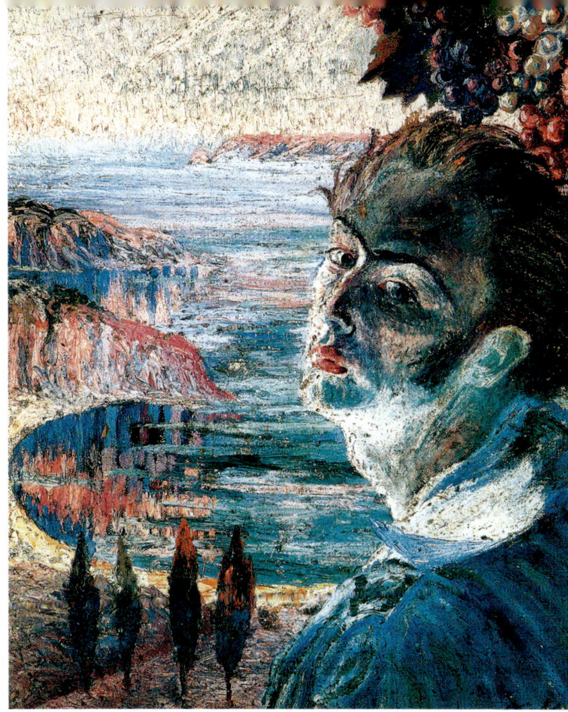

Even as a 17-year-old, Dalí's talent as a painter was evident in Impressionist pictures like this *Self-Portrait*.

Self-Styled Genius

"The two luckiest things that can happen to a contemporary painter are first to be Spanish and second to be called Dalí. Both have happened to me." Seeking greatness and fame, and driven by a desire for recognition, Dalí proclaimed himself the savior *(salvador)* of modern painting. But for all his theatricality, there was no mistaking the seriousness of his ambition. A passion for work was the real motivating force behind his output: a master craftsman, Dalí was totally dedicated to his art.

"Dalí's imagination affects me like an outboard motor that's constantly running."

Pablo Picasso

"I'm an Impressionist"

Back in the early days, the principal influence on Dalí's artistic development was the Spanish artist Ramon Pichot, who was beginning to establish a reputation as an Impressionist painter in Paris. His work is little known today, and he is now remembered only as a friend of Picasso. But for the young Dalí, his works were a revelation. During a summer visit to the Pichots' country home, the family put oil paints, a canvas, and a studio at Dalí's disposal, and encouraged him to get on with it: "These clean, shiny tubes represented a

Dalí with his uncle Anselm Domènech in front of *Harlequin and Small Bottle of Rum* (1925).

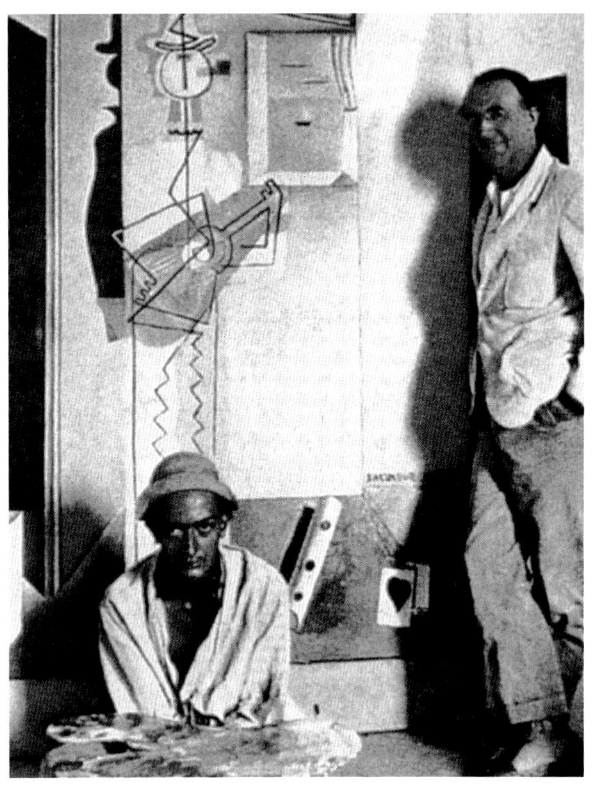

whole world of effort and longing for me, and I looked at them and stroked them with hands trembling with excitement, as lovers do in my imagination. ... These paints seemed to radiate a whole future full of hope and happiness. How happy I shall be, the day when I can actually turn out the things I've imagined, the things I've felt and thought up." He now threw himself seriously into the task of becoming an Impressionist painter.

Early Signs of Talent

Dalí's talent quickly came to light, and from 1916 was given every encouragement. For six years he had drawing lessons with Juan Núñez Fernández at the state art school in Figueres. According to Dalí's account thirty years later, he learnt more here than from any other teachers he ever had. At the end of the first year at art school, he gained a *diploma de honor*, and at fourteen took part in his first group show, at the town's theater. The young Catalan showed talent in another field as well: writing literary texts and composing critical essays. He produced a series of articles on the "great masters of painting"—written with remarkable style—for the school magazine *Studium*, which he and some friends had founded. The subjects were the painters Dalí most admired: Goya, El Greco, Dürer, Leonardo, Michelangelo, and Velázquez.

Experiments in Modernism

From 1921 to 1926, Dalí studied at the Royal Academy of Fine Arts in Madrid. His uncle, Anselm Domènech, who ran a bookshop in Barcelona, supplied him with the leading art periodicals, which extended his horizon beyond Impressionism to the contemporary international art scene generally. Although the lecturers in Madrid did not know much about the avant-garde, the young student endeavored to keep up with modernism. During these years, he experimented with various styles, trying Pointillism (*The Bathers of Es Lanér*, 1923) and Cubism (*Cubist Self-Portrait*, 1923). In his early twenties, he also tried a neo-classical style similar that developed by Picasso (*Portrait of My Father*, 1925), and then a realism reminiscent of Vermeer (*The Girl of*

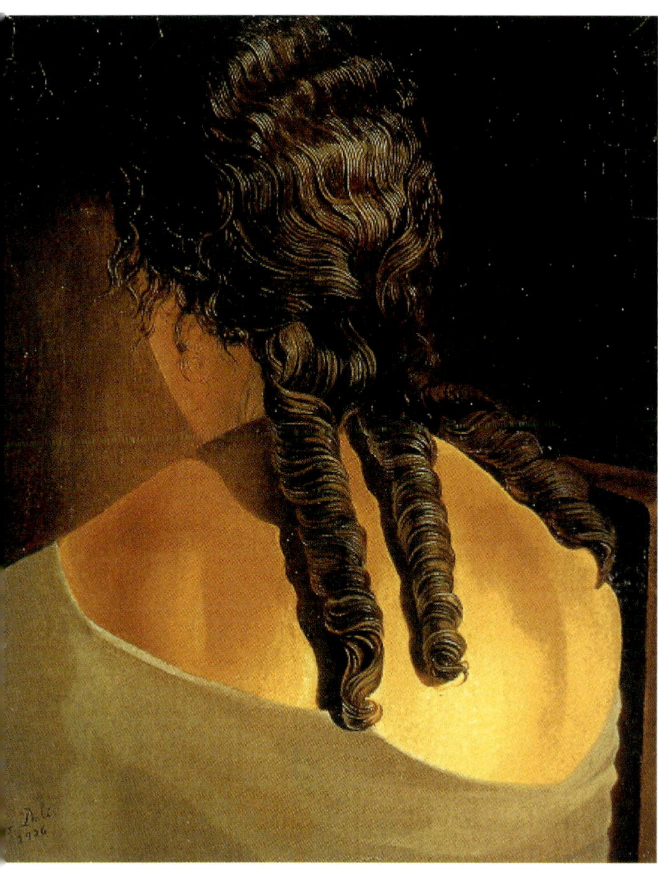

His sister was a predominant motif in his early work, which therefore tends to get labeled as the "Anna Maria Period." This 1926 painting shows her as a *The Girl of Figueres*.

Figueras, 1926). His attitude to art had an altogether anarchic ring when he boldly asserted "you have to paint without any kind of aesthetic doctrine, paint for painting's sake, without putting up with any constraints."

Dalí was very disappointed in the way the craft of art was taught at the academy. But he applied himself with industry and great energy—a characteristic of his whole career—and, coupled with a compulsion for perfection and a liking for experiment, he laid the foundations of technical and compositional mastery very early on. Associated with this was a conspicuous honing of his skills as a draughtsman. The young Dalí was well aware that only someone who has thoroughly mastered his craft can take things much further.

Going His Own Way

His academic studies appearing more and more irrelevant, in 1926 he brought them to an end. He now pursued his own ambitions, painting and preparing for exhibitions. The first group shows in Madrid and Barcelona in the early 1920s had been crowned with success. Observers were unanimous: the young Catalan had outstanding artistic potential. Among the works he exhibited were those in a realistic style, most notably the portraits of his sister Anna Maria, Dalí's model in the early years. Among the twelve paintings he did between 1923 and 1926 is the remarkable painting of *Girl Standing at the Window*, where Anna Maria is shown in a graceful pose in Dalí's favored rear view. From 1926 on there followed a substantial series of paintings and drawings of his friend, the writer García Lorca, where Lorca's head generally merges with the painter's.

The Surrealist group *c.* 1930.
L. to r.: Tristan Tzara, Paul Eluard, André Breton, Hans Arp, Salvador Dalí, Yves Tanguy, Max Ernst, René Crevel and Man Ray.

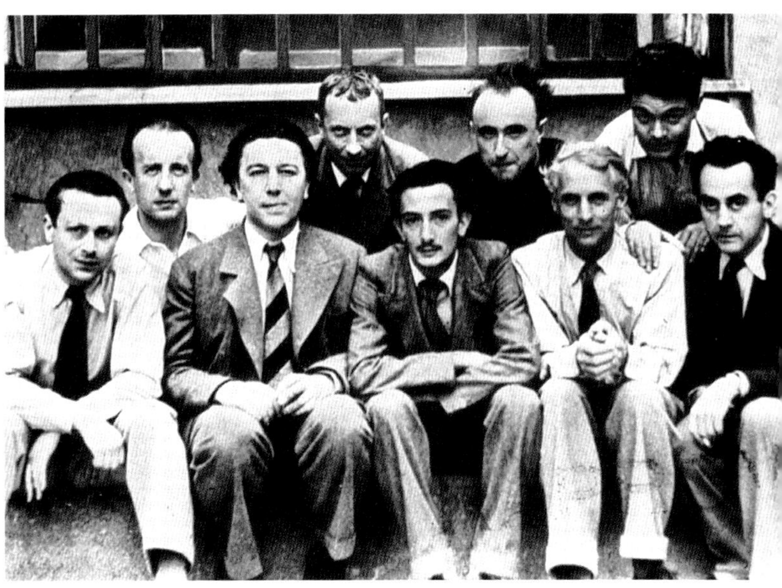

Gallery owner Pierre Loeb had been considering taking Dalí on very early on, but was waiting for him to develop a strong voice of his own rather than constantly leaping from style to style. "I am sure you'll find *one style,*" wrote Loeb, "and with your talent I am convinced you have an outstanding career ahead of you as a painter."

The Discovery of Surrealism

Dalí now discovered the theories and images of Giorgio de Chirico's Metaphysical Style, and greatly admired the work of Tanguy, Magritte, and Mirò. The Surrealists' spokesman, the poet André Breton, "immediately became something of a second father" to him. When in 1927 he opted for Surrealism—whose intellectual windows he pushed wide open and so breathed new life into, according to Breton—Dalí's work underwent a profound change. His pictures became more provocative: he was keen to make his own contribution to Surrealism's attacks on the values of bourgeois society and traditional reality.

In 1928, Dalí submitted his newly finished *Unsatisfied Desires* to the annual autumn salon in Barcelona, and duly caused uproar. The picture features pink, organic-looking shapes reminiscent of body parts against a light-colored background. The left one is a hand with fingers (one outstretched) with a mouth or female sex between them. The shape on the right displays a flag like a tongue sticking out of a tiny opening.

The picture gave rise to all kinds of responses. The Maragall Gallery said that, in order to preserve the

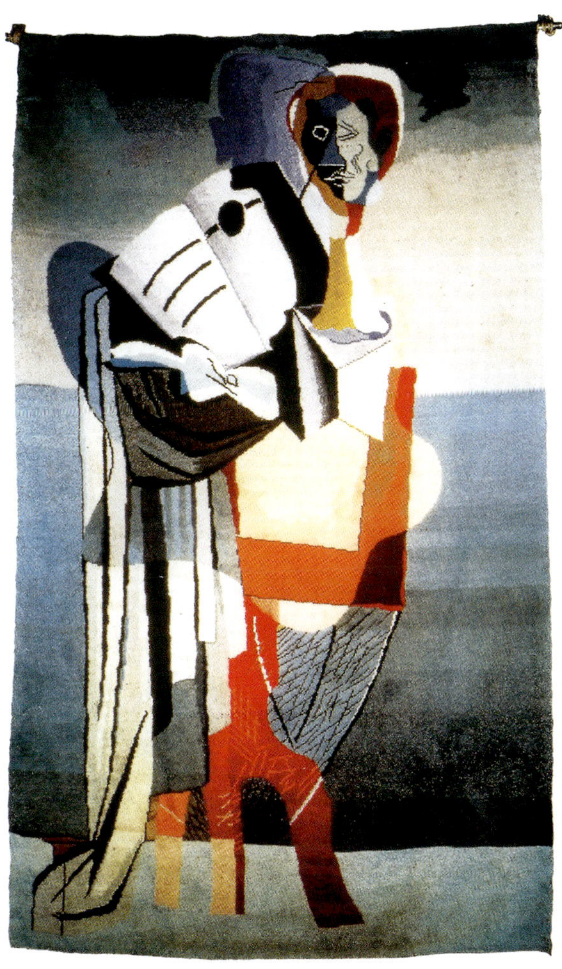

In his early years, Dalí experimented with the latest painting techniques, as in this *Cubist Figure* of 1926.

gallery's reputation, it would be unable to exhibit the picture. Moreover, it wouldn't do Dalí's career in the art world any good to show the work. Dalí's view was of course quite the opposite: he was aware that a controversial image could be thoroughly advantageous to his success. But even gallery owner and champion of contemporary art Josep Dalmau—who had previously exhibited Impressionist, Fauvist, and Cubist artists in Spain, including Matisse, Picasso, and Miró—was very concerned about the painting. He proposed covering the offending parts of the painting so as to avoid the risk of having his gallery closed by the authorities! Dalí protested with a lecture: "Catalan art today vis-à-vis the latest forms of expression of youthful intelligence."

In 1927 and 1928, Dalí wrote a series of essays on art in which he firmly aligned himself with the Surrealist movement. Like his literary writings, they were published particularly in the Barcelona periodical *L'Amic de les Arts* and the international *Gaceta Literaria*, to which he now regularly contributed articles and drawings.

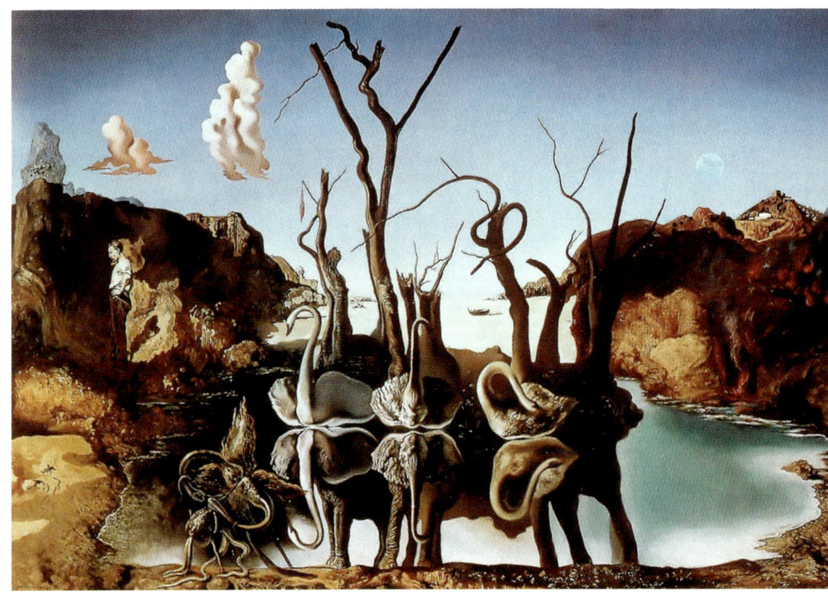

Swans Reflecting Elephants (1937) attests to Dalí's enthusiasm for the old tradition of puzzle pictures.

Artistic High Points

The discovery of Freud's writings represented an inexhaustible source of insights for Dalí, and led on to the most outstanding period of his artistic career. Using a mixture of Freudian symbolism (unmistakable, for example, in the very phallic nose in several of his works) and his own idiosyncratic symbolism, he worked fears, dreams, and visions into his paintings, putting into practice what the *Surrealist Manifesto* had demanded, namely a yielding to the psychic automatism of unconscious associations. In Dalí's view, that meant ignoring moral taboos of any kind. He thus devoted himself to painting sexual content, and *Apparatus and Hand* launched a long series of paintings, drawings, and writings on the subject of masturbation. *The Great Masturbator*, painted in the seclusion of his studio in Figueres after the first encounter with Gala, became one of his most famous paintings. "It shows a large head soft as wax, with very rosy cheeks, long eyelashes and a long, impressive nose pressed to the ground. The face has no mouth, a huge grasshopper occupying the position instead. The decaying belly of the insect is full of ants. Several of these ants are scurrying around where the mouth of this alarming face ought to have been. The head terminates in structures and fin-de-siècle style ornamentation." In his autobiographical *The Secret Life of Salvador Dalí*, he confessed to being a compulsive masturbator, and described time and again how closely his enthusiasm for art was connected with sexuality, there being something ecstatic about both.

The Great Masturbator was exhibited at Camille Goemans' gallery with ten other paintings. Dalí had thereby attained his goal of a solo show in Paris, which was still the center of the avant-garde scene and so the focus of

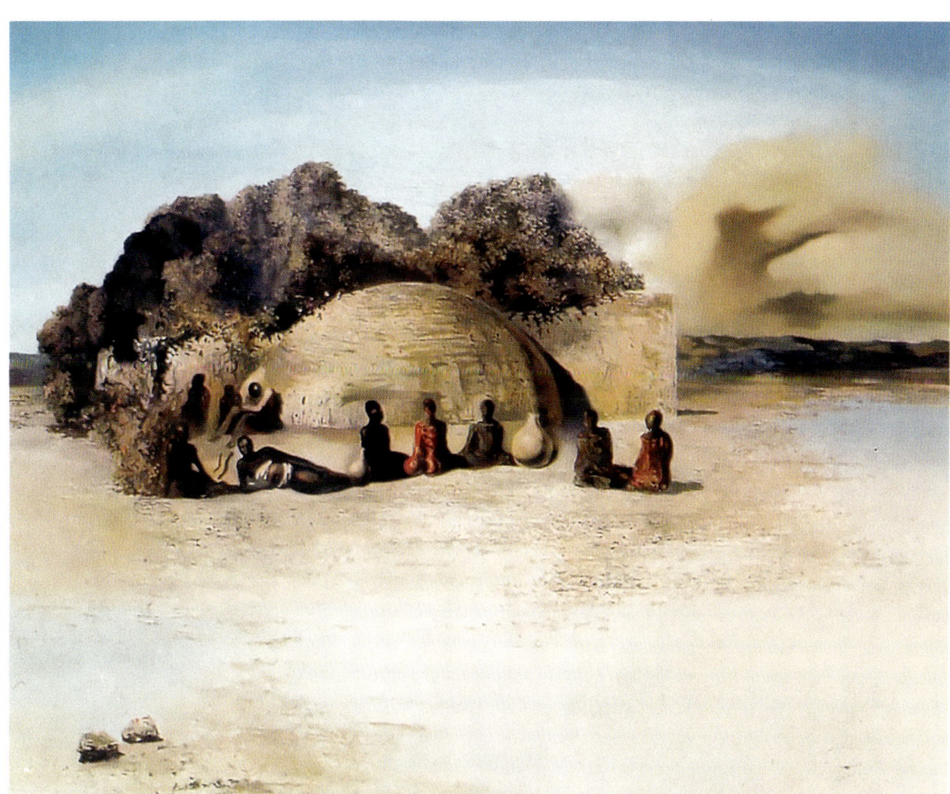

Dalí's Paranoiac Visage from 1931, was inspired by a photo of an African village.

his longings. Breton bought the work even before opening day. He also wrote the foreword to the catalog, proof of how seriously the founder of Surrealism took Dalí, who was eight years his junior. "Dalí's work, the most hallucinatory ever produced to date, constitutes a real threat. Absolutely new creatures, visibly with evil intentions, are on the march."

The "Conquest of the Irrational"

In the summer of 1930, Dalí invented a method he called "critical paranoia," which he described as "a spontaneous method of irrational knowledge based on systematic objectivization and fantasizing interpretations." Dalí enthusiastically used "critical paranoia" for creatively implementing "mostly compulsively dangerous ideas." The aim was to paint or draw delusional pictures with a degree of clarity that made them seem real. His intention was to place viewers in the same delirious state as the artist, to "systematize confusion and contribute to the complete discrediting of the world of reality." He thus went beyond the automatism recommended by Breton in his first manifesto, replacing it with the imperative of the unconscious.

Closely connected with the method was Dalí's interest in "anamorphoses," which have a tradition going back to the 16th and 17th centuries. In an anamorphosis, an image is completely transformed when seen from a particular angle. "Thanks to an unambiguously paranoiac procedure, it has become possible to get a double image in the mind—the representation of an object that, without the smallest figurative or anatomical change, is at

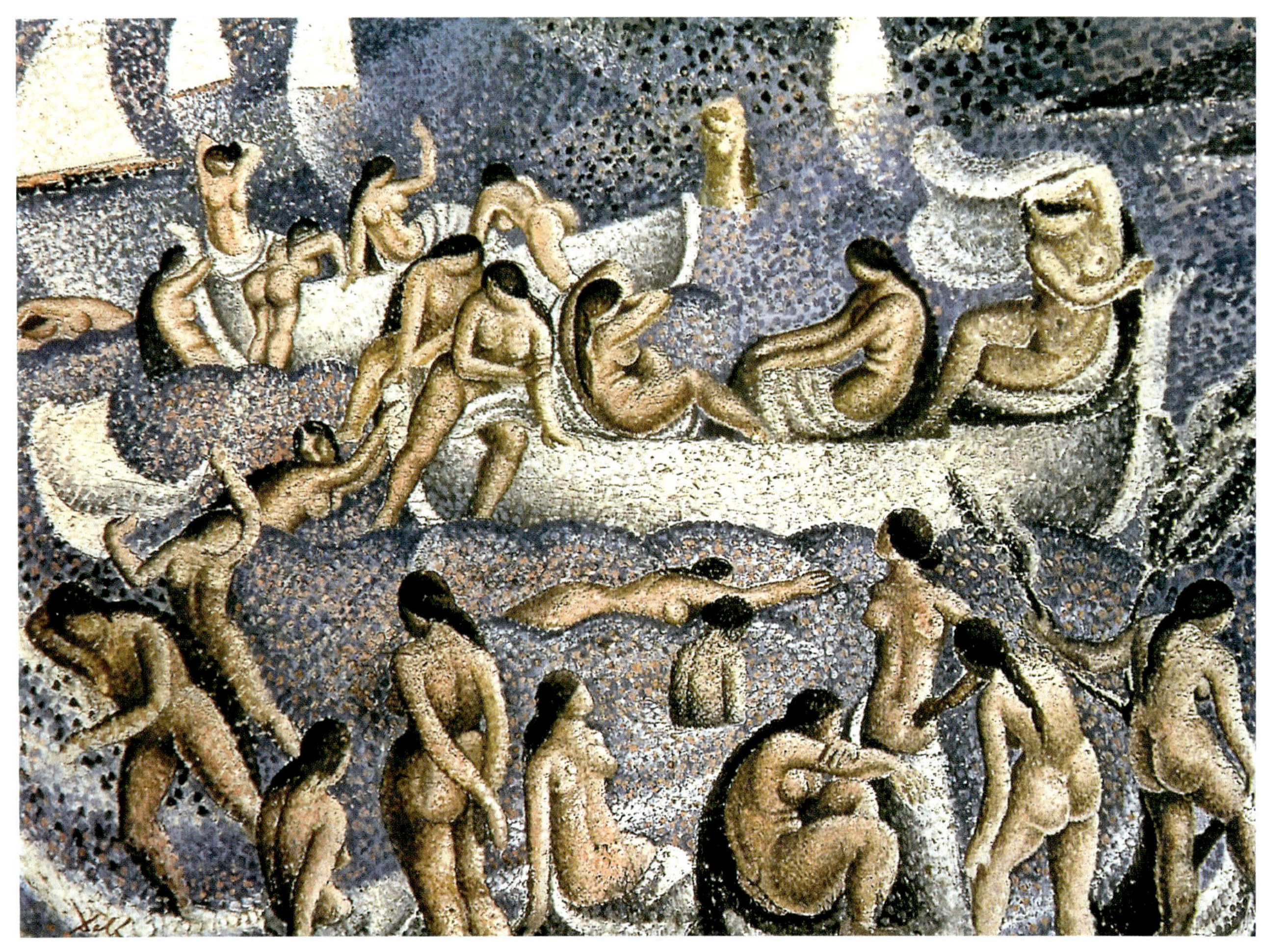

Dance of the naked body *The Bathers of Es Llanér* on the beach at the fishing village of Cadaqués was an early Pointillist study by Dalí dating from 1923. It shows the same female figure in 24 different graceful poses and movements in the sea. The picture is reminiscent of works by contemporaries such as Picasso and Matisse.

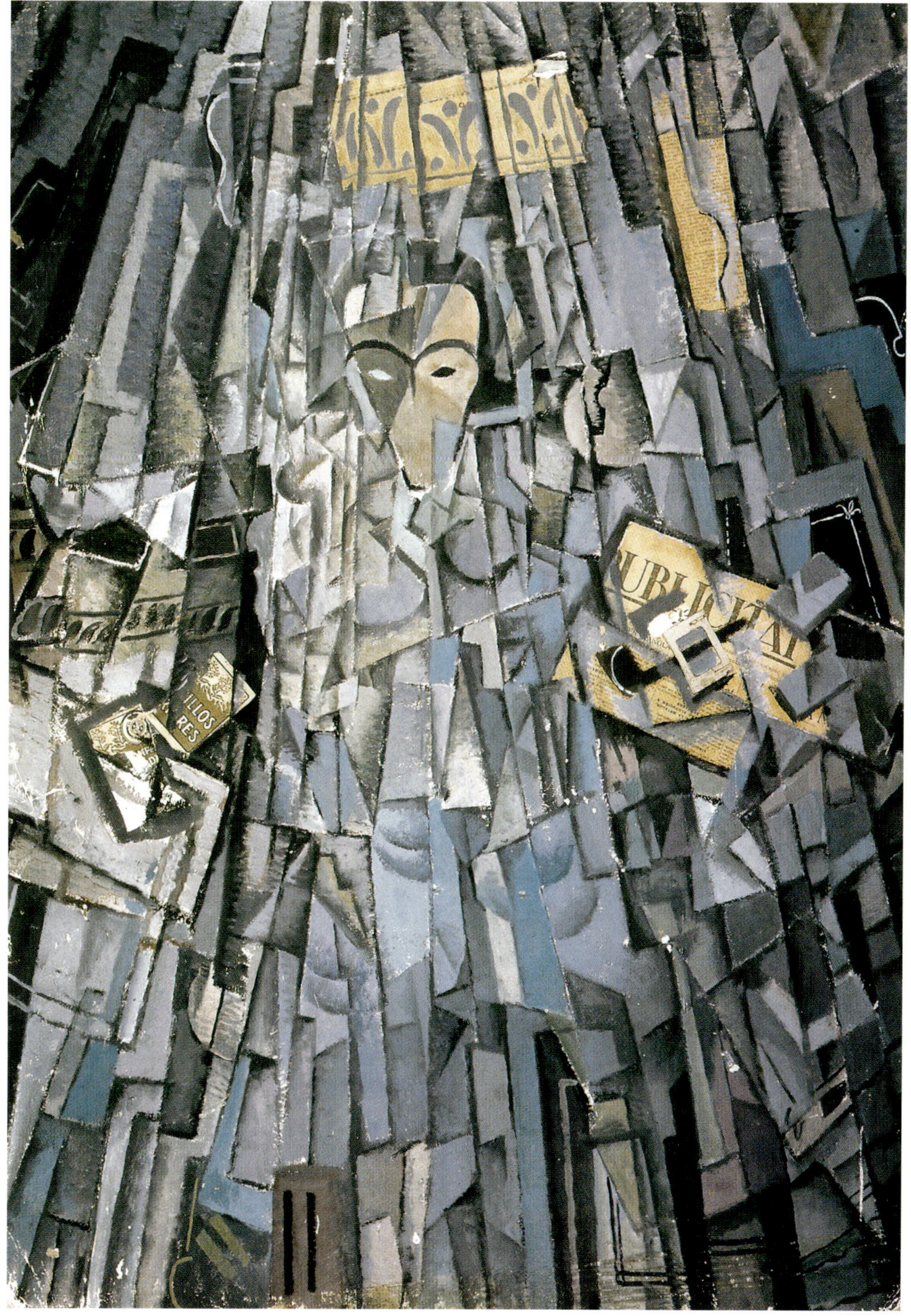

Joining the avant-garde After exploring Impressionism and Pointillism, Dalí tried his hand at Cubism. He fragmented people and things in his pictures and reassembled them according to the rules of geometric figuration. His *Cubist Self-Portrait*, a play of colors in various shades of blue with ochre highlights, was produced during his student years in Madrid.

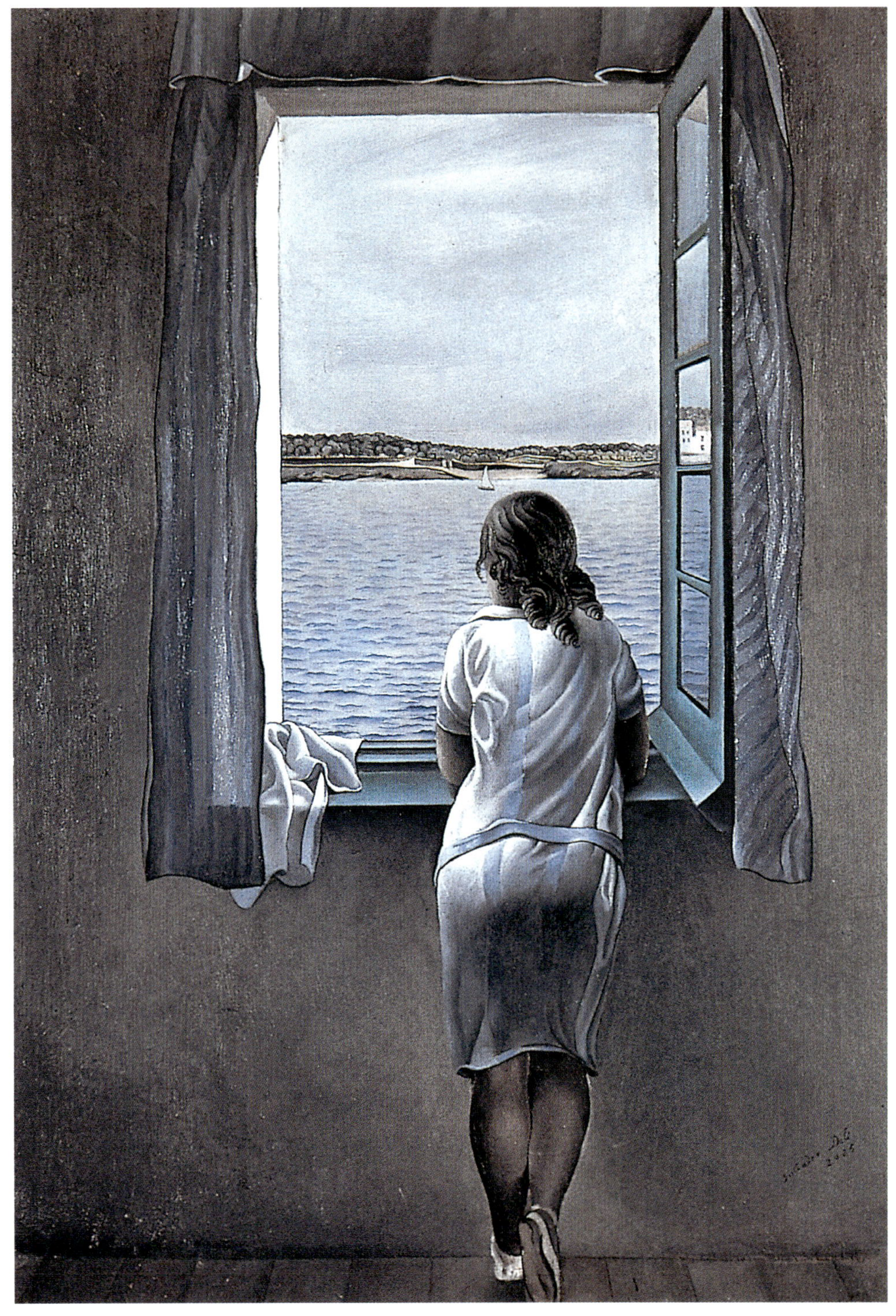

View out of the window In his early paintings, Dalí switched from style to style. *Girl Standing at the Window* is reminiscent of Vermeer's realism. The work shows his sister Anna Maria at their parents' house in Cadaqués. In 1954, he transformed it into one of his most erotic paintings *Young Virgin Auto-Sodomised by the Horns of her Own Chastity* (page 31).

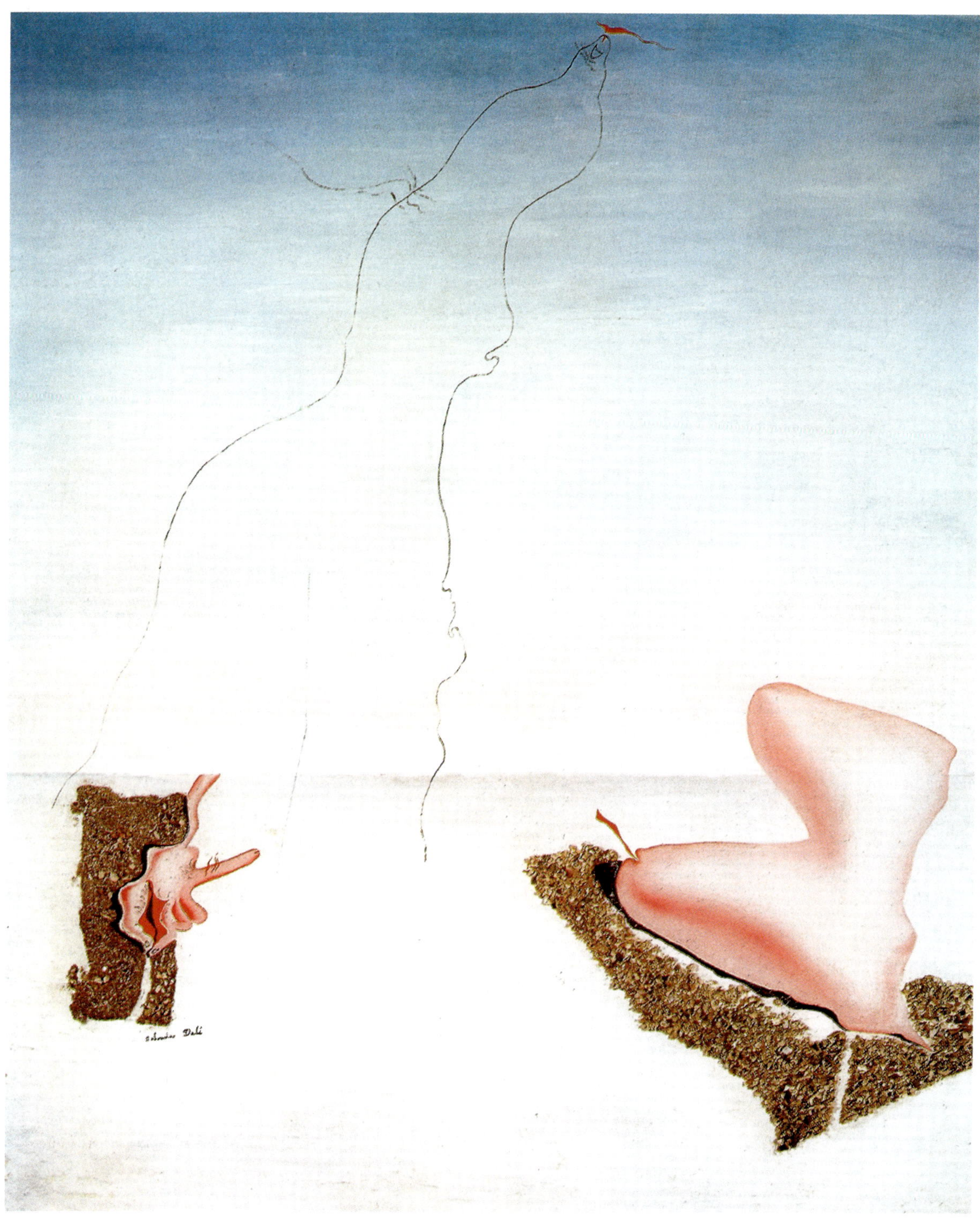

Unsatisfied desires Dalí submitted his latest painting as one of two works for the Autumn Salon in Barcelona in 1928. The desire mentioned in the title was interpreted as an outrageous sexual allusion, so that the director of the Salon refused to accept the work for the exhibition.

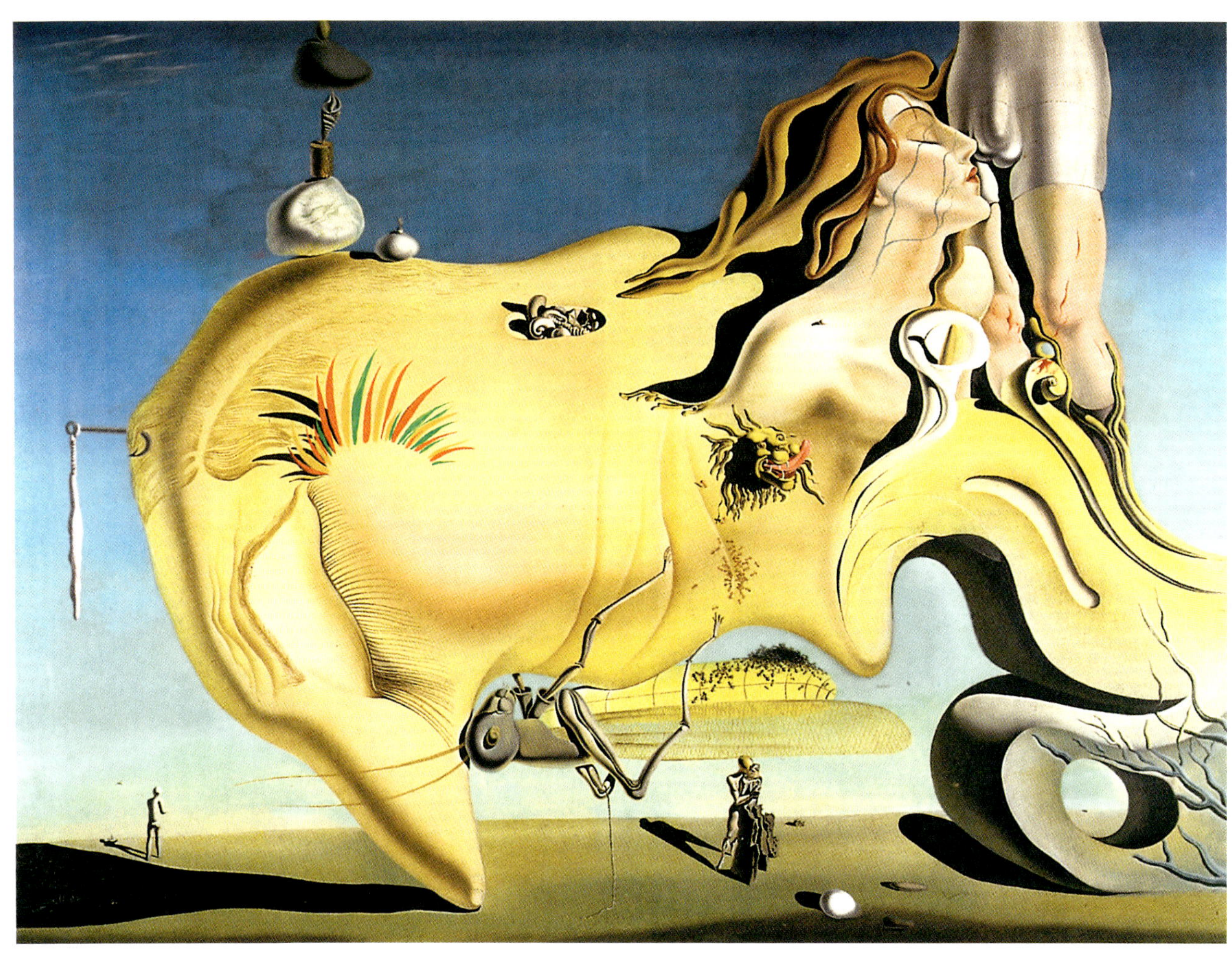

Merciless Dalí put down on canvas his neurotic urges and sexual restlessness in the name of psychoanalysis. The results fired the Surrealist movement. As an art-historical allusion, *The Great Masturbator* evokes Chirico's painting *The Great Metaphysician*, which Dalí replaces with something more human and banal.

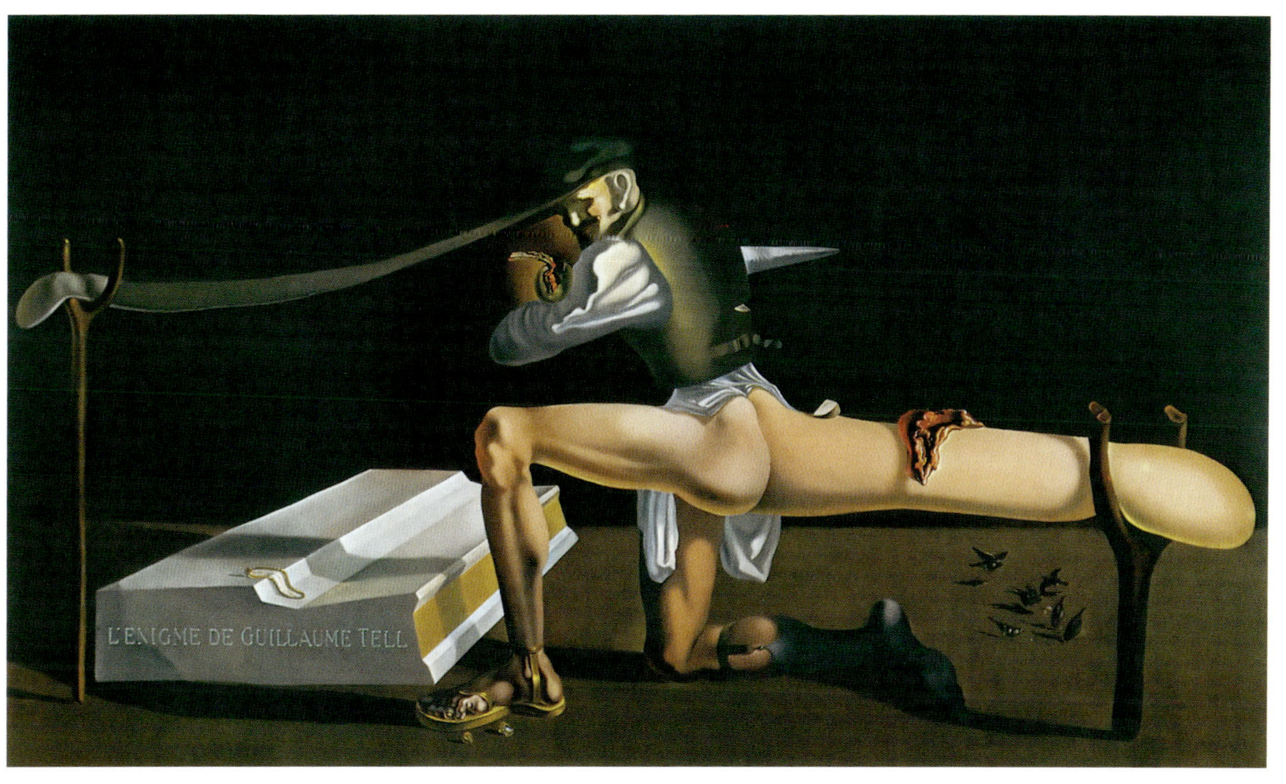

Double reckoning The *Enigma of William Tell* depicts a father holding his son in his arms with threatening intent. The picture combines autobiographical elements with political connotations. The latter were taken by Surrealist spokesman André Breton as deliberate provocation. He saw the representation of Lenin as an "anti-revolutionary act," and demanded that Dalí be kicked out the Surrealist group.

Millet's famous painting of *The Angelus* (1857–59) inspired a series of paintings by Dalí.

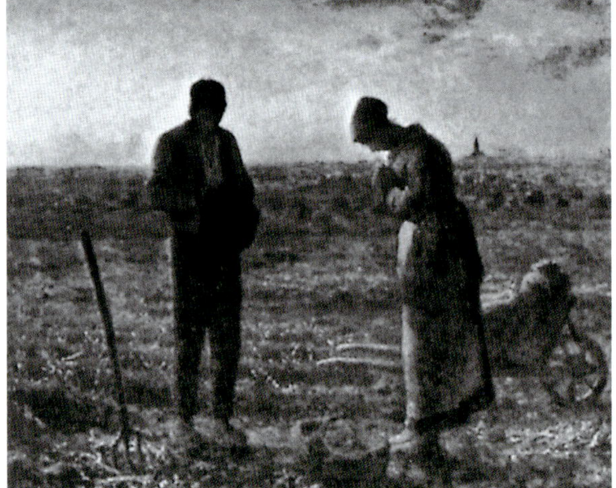

One of many versions of the Angelus motif: *Atavism of Twilight* (1933–34).

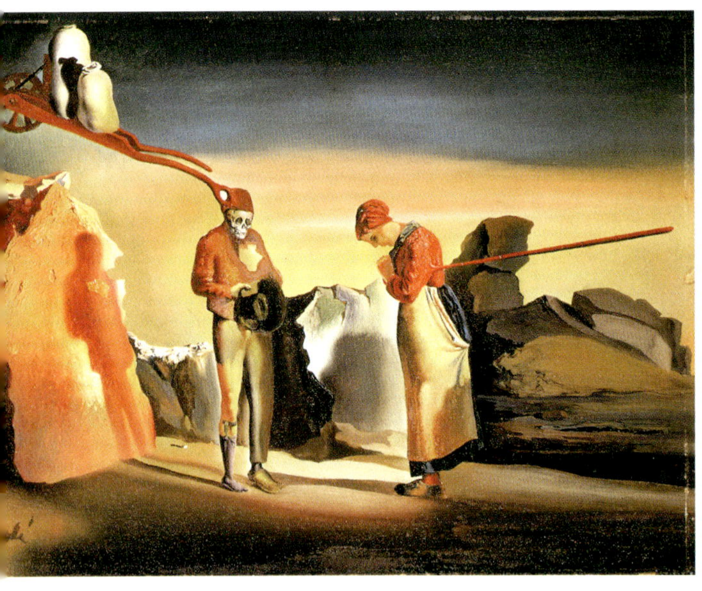

the same time a representation of another completely different object, which is itself devoid of any kind of distortion or anomaly that would infer arrangement."

The Persistence of Memory, which dates from 1931, was the first picture to introduce his famous "soft watches," which henceforth re-appeared as frequently as the head from *The Great Masturbator* (1929). Another item to make an appearance in these years was the "Angelus motif," which likewise turns up sporadically in later works. As he did so often, Dalí used a painting from the history of art as a starting point, which he then transformed by means of critical paranoia.

Jean-François Millet's *The Angelus* (1857–1859), with the "two motionless silhouettes" of peasants at prayer, had caused "great unease" in Dalí ever since childhood. Looking through the tinted spectacles of Freud's dream theory, he tried to get to the bottom of his obsession: there had to be a more significant content behind the obvious one. Dalí duly ascribed an erotic meaning to it, making Millet's male peasant a son lusting after his mother. The hat he interpreted as a symbol of sexual arousal, which he conceals with the hat, expressing a bashful attitude to his masculinity. Even the fork stuck in the ground and the wheelbarrow are interpreted as symbols of sexual relations. Dalí decided that the painting reflected his deepest fears and disappointments. In his self-analysis, the motif of the devout peasants was discovered to be a significant vehicle of his Oedipus complex. When he found out twenty years later that Millet had originally placed a coffin containing the body of a dead son (the object of their prayer) between the peasants, Dalí considered his premonition confirmed: "Everything is now clarified! My critical para-

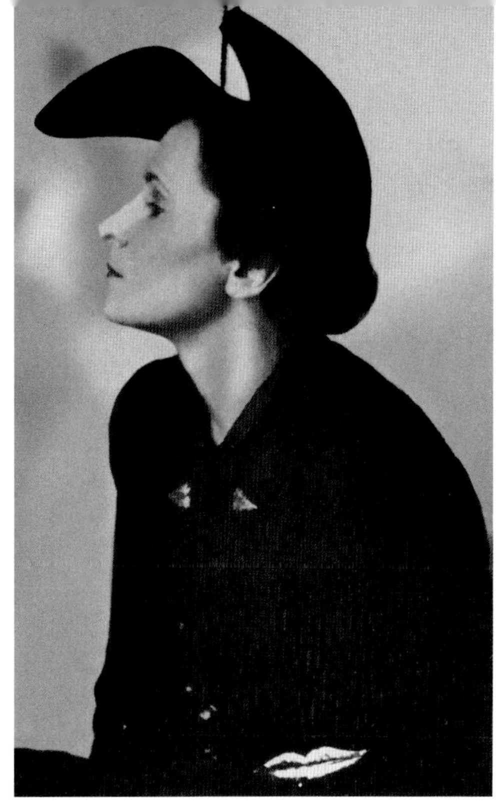

Gala wearing Elsa Schiaparelli's *Shoe Hat*, made to a design by Dalí.

noiac genius recognized the essential point." Dalí's parents also mourned a son who died before Salvador was born.

Expelled from the Surrealists

From the mid-1930s, Dalí found himself at odds with the other Surrealists. His political views were the main cause, though his paintings were also a source of endless debate. The irreverent *Enigma of William Tell* shows Lenin with a bare backside, one buttock bizarrely long which was enough to bring the many Communist-minded artists in the movement to the barricades. In 1934, Breton convoked an extraordinary session of the Surrealists in order to sit in judgment on Dalí's supposed Hitlerist sympathies. Dalí described himself as an apolitical person—which did not prevent him from admiring individual aspects of Hitler's personality and praising his "paranoiac potential." He turned the "trial" into a farce. With a thermometer in his mouth and wearing several layers of clothing that he kept taking off and putting on, he pontificated about Hitler's "four eggs and six foreskins," totally undermining the gravity Breton had meant to confer on the occasion. He also cited Breton's own manifesto, saying that he was only recording his dreams in pictures as faithfully as possible. Dalí finished by saying to Breton: "If I dream tonight I'm fucking you, tomorrow morning I shall paint all our best fucking positions with the maximum wealth of detail."

Though nothing came of it at this date, some years later Breton did finally expel Dalí from the Surrealist group when he repeatedly made racist remarks. In his article "Latest Trends in Surrealist Painting," Breton declared: "In February 1939, Dalí said that ... all the current unrest in the world was of racial origin and the best solution would be an agreement between all white races to force the dark races into slavery. ... After that, I see no possibility of his message still being taken seriously among independent minds." Dalí's growing reputation was no obstacle to the expulsion. He had long been going his own way.

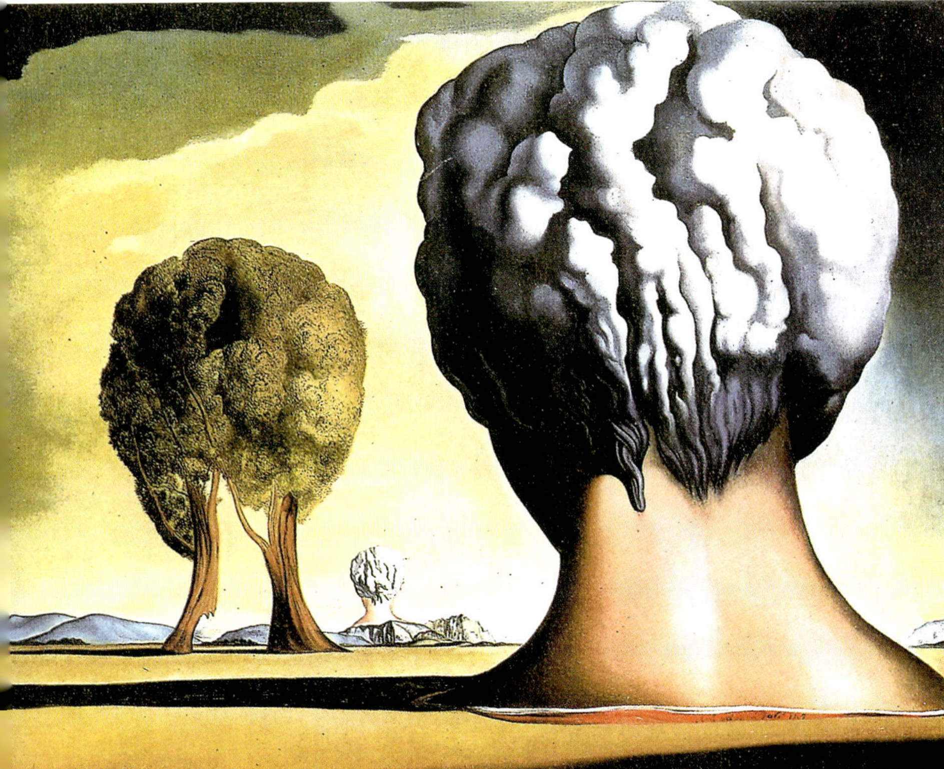

The Three Sphinxes of Bikini followed US atomic bomb experiments on Bikini Atoll in the Pacific.

Dream-Inspired Objects

Dalí created not only a large proportion of his most important pictures during the 1930s, but also some his best-known three-dimensional objects, which are also a profound a breach with conventional reality. Works such as his *Lobster Telephone* and *Retrospective Bust of a Woman* are akin to *objets trouvés*, ready-mades, or found objects, the first example of which was Marcel Duchamp's bicycle wheel mounted on a chair (1913). Dalí's *Aphrodisiac Jacket* was later described by its inventor as one of the most glorious forerunners of later Pop Art objects—a dinner jacket equipped with glasses containing a liqueur with undefined aphrodisiac effects. In 1937, Elsa Schiaparelli turned his ideas for Surrealist objects into Parisian *haute couture*, designing, among other things, a suit with pop-out drawers. Dalí himself made a perfume bottle for her in the shape of a golden shell, a shoe hat, and various fabrics and garments. The following years were filled with a variety of activities. He designed Surrealist shop window displays and a pavilion for the park at the World Fair, and did work for ballet, film, the media, advertising, and design.

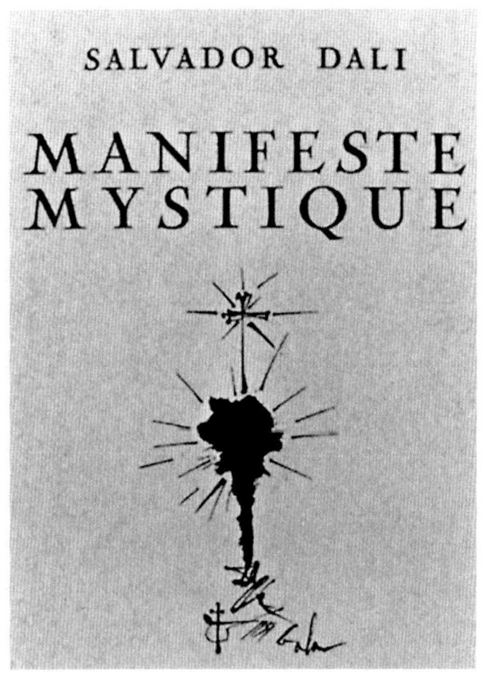

Cover page of the *Mystic Manifesto* (1951).

Change of Paradigms

Up to World War II, Dalí had chiefly been interested in psychology. His interest thereafter turned to science, with Albert Einstein joining Freud as one of his all-time heroes.

After atomic bombs were detonated in New Mexico, and then over Hiroshima and Nagasaki, Dalí embarked on an "atomic" or "nuclear" phase, resulting in works such as the *Melancholy, Atomic, Uranium Idyll* and *Three Sphinxes of Bikini*. "The atomic explosion on 6 August 1945 shook me seismographically. From then on, the atom was my favorite subject. Many of the landscapes I painted in this period express the great fear triggered off in me by the announcement of that explosion." He was still using atomic physics as a model in later paintings. *Galatea of the Spheres* of 1952 is one of the paintings that testify to his interest in the modern physics—Gala's head is dismembered into numerous particles.

In his *Mystic Manifesto* of 1951, Dalí proclaimed his return to the Catholic Church and his new belief in mysticism. For his painting, this meant subject matter from Christian tradition and its iconography, themes to do with birth and death, and also themes relating to Greek mythology and classical literature. Associated with the new respect for tradition was the application in his paintings of design principles such as the golden mean and symmetry, as well as the use of the expressive gestures of Mannerism. Only in his watercolors, lithographs, and etchings did he continue to allow himself absolute freedom.

Dalí's *Madonna of Port Lligat* was among the first of his "religious" works. Dalí claimed the painting was a "compendium" of his development as an artist, and also a foretaste of his new classical style of painting. Inspired by the models of atomic physics, and by the new conception of matter as a dynamic relationship of forces, he has all the elements in the picture "floating" in apparent

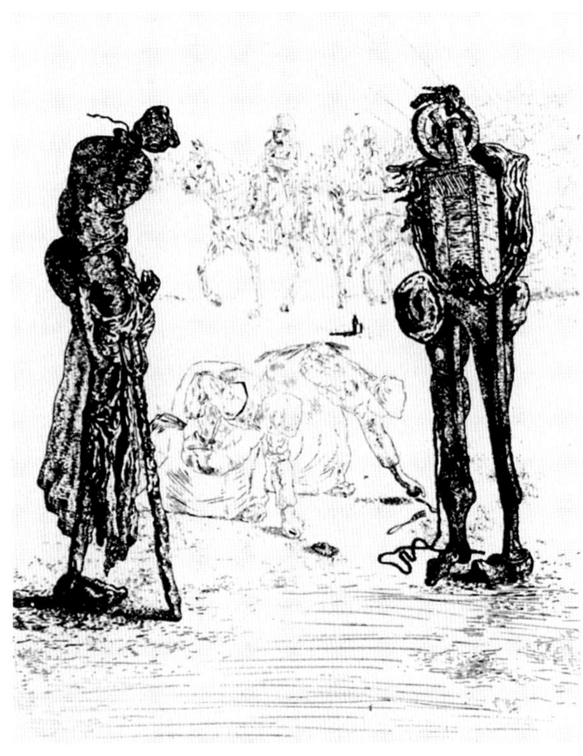

Dalí did illustrations for Lautréamont's prose poem *The Songs of Maldoror* (1869) for Geneva-based publisher Albert Skira.

weightlessness. He presented the first version of the Madonna to Pope Pius VII during a private audience. He painted a second, larger version (3.6 x 2.4 meters/ 12 x 8 feet) one year later, in 1950. The Madonna picture was inspired by a Piero della Francesca *Madonna and Child*. The unusual architectural elements are likewise Renaissance-inspired, though broken into geometrical shapes.

The picture was one of the series of conspicuously large-format works Dalí now embarked on. He took on an assistant for the purpose, in the best tradition of old masters, and for the next thirty years the set painter Isidor Bea helped him prepare and execute his pictures.

Inspiration and Experiment

Dalí illustrated a great number of literary works. An early example dates from 1934, when he did forty etchings for Lautréamont's *Songs of Maldoror*. The work was published by distinguished Swiss art publisher Albert Skira, for whom Picasso and Matisse also did illustrations. A commission from the Italian government for the 500th anniversary of Dante's birth kept Dalí busy for almost ten years: his watercolors for the *Divine Comedy* now rank among the most important works of illustration in the 20th century.

Dalí was also very inventive in the field of printed graphics. He treated lithographic plates with rhinoceros

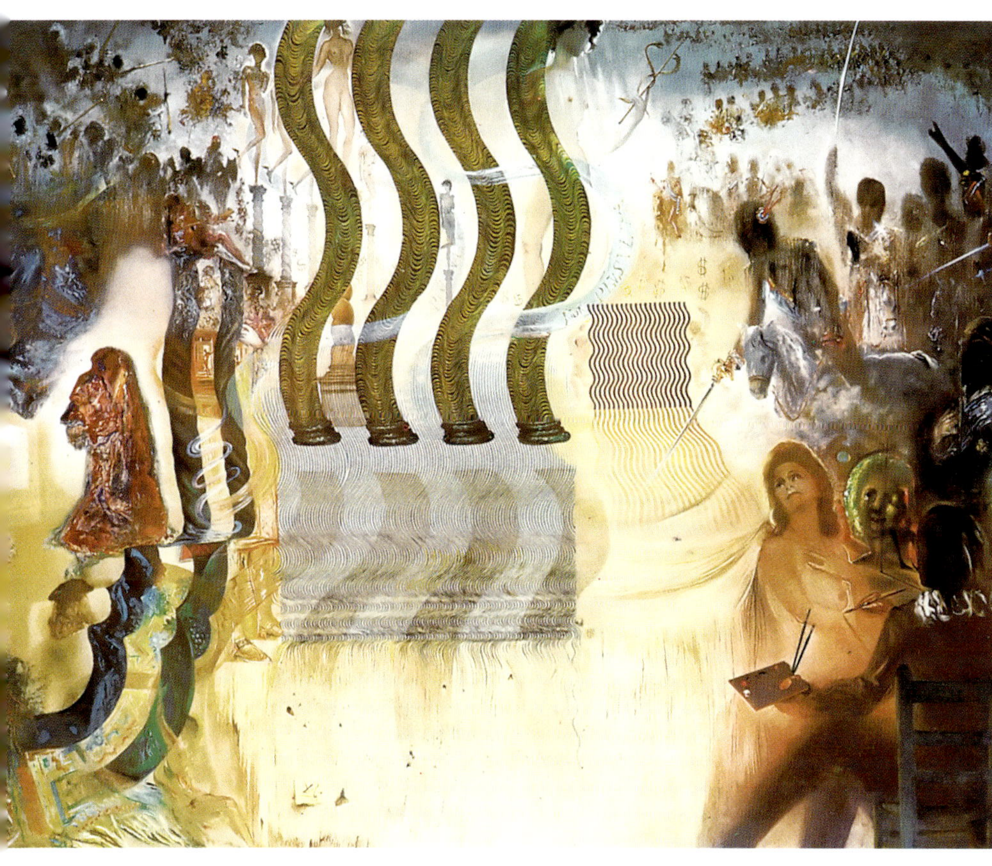

A late work by Dalí:
The Apotheosis of the Dollar
(1965)

horns or peppered them with a shotgun. On such occasions he organized public happenings that made excellent public relations: "The great event took place on a pontoon bridge over the Seine on 26 November 1956, where, surrounded by 100 sheep, I fired lead bullets dipped in lithographic ink at the plate, thereby generating wonderful splashes. I recognized immediately an angel's wing full of dynamism, constituting the peak of perfection." He was wonderfully pleased with the idea of a specially designed bomb: the prints would achieve wonderful results.

Dalí's Pop Art

Dalí experimented with latest laser techniques in the 1960s in a quest for three- and four-dimensional art. The result was what he himself called "Dalí's Pop Art," inspired by the contemporary movement in the United States. The grandiose painting *The Battle of Tetuán* was among them: he said it was the greatest piece of kitsch he had ever produced. The style was 19th-century history painting, in this case the unfinished battle scene by Catalan painter Mariano Fortuny. Kitsch or not, the work was bought by millionaire Huntingdon Hartford for his Gallery of Modern Art in New York, which in 1965 organized a huge Dalí exhibition of 200 paintings and drawings, plus printed graphics, sculptures, and objects. And that was only one show among many, for the artist had major retrospectives in Europe and America. Dalí's fame was now truly international.

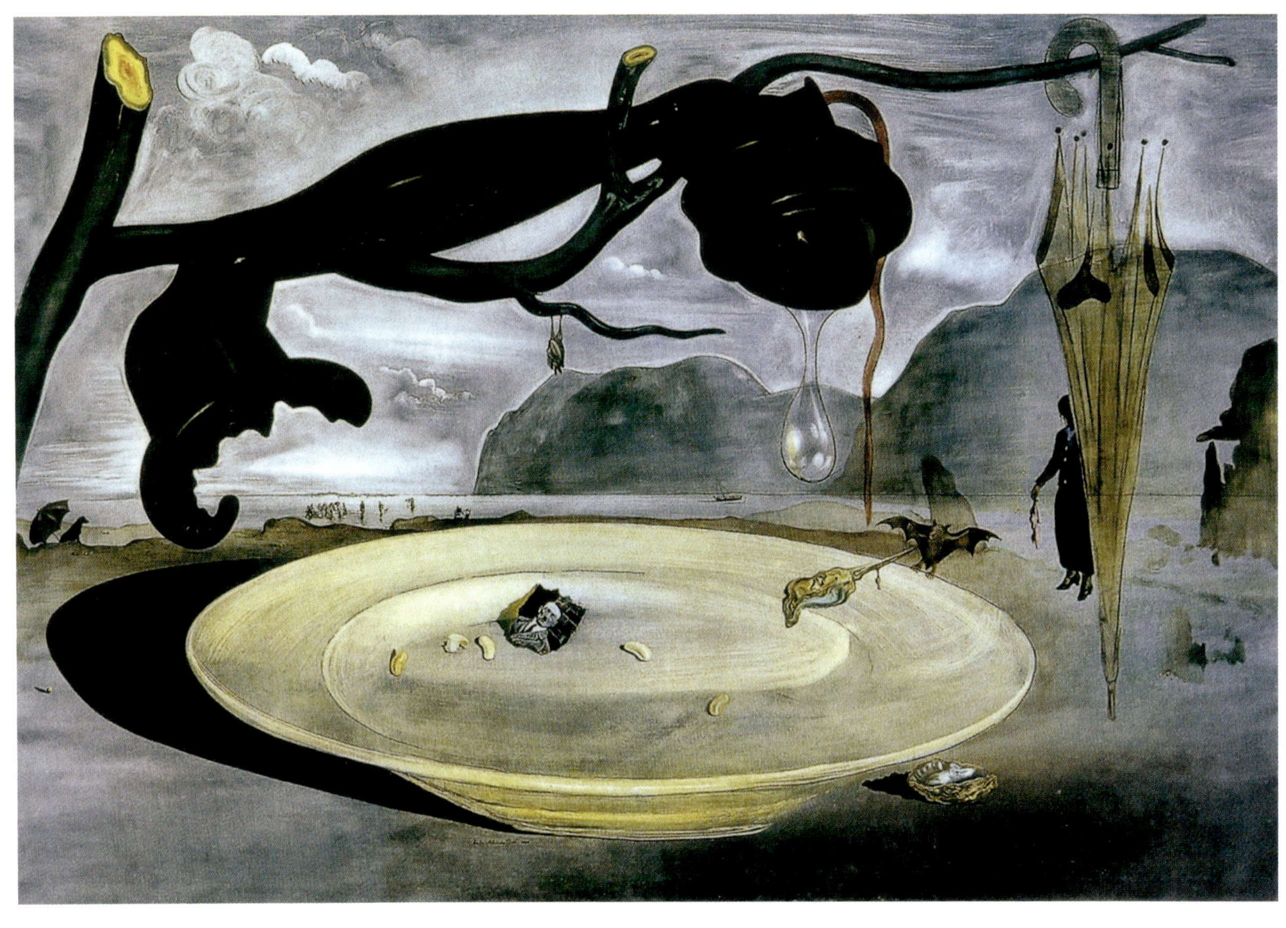

Faulty connection The motif of the telephone receiver in *The Enigma of Hitler* refers to the negotiations between Chamberlain and Hitler. The Second World War broke out shortly after this picture was painted, which prompted Dalí in hindsight to interpret his picture as prophetic. The Surrealists considered Dalí's interest in Hitler as proof of his political sympathies with the dictator.

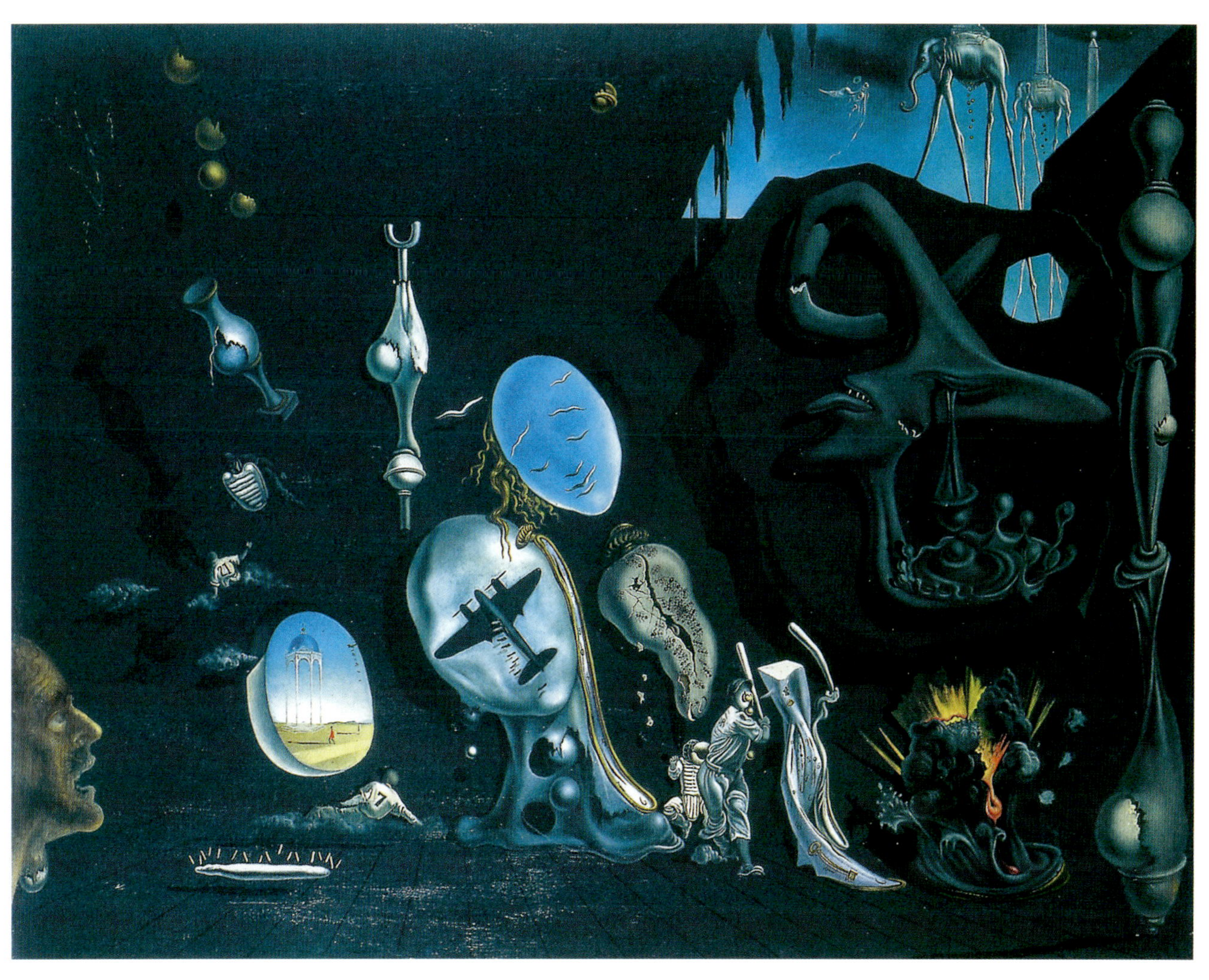

Explosive The first atom bomb (called Little Boy) was dropped on Hiroshima on 6th August 1945. Dalí's painting *Melancholy, Atomic, Uranic Idyll* was painted immediately afterwards. It marked a new phase in his output that he called "nuclear" or "atomic" painting.

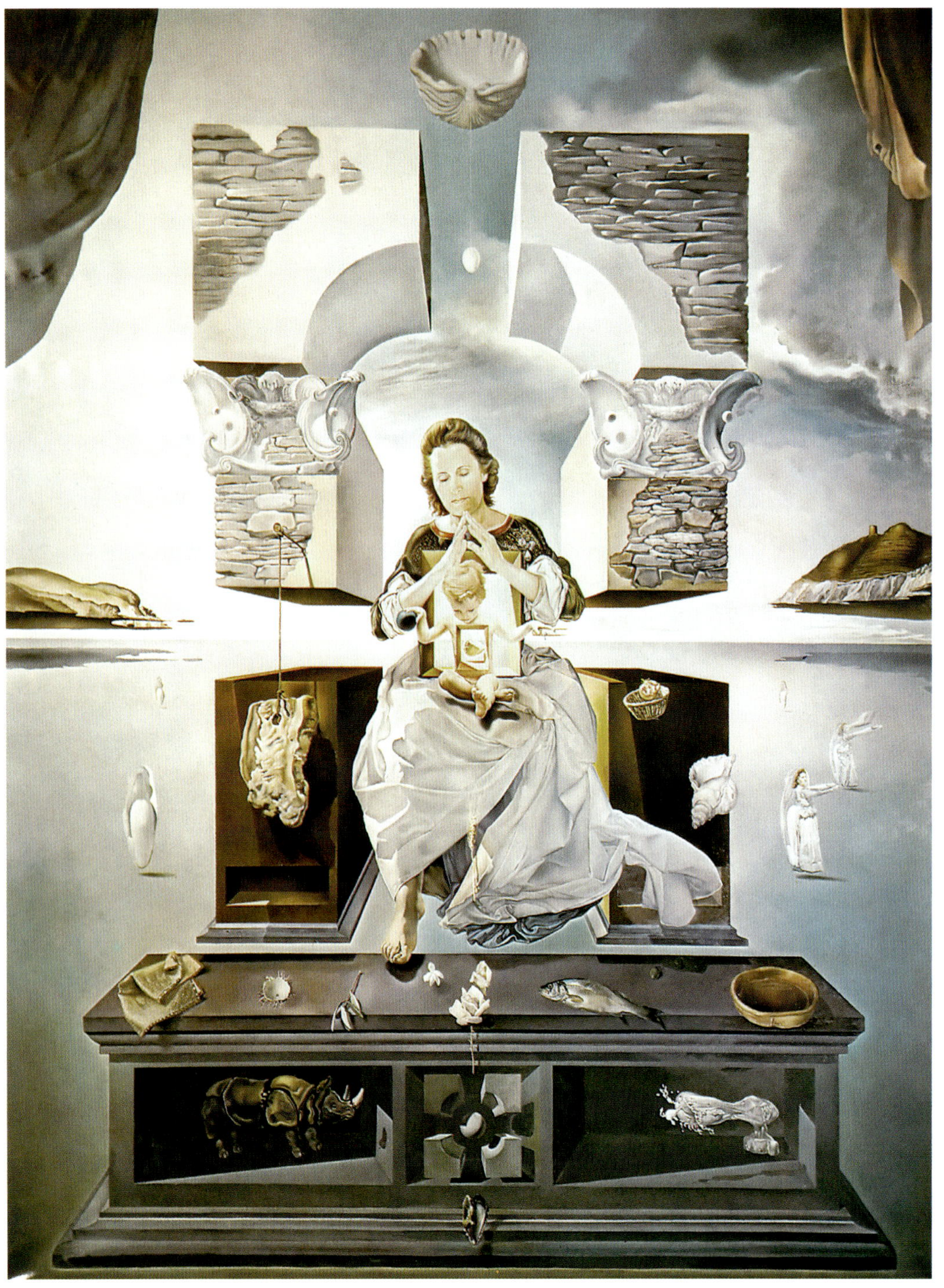

The artist as a mystic In the 1950s, Dalí took a new shine to the Italian Renaissance and painted religious works such as *The Madonna of Port Lligat*. Two versions from 1949 and 1950 (this picture) show Gala as a model for the Mother of God. Dalí presented the first version of the painting to Pope Pius XII during an audience in November 1949.

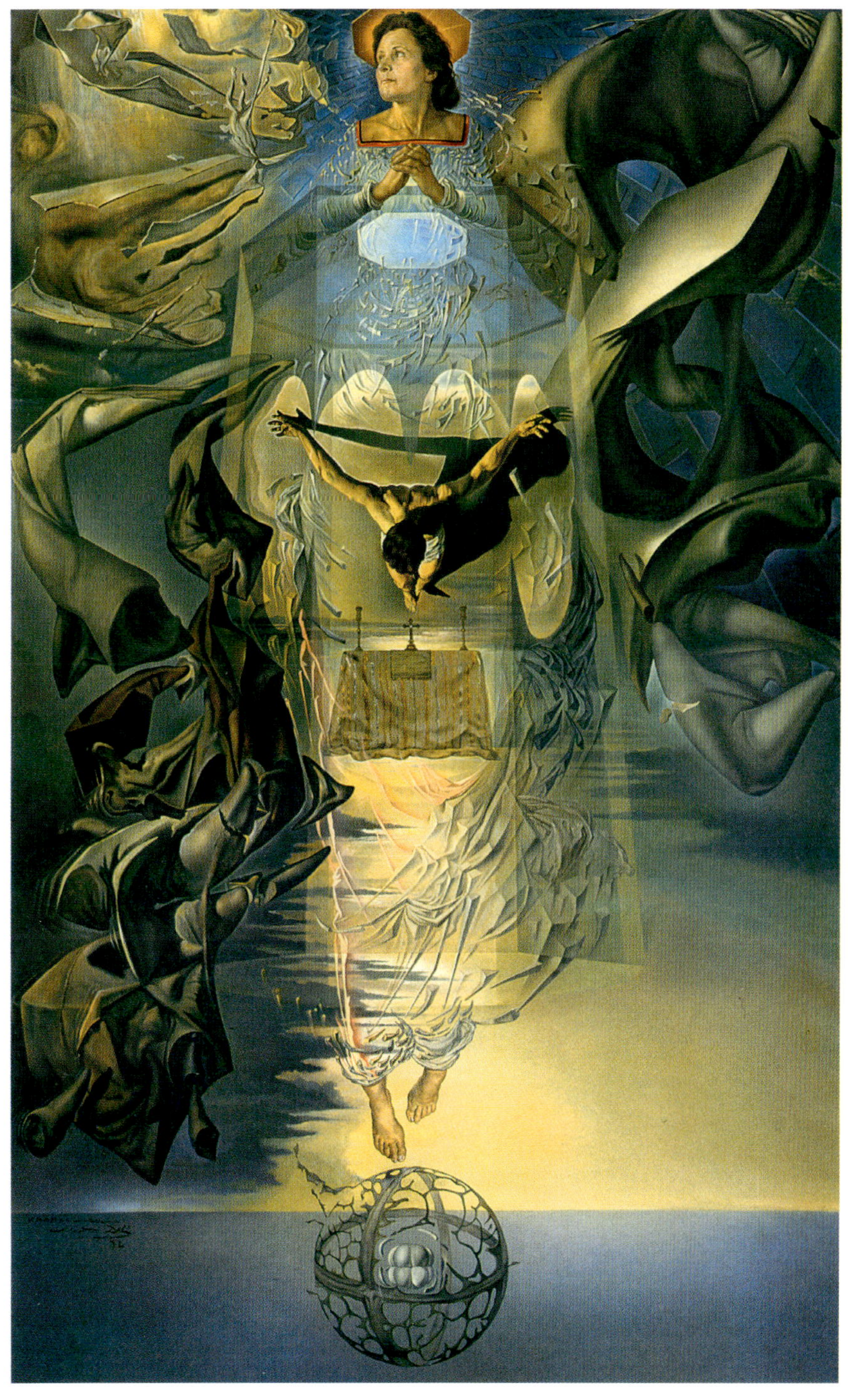

Exaggeration "If Nietzsche's *übermensch* is not perfect, there is a Nietzschean *überfrau* in the resurrection of the Virgin. She ascends to heaven, borne aloft by angels of anti-matter." Thus spoke Dalí about his painting *Assumpta Corpuscularia Lapislazulina* of 1952.

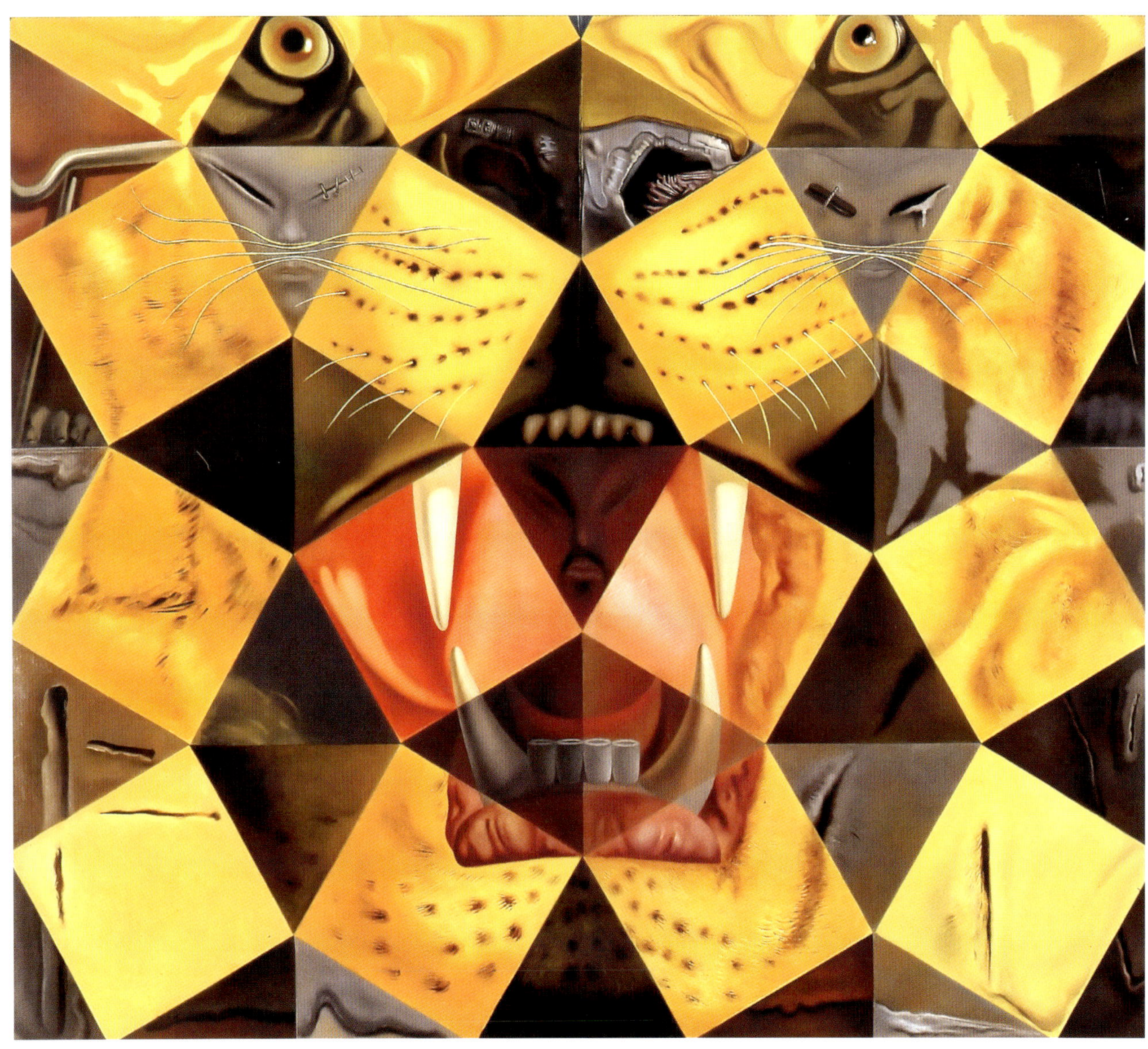

Abstraction and Subject Matter *Fifty Abstract Paintings Which as Seen from Two Yards Change into Three Lenins Masquerading as Chinese and as Seen from Six Yards Appear as the Head of a Royal Bengal Tiger*, 1963—a year in which Dalí attempted to attract attention with his self-titled *Dalí's Pop Art*.

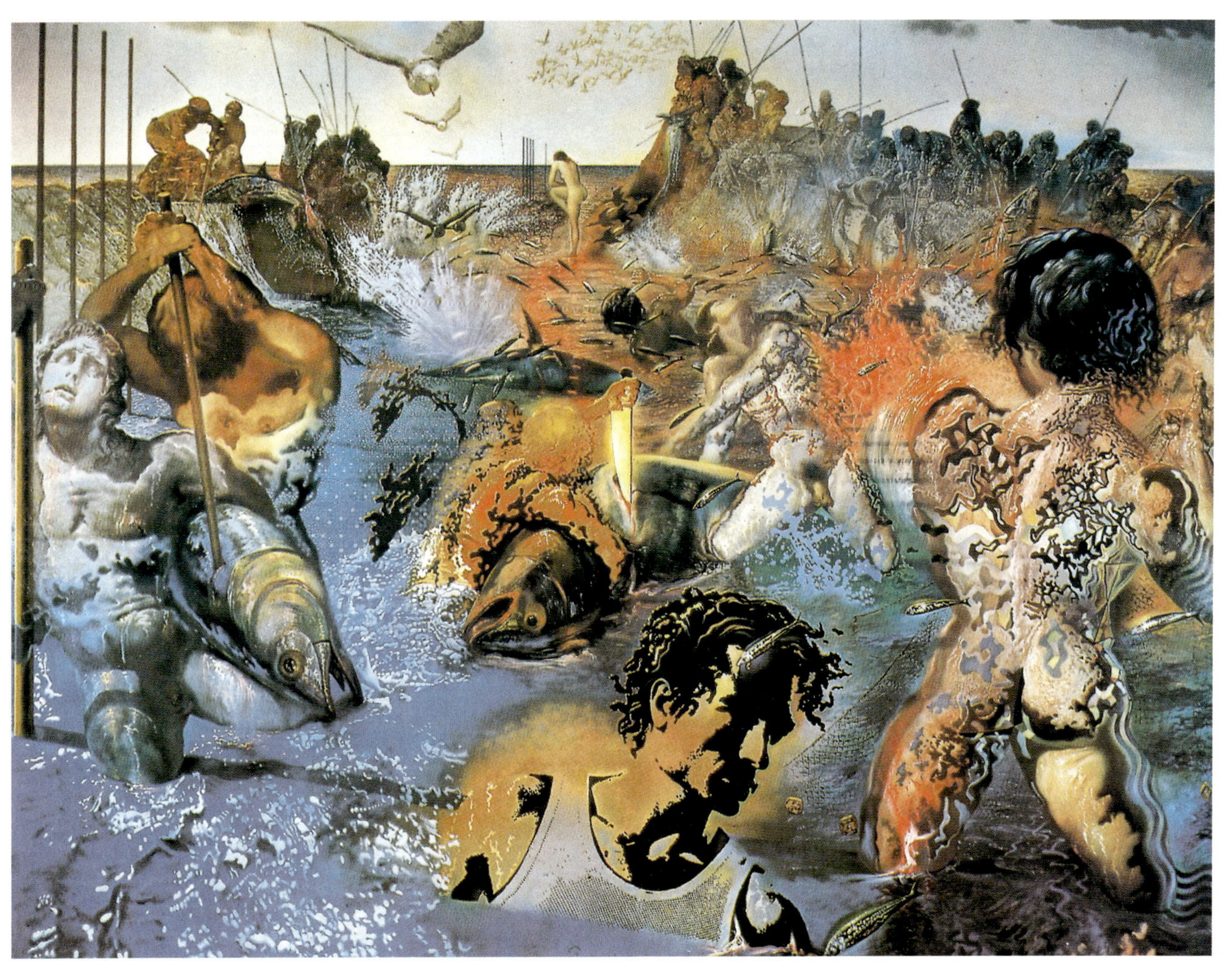

304 x 404 cm Dalí worked on his painting of *Tuna Fishing*, which is overwhelming even in its dimensions, for two whole summers (1966 and 1967). It is "the result of all his painting studies and experiments, a cosmological explosion, evolved from the original chaos of pure, liberated energy." (Robert Descharnes)

Life

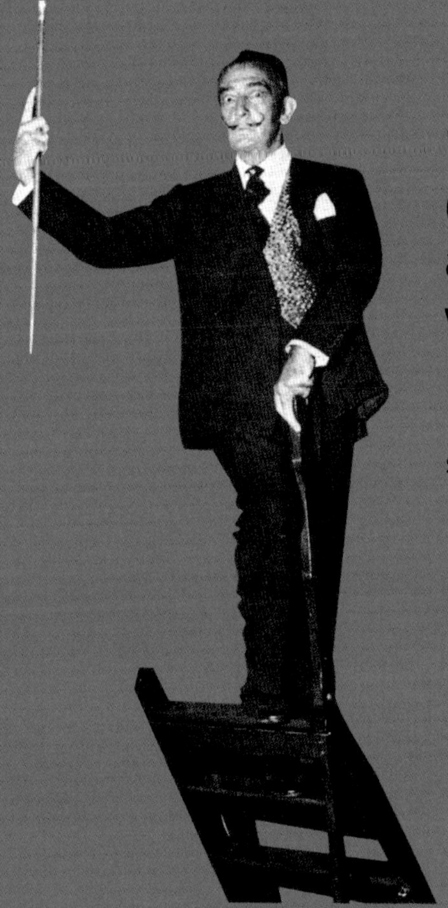

“I’m a polymorphous, dyed-in-the-wool, and anarchistic weirdo.”

Salvador Dalí

A Very Public Secret Life

What was the real Dalí like? The man painting provocative pictures, the man behind the mask forever acting out the "Great Paranoiac" with such huge success? It's worth taking glance behind the scenes of a life that began in 1904 and lasted most of the century.

A Name to Conjure With

Salvador Felipe Jacinto Dalí y Domènech (his full name) was born in 1904 as the second son of Don Salvador Dalí y Cusí and Felipa Domènech. The eldest son, Salvador Galo Anselmo, who was born on 12 October 1901, had died twenty-one months later of an "infection of the stomach and intestines," as the death certificate notes. A mere nine months and ten days later the "real" Salvador was born. The re-use of the first name as a sign of family attachment was not without profound consequences: Dalí henceforth always nourished the feeling of being just a replacement for his deceased brother. He accused his parents of a "subconscious crime." It's a story that he deployed for the rest of his life as a justification for his eccentric behavior.

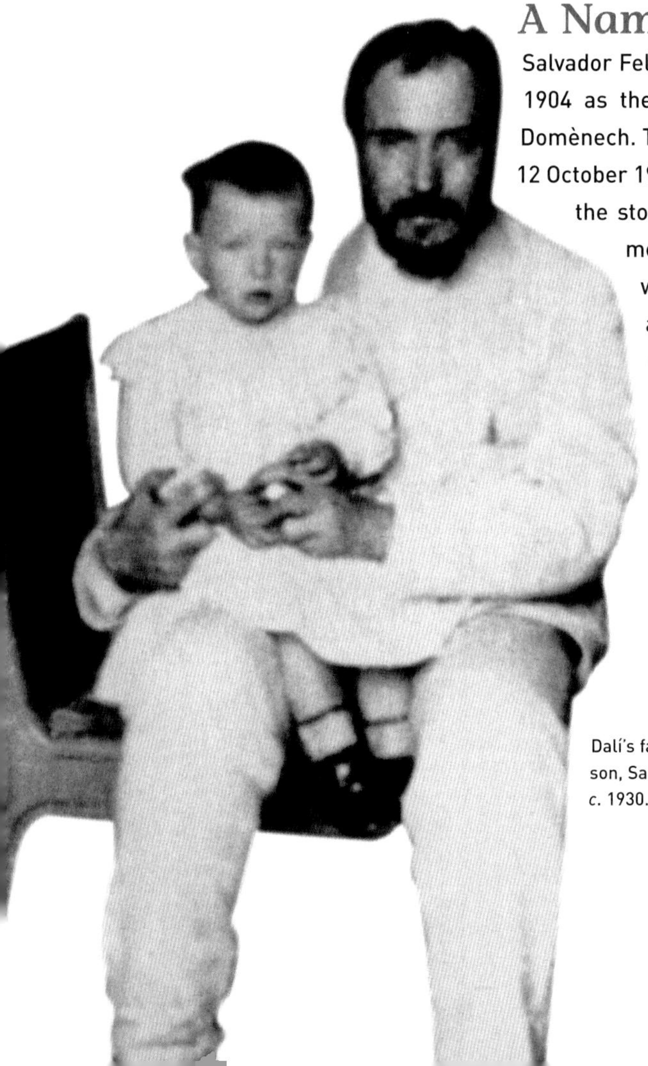

Dalí's father with his firstborn son, Salvador Galo Anselmo, *c.* 1930.

"An honest attempt at a self-portrait"

> **"I've never seen such a perfect example of a Spaniard. What a fanatic."**
>
> **Sigmund Freud**

When in exile in Virginia, Dalí wrote a 400-page autobiography he called *The Secret Life of Salvador Dalí*, in which he describes his childhood, his study years in Madrid, and the early years of fame up to the time of his departure to the United States in 1940. His memoirs are highly entertaining and amusing; but one thing they are decidedly not is a reliable account of what actually happened in the first thirty-eight years of his life. Facts are mixed with untrue claims and plain fantasy, and many of the childhood experiences dovetail all too incredibly with his later career. Meantime, Dalí claims emphatically that, of course, he is accurate and sincere in every detail. So what's it all about? The book is in fact a bold and highly original image of Dalí as he wanted to be seen by posterity—a skilful piece of public relations in the relentless creation of the Dalí legend.

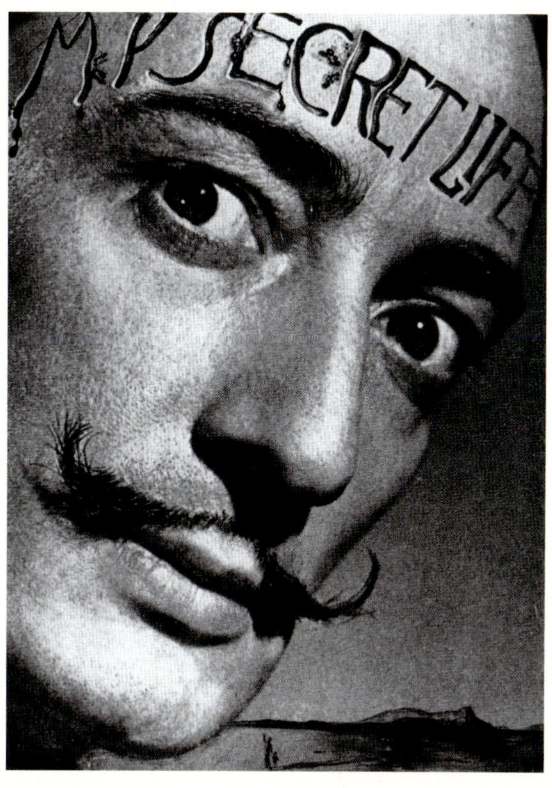

Father and Son

According to Dalí, father and son were continually in dispute, and in 1929 there was a severe breach. His father read in a Barcelona newspaper an article about Dalí's *The Sacred Heart* containing a quotation by Dalí, in French, that sounds like willful provocation: "Sometimes I spit at the portrait of my mother just for fun." This vituperative remark was no doubt intended as Dalí's passport to the Surrealist group, but his father took it as an appalling insult to his deceased wife. Without further ado, he threw his son out of the house and informed him by letter of his "irrevocable banishment from the family home."

Dalí's painting *The Sacred Heart*, with the inscription "Sometimes I enjoying spitting at the portrait of my mother."

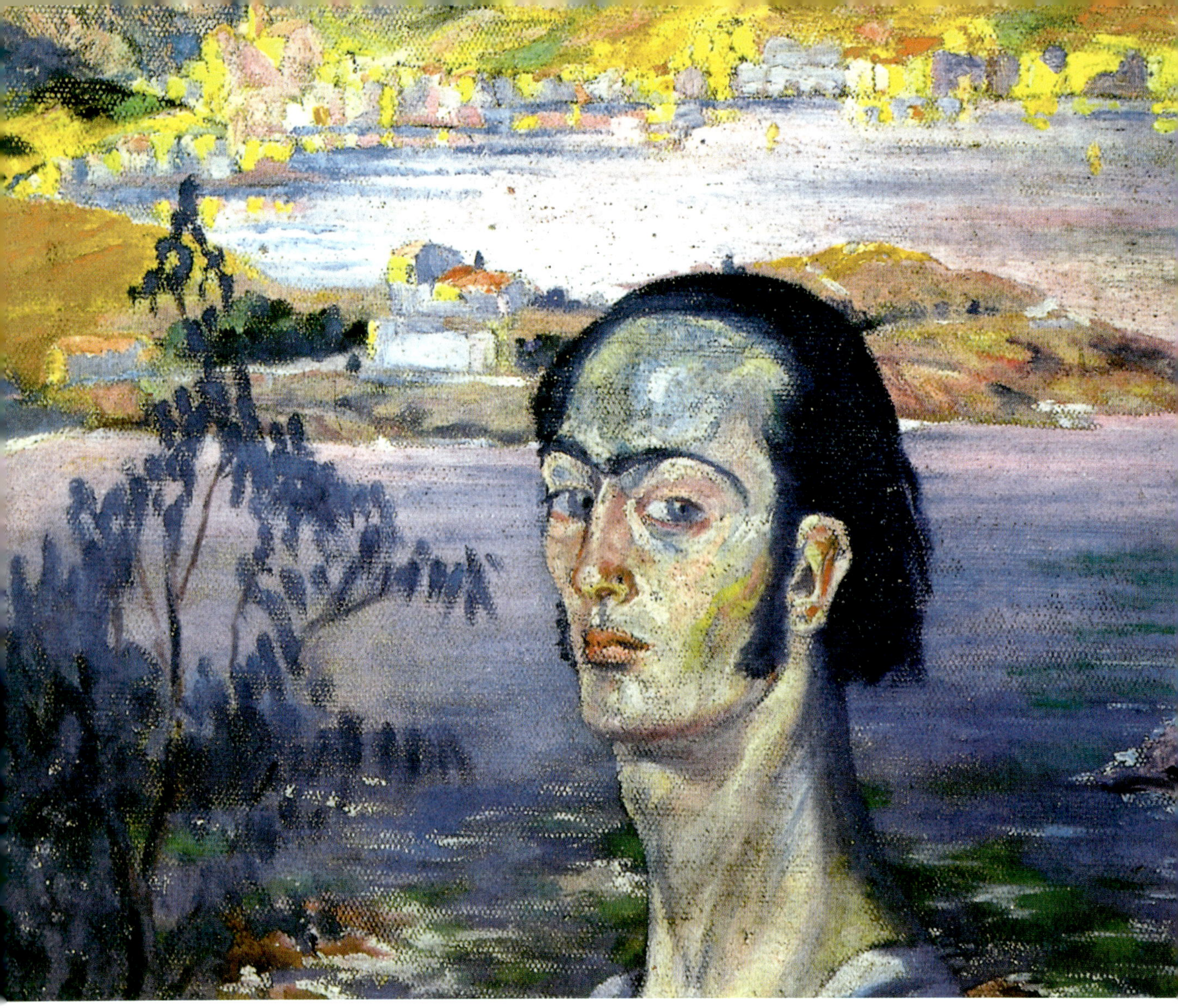

The *Self-Portrait with Raphaelesque Neck* dates from shortly before Dalí became a student in Madrid. The curved neck à la Raphael is combined with attributes of masculinity. The long sideburns earned him the nickname "Señor Pastillas" among his fellow Spaniards.

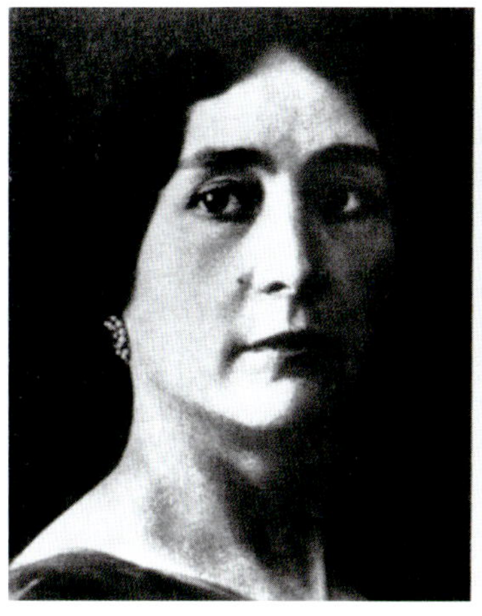

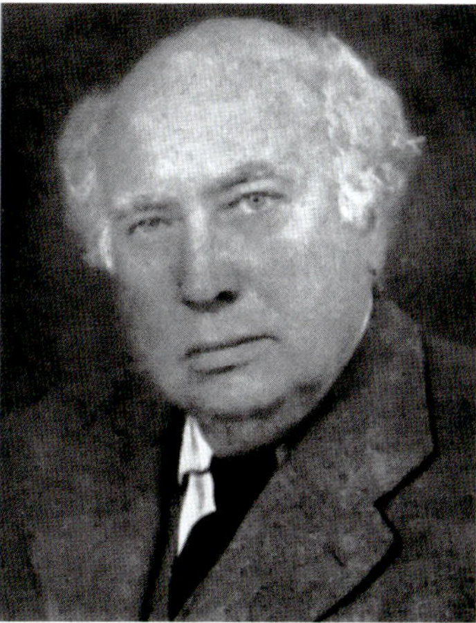

Dalí's parents, Don Salvador y Cusí and Felipa Domènech y Ferrés.

Becoming a Genius

Eccentric, narcissistic, and always striving after the maximum possible effect: that's the Dalí we are familiar with. But let's look back at his early days, his childhood and youth in Catalonia, where much that would distinguish his later character had its origins. Let's follow his years of study in Madrid, the years of fame in Paris and New York, and finally a life that he spent largely in his homeland, with Gala always at his side.

Childhood and Youth

Born in Figueres, Catalonia, on 11 May 1904, Salvador Dalí grew up in the sheltered circumstances of a middle-class family. Photos from his childhood testify to an idyllic, harmonious family life. His father, Don Salvador Dalí y Cusí, was a lawyer and public notary in Figueres, and despite his well-known irascible temperament was a highly regarded figure in

"All the eccentricity, which I assert is ordinary, the incoherent exhibitionism, is nothing but the constant tragedy of my life."

Salvador Dalí

His deceased brother would haunt him all his life. The *Portrait of My Dead Brother* (1963) is therefore suitably spooky.

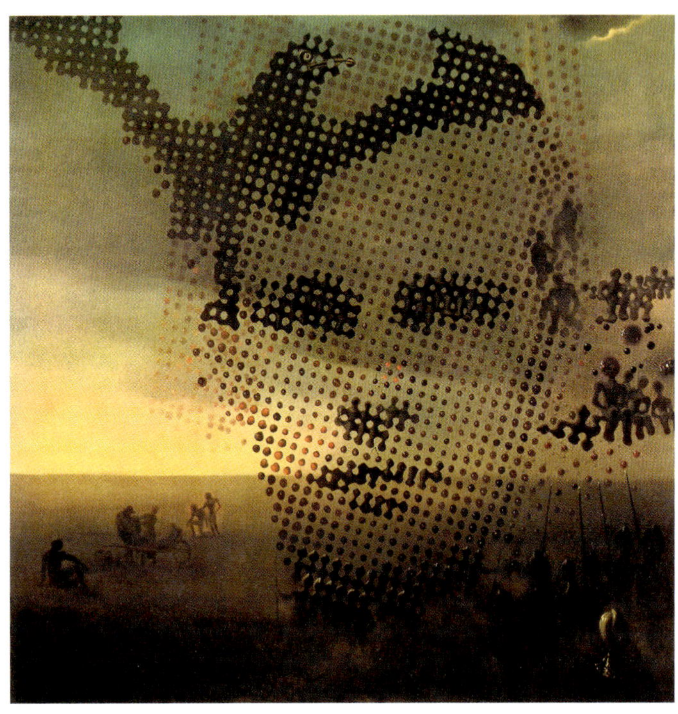

the town. His mother, Felipa Domènech, was always particularly concerned for her son, did everything he wanted, and often let him have his way. Retrospectively, Dalí described his relationship with his mother as extraordinarily affectionate: "What would you like, my love? What can I get you, my love?" were always the first questions little Salvador was awoken with every morning. Living with the family was his mother's sister (Salvador's *Tieta*), his grandmother, and (from 1908) a little sister, Anna Maria, who would become his first model.

Whereas young Salvador was assured of his mother's affections, the relationship with his father was very difficult. His father was "a giant in strength, intemperateness, authority and peremptory love," which made things hard all his life. Looking back at the days of his childhood, Dalí depicted in detail the identity trauma occasioned by the death of his brother, a death that was ever-present in Dalí family life. His father—to Dalí, a hard man of unyielding stubbornness—always made him feel that he could not forget his firstborn son: "When he looked at me, he saw my brother as well as me. ... My soul churned in pain and anger beneath this constantly probing. ... And for a long time I had a bleeding wound in my side that my unfeeling, insensitive father, heedless of my sighs, continually opened with his impossible love for a dead boy." Dalí's need to assert himself anywhere and everywhere sprang from this feeling.

When Dalí was four, his father sent him to school. "I spent ... my first school year together with the poorest children in the town, which was very important, I believe, for the development of my natural delusions of grandeur. I became increasingly accustomed to ... considering myself, the rich child, as something very precious." In his "memoirs," he describes a situation in which he unexpectedly became the center of attention and thereby experienced a "strange feeling" that demanded repetition. It was a first sign of his later insatiable need for being the center of attention.

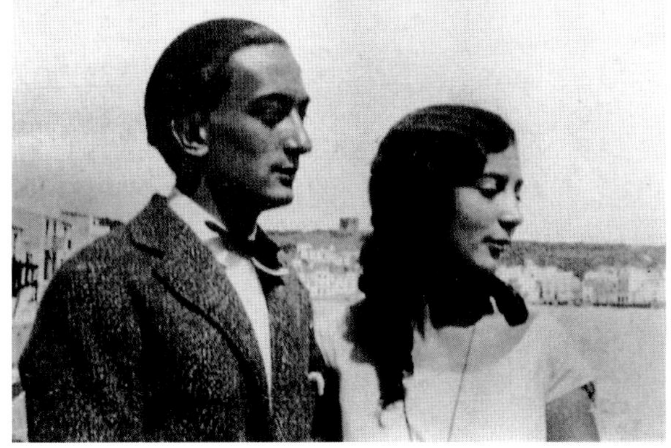

Dalí with his sister Anna Maria in Cadaqués, *c.* 1925.

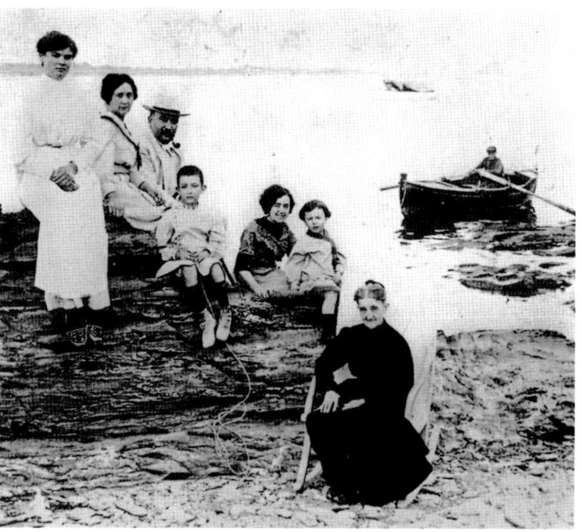

The Dalí family on the beach at Es Llanér, *c.* 1911. From left to right: Aunt Maria Teresa, the artist's mother and father, Salvador Dalí, the mother's sister, Salvador's sister Anna Maria, Grandmother Anna.

While he says that he tried to assert his specialness, he also describes himself as a dreamy and extremely shy child: "The slightest notice made me blush up to my ears. I spent the time hiding and being alone." During school lessons, he was unenthusiastic, apathetic, and absent-minded. He looked out of the window lost in his thoughts, or became absorbed in a reproduction of Millet's *Angelus* hanging in the corridor. Only one subject filled him with enthusiasm—drawing, where his boundless imagination was encouraged and he could translate his "visions" into reality.

A long-harbored desire was finally fulfilled by his parents when a small utility room in the attic became a studio, which Salvador could turn into his own little world. "Once I was in the attic, I noticed that I was unique again. ... The whole panorama towards the Badia de Roses seemed to respond to me and be dependent on my looking." We find here the first manifestations of the poseur. "I could talk ad infinitum about everything I went through in my laundry tub, but one thing is certain—the first pinches of the salt and pepper of my humor date back to there. I started testing and observing myself, accompanying genial twinklings of the eye with a slight, malicious smile, and vaguely and indistinctly I knew that I was playing the role of a genius. 'Oh, Salvador Dalí! You know now: if you play the genius, you'll become one.'"

A Student in Madrid

After leaving school—to prepare for the university career his father had mapped out for him, Dalí had been to state and private schools at the same time—his father agreed he could go on to the Royal Academy of Fine Arts in Madrid. A qualification from the most highly regarded art academy in the country offered the best prospects for a teaching post, and so his father could at least hope for a secure career for his son. In September, father and sister accompanied Salvador to Madrid, where he was to take the entrance exam. Anna Maria remembered the stir that her brother's appearance caused: shoulder-length hair and long sideburns, an ankle-

Dalí with shaven head, after being thrown out of the family home.

First-year students at the San Fernando art college, 1922/23. Dalí kneels in the middle of the picture, his head propped on his hands.

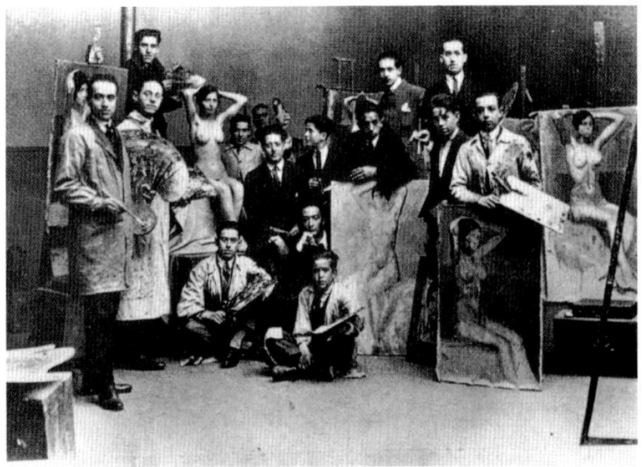

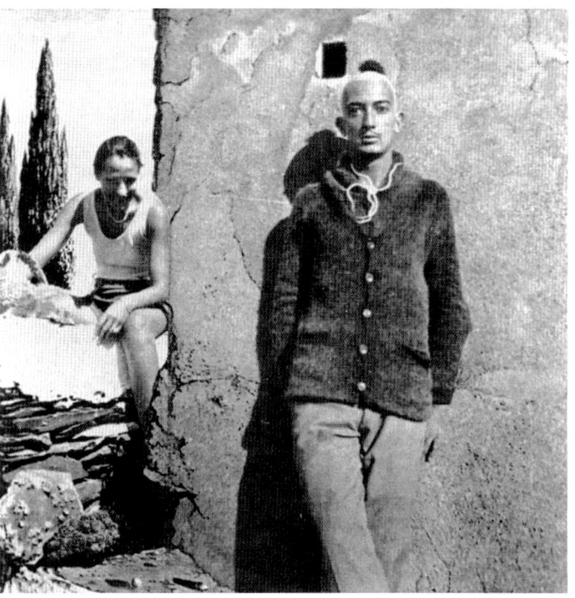

length cape, and a walking stick with a gilt knob. Although Dalí's drawing of a plaster cast of *Bacchus* by Jacopo Sansovino did not comply with the academy's specifications—it came out far too small—it was so perfectly done that he was allowed to enroll.

As a student in the faculty of painting, sculpture, and graphics, one of the teaching departments of the academy, Dalí worked industriously and in seclusion. During the week, he spent his time on subjects such as perspective, anatomy, the history of art, and sculptural drawing, while in the evenings he went back to his room and painted. He spent the weekends at the Prado, where he studied for himself and was within arm's reach of the artists he admired, notably Bosch, El Greco, and Goya. In society, the young Dalí remained insecure, and his fellow students were unanimous in describing him as "literally sick with shyness." The situation changed when he got to know Federico García Lorca, Luis Buñuel, and other members of the artistic and literary avant-garde in the Residencia de Estudiantes, the most liberal cultural center and student hostel at the time. Lorca, Dalí, and Buñuel represented three of Spain's most creative talents of the day, and they became firm friends. They collaborated closely in the fields of film, theater, and literature; Dalí, for example, designed the stage sets and costumes for Lorca's groundbreaking play *Mariana Pineda*. Dalí and Buñuel—a born rebel—meantime did the screenplay for two films. Like Lorca, Buñuel was sociable and belonged to several literary groups in the capital. The three young men enjoyed their student years to the full, and frittered away their parents' money in cafés and bars with limitless liberality. Lorca's personality in particularly made an "immense impression" on Dalí. They spent the summers with Dalí's family in Cadaqués, where the universally talented

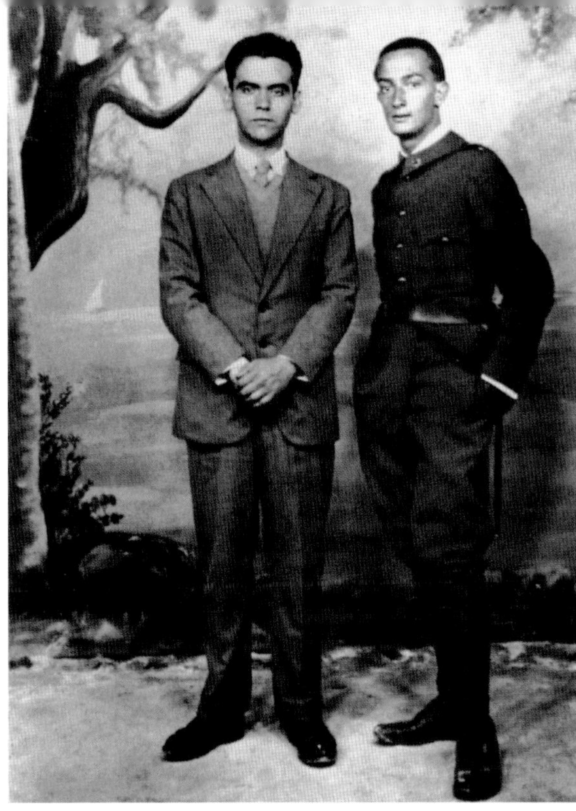

Dalí with his friend, writer García Lorca, during military service in 1928.

young Andalusian proved outstandingly good company, giving improvised poetry readings and piano concerts. He composed a 113-line *Ode to Salvador Dalí,* which was immediately recognized as a significant literary achievement:

"O Salvador Dalí, of the olive-colored voice! Not your imperfect youthful brush, not your paint, which revolves around the paint of your age, do I praise—I praise your longing for boundless eternity ... Yet above all I sing an outlook that we share, that unites us in the dark and in the golden hours. Not art is the light that blinds our eyes; first and foremost it is love, friendship—even fighting."

Lorca was homosexual, and, as Dalí wrote later, "madly in love with me. He twice made passes at me ... I was very cross because I wasn't homosexual and had no desire to comply. Anyway, it hurts. So it didn't work. But the prestige was enormously flattering. I felt deep down that he was a great writer and that I really owed him a little of the unmentionable hole of the Divine Dalí."

Dalí had already been suspended for a year for supposedly inciting up a protest against a professor at the academy, and in 1926 he was finally expelled. He was already admitted to the final examination when he deliberately provoked his exclusion by asserting, in front of the examination board, that "none of the professors of the academy of San Fernando are up to assessing me." A statement he made many years later came closer to the motivation for his refusal: "I wanted to have done with the School of Fine Arts and the dissipated life of Madrid once and for all. I wanted to be forced to escape all that and go home to Figueres and work for a year. Then I wanted to persuade my father that my studies should be continued in Paris."

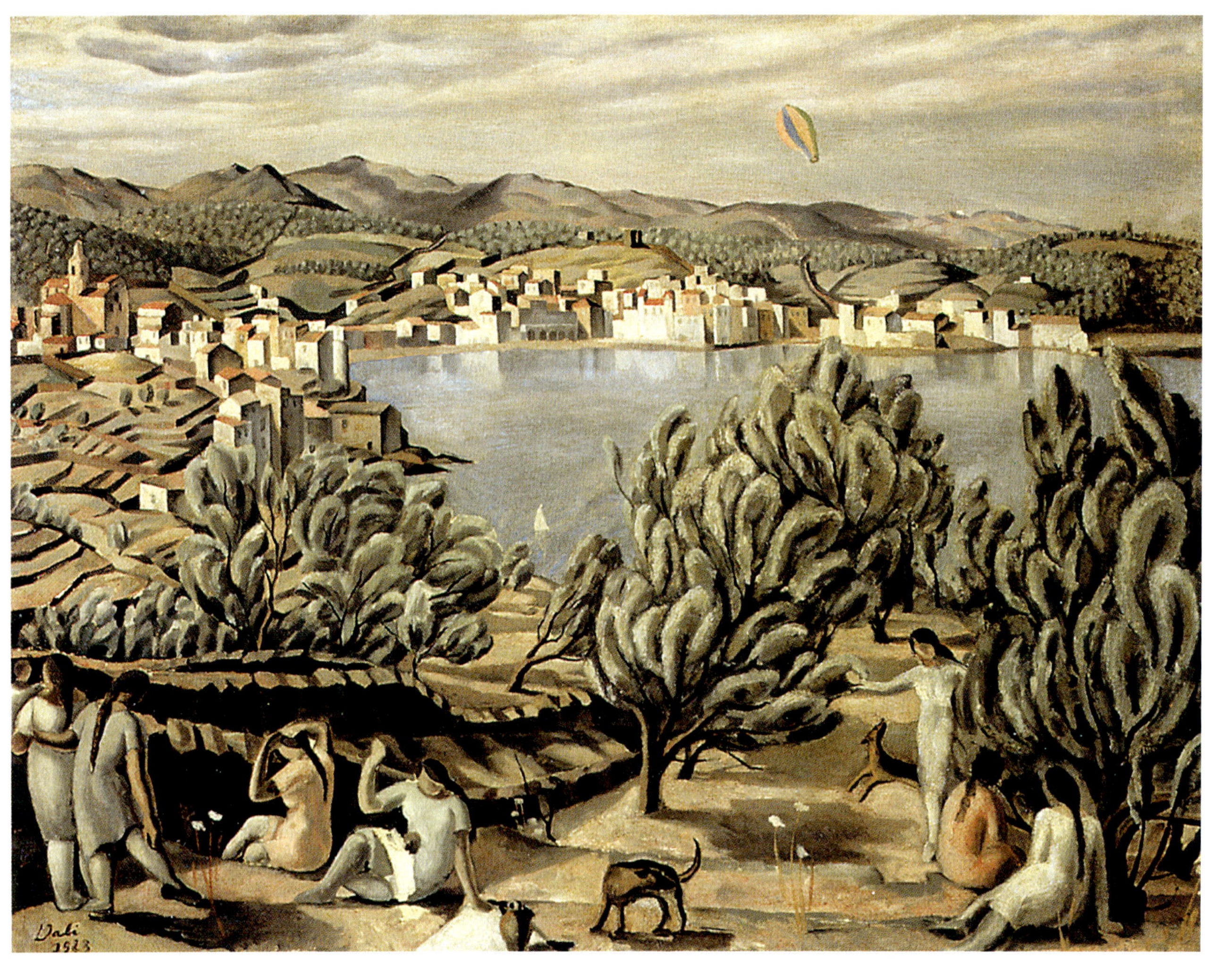

A peaceful world *Cadaqués* shows the fishing village on the Costa Brava in idyllic summer conditions. This was where his father came from and where Dalí spent his leisurely summers in the family holiday home. He painted a harmonious and peaceful picture with a calm sea and young girls enjoying themselves.

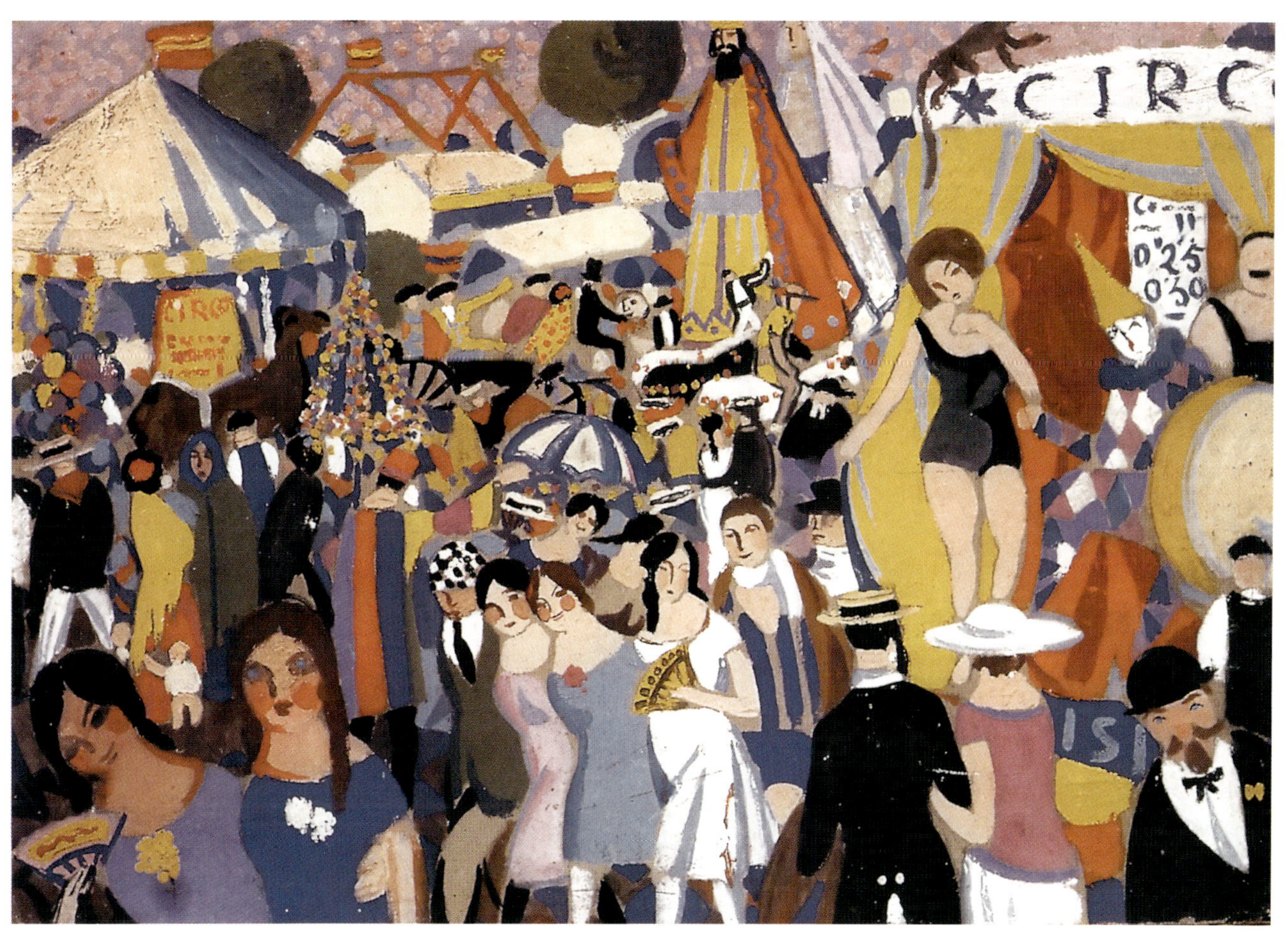

The magic of Figueres An important motif in Dalí's pictures is Figueres, where he first started painting and where his last "work" still stands today, the Teatre-Museu Dalí. Along with numerous landscape compositions, in the 1920s he also did scenes of popular festivals such as the Santa Cruz festival in Figueres.

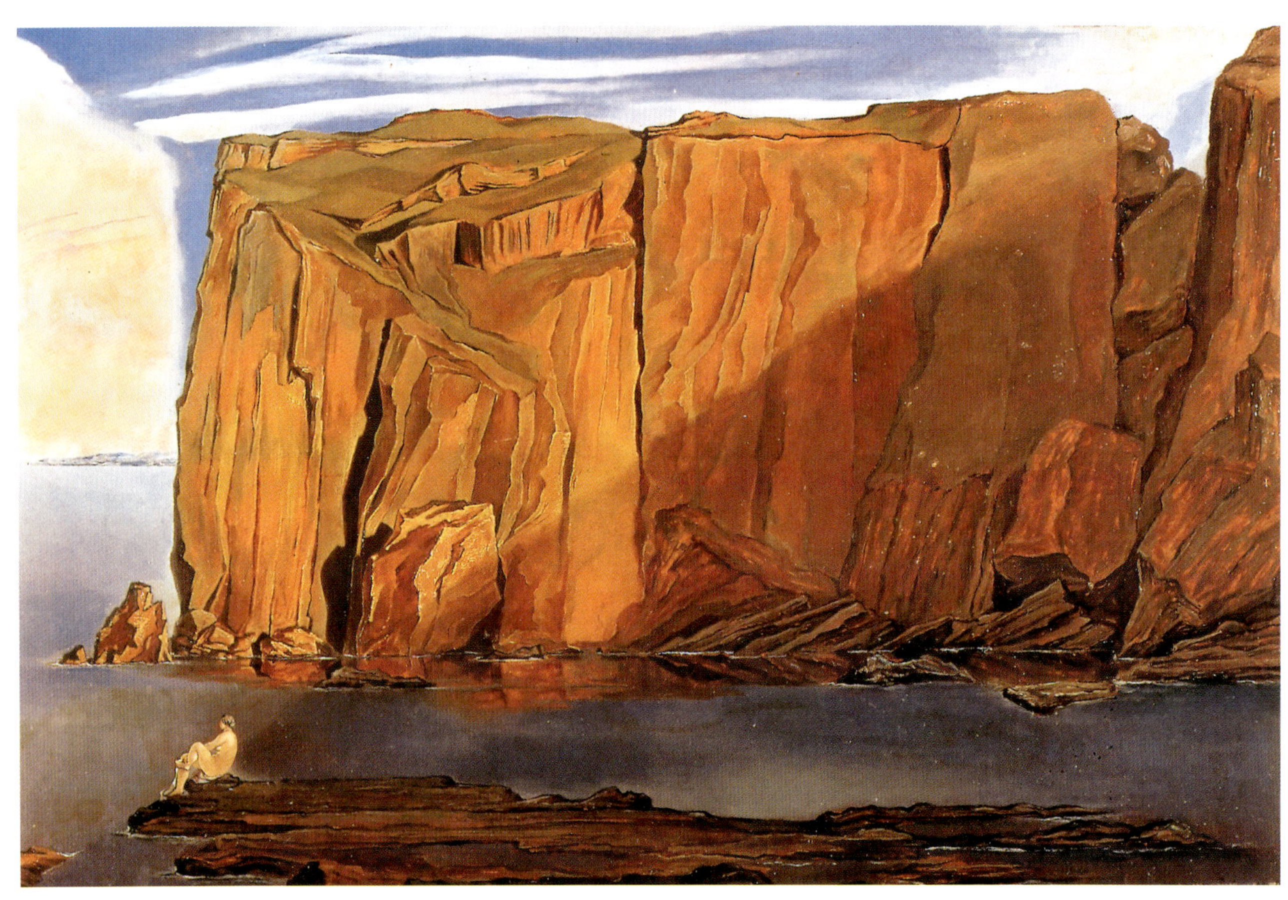

A bare landscape Countless pictures by Dalí record the bare landscape of his native region. The real-life counterpart of the imposing cliff in *Penya-Segats (Woman by the Cliffs)* is the "fissured rocks" (Penya-Segats) near Cadaqués.

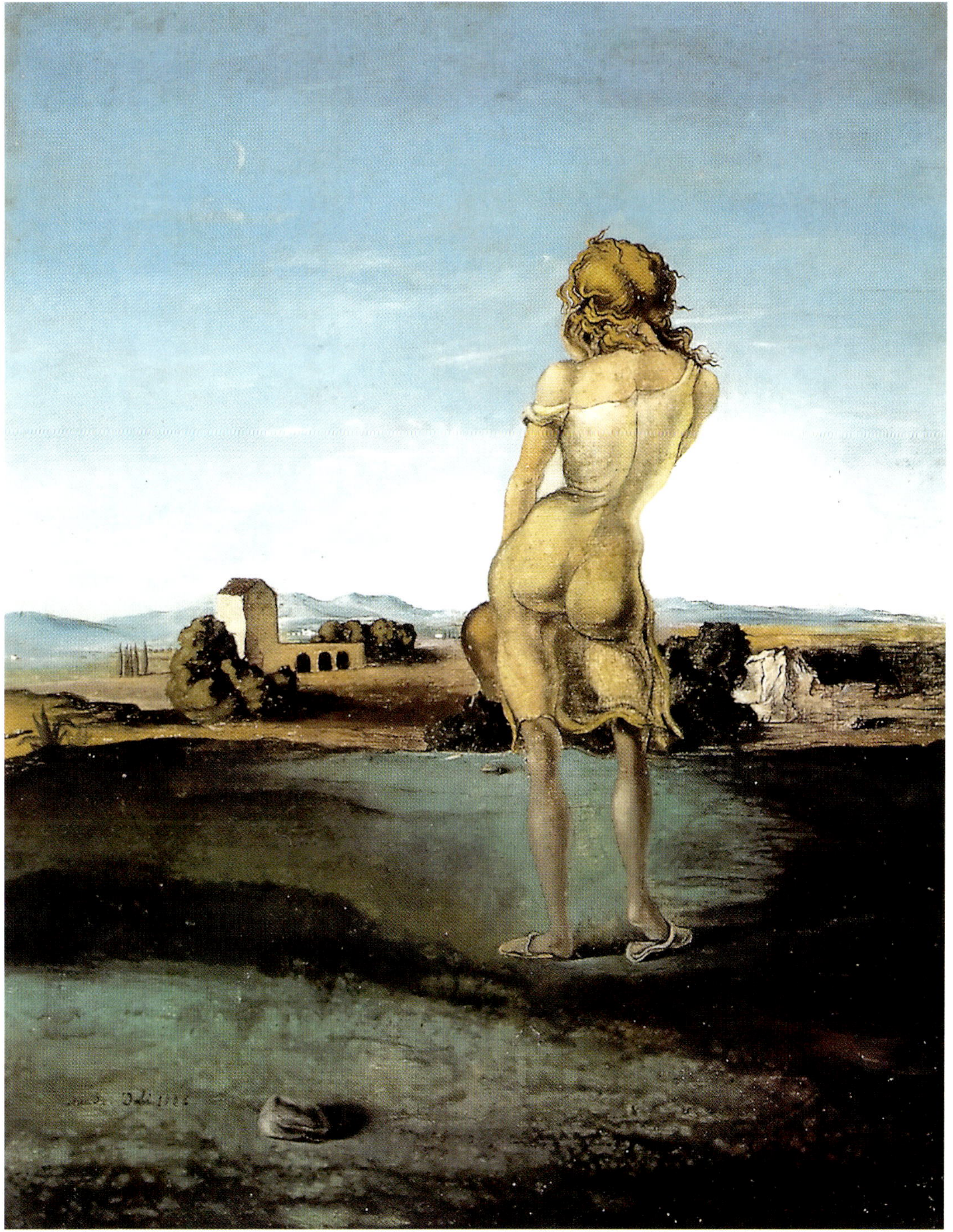

"As if I had an audience with the Pope" Dalí first went to Paris in 1927, visiting Picasso, whom he admired. He proudly reported: "I had brought a small picture with me, which I'd carefully packed – the *Girl from Ampurdán*. He looked at it for a quarter of an hour and made no comment at all."

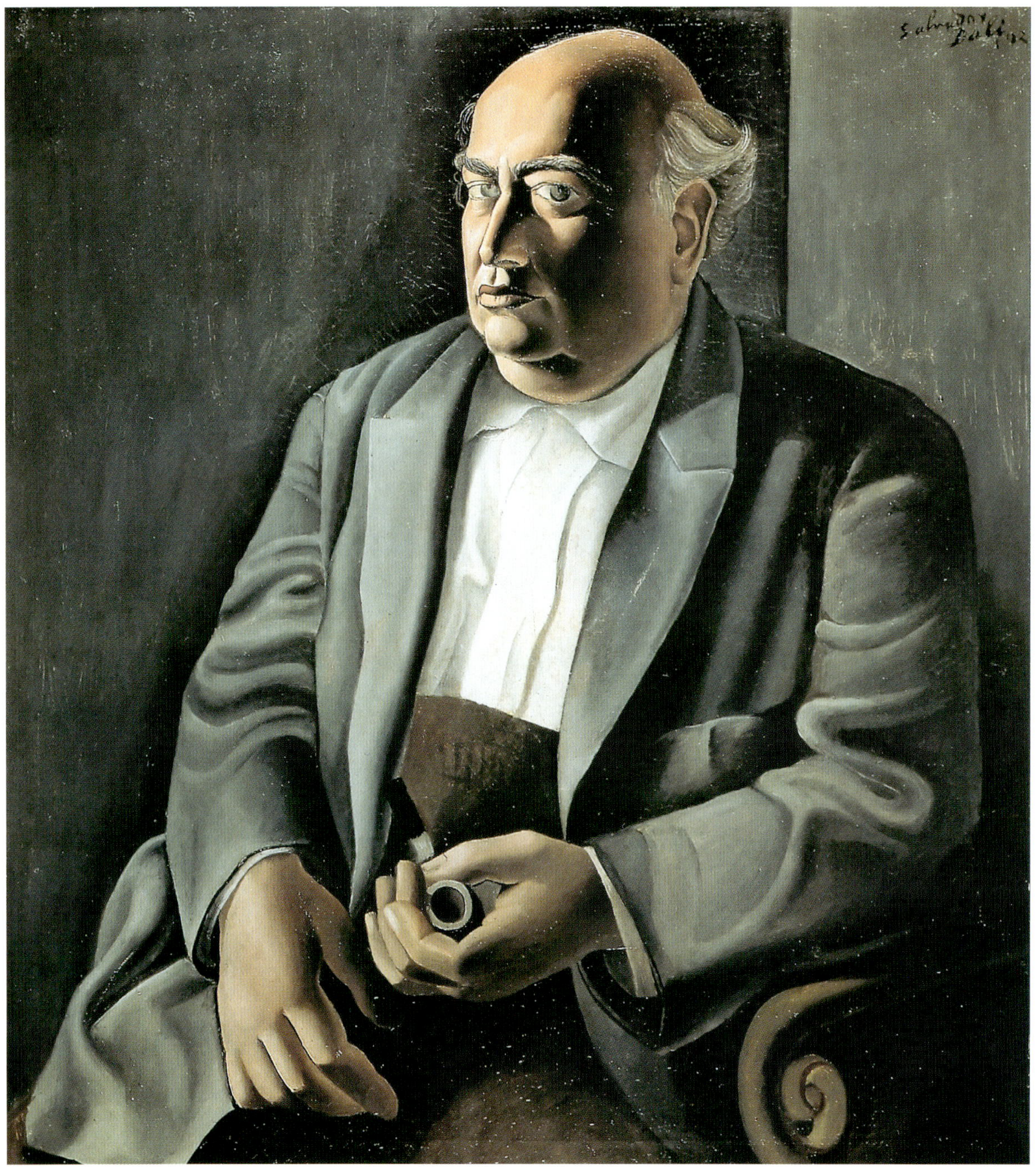

An austere father The *Portrait of My Father* was painted in 1924, when Dalí was asked to leave the academy for protesting against the appointment of a professor and for supposedly inciting disorder. "All his hopes that I would take up a career in the public sector were dashed ... in my father's facial expression is the pathetic bitterness that consumed him in those days," Dalí wrote about a preliminary drawing for this picture.

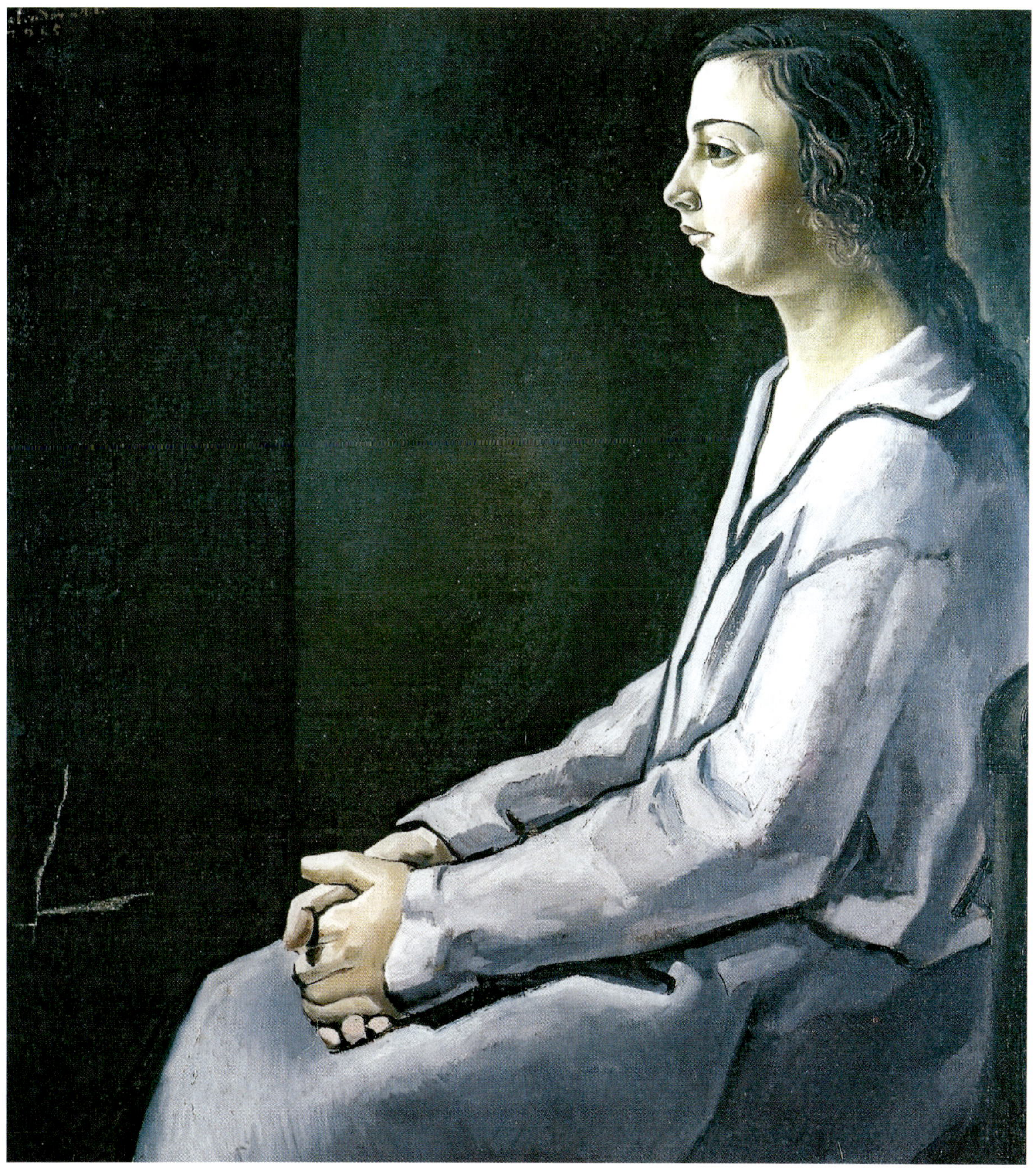

Anna Maria "The clothing in *Portrait of the Artist's Sister* is rendered with warmth and exuberance in equal measure that distinguishes it from the treatment predominant around the head, which is painted with cool severity. Could this be because, when he is not painting human figures, ... the artist casts off all constraints and allows his temperament free rein? ... Wouldn't this distinction be completely romantic?" *La Publicitat*, November 20, 1925

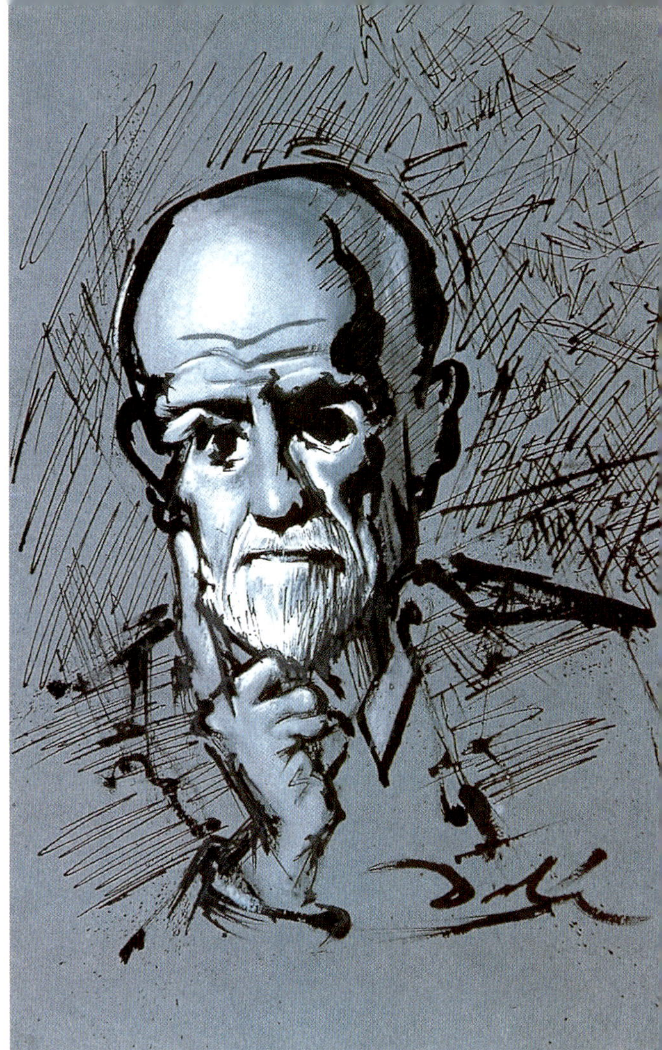

The *Portrait of Sigmund Freud* was done during a meeting with Freud in 1938.

A Fateful Year

But for the time being, Dalí was obliged to do two years of military service. That ended in 1929, which was a profoundly important year for his subsequent career: he joined the Surrealists and he made the acquaintance of Gala, with whom he spent the rest of his life. Directly connected with these events was the rupture with his family. Dalí's father was horrified by his son's liaison with a married woman. When he read Dalí's *The Sacred Heart*, and what to him was the sacrilegious insult to his wife, Felipa Domènech, in the inscription on it ("Sometimes I spit at the portrait of my mother just for fun"), he then and there decided to sever all contact with his son. He changed his will, bequeathing his whole estate to his daughter, Anna Maria. He wrote to Lorca and Buñuel justifying his action: "My son does not have the right to embitter my life. Cadaqués is my spiritual refuge and ... above all it's where my wife is buried, and it will be destroyed if my son soils it with his unseemly behavior."

Dalí's mother died at the age of forty-seven as a result of an operation for uterine cancer. It was a heavy blow to the young Dalí. His father found a new wife in the sister of his deceased wife, Salvador's *Tieta*. Dalí tried later to justify the picture via the Surrealist principle. He had, he said, only followed the dictates of the unconscious, claiming that one "curses people in dreams whom one respects when awake. And dreams of spitting at one's mother." He went on to say that in many religions "the act of spitting has a sacred aspect." But however he tried to justify it, father and son did not see each other for six years. It was many years before there was a complete reconsiliation.

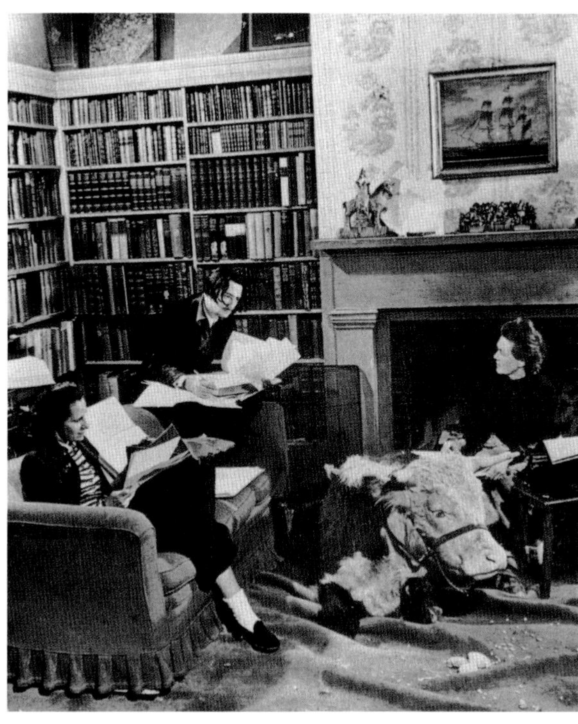

Dalí reading his autobiography *The Secret Life of Salvador Dalí* to Gala and Caresse Crosby.

Turbulent Times

Meantime, Dalí and Gala spent their first "love years" in the seclusion of their new home at Port Lligat on the Catalan coast, which from now on would become the focus of the couple's life. Depending on the season, they traveled to Paris to look after Dalí's business affairs and to fulfill their social obligations. But once the Spanish Civil War broke out in 1936, the Dalís (they were married by then) avoided spending time in Catalonia, visiting Italy, the south of France, Paris, and New York instead. In 1938, Dalí visited Freud, whom he so venerated. Freud, now eighty-two, had been driven out of his native Vienna by the Nazi takeover of Austria, and was living in exile in London. The encounter was arranged by Stefan Zweig, a great admirer of Dalí, who in his view was "the only painter genius of the age and the only one who will outlast it." Zweig wrote to the great psychoanalyst, with whom he was on friendly terms: "But I think a man like you should see the artist on whom you have had more effect than anyone and whom I have always considered it a privilege to know and appreciate." After the encounter, Freud wrote to Zweig to thank him: "Really, I have to thank you for the happy accident that brought me my visitors yesterday. Up to then I had been inclined to see the Surrealists, who appear to have appointed me patron saint, as absolute ... fools. The young Spaniard with his trusting, fanatical eyes and his undeniable technical mastery has prompted a different estimation."

Another catastrophe of war was soon upon them. On 1 September 1939, Hitler invaded Poland, and two days later Britain and France declared war on Germany. Dalí and Gala abandoned Paris in haste and rented a large

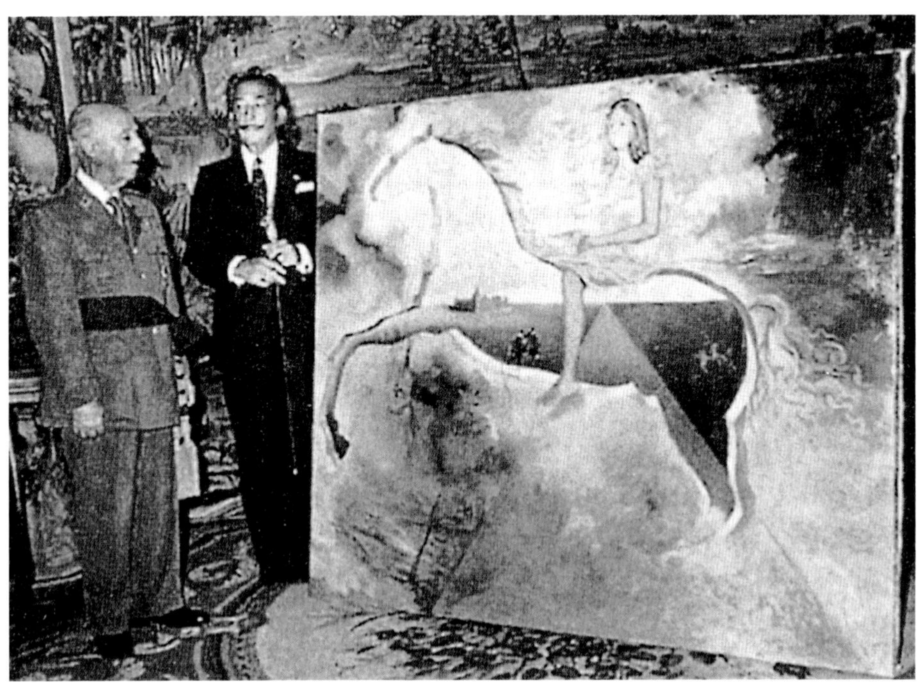

Dalí giving Franco an equestrian painting that shows the general's granddaughter.

colonial-style villa in Arcachon near Bordeaux. They were not the only ones escaping Hitler's troops there: Marcel Duchamp, Coco Chanel, Léonor Fini, and other artists and intellectuals were also in Arcachon. Then after German troops marched on Paris in June 1940 and were heading for Bordeaux as well, the couple left Arcachon, too. Leaving Gala in Lisbon to prepare their journey to America, Dalí made a detour via Figueres, to say goodbye to his family. War had left its mark there as well: his sister Anna Maria had been tortured by the Communist-run Military News Service (SIM), temporarily deranging her, so that she had to be force-fed. Moreover, the house in Figueres had been damaged by bombs and plundered.

In America, Dalí and Gala first stayed with Caresse Crosby, a friend from Paris, who in 1936 had bought a huge mansion to house all her artist friends. Writer Henry Miller was living there at the time with diarist Anaïs Nin, who had supported her writer friend for years. There, in Hampton Manor, Virginia, Dalí wrote his "memoirs." *The Secret Life of Salvador Dalí* was published by Dial Press of New York in 1942 as a translation from French. The book was a huge success. In fact, the years in America were Dalí's great breakthrough—he was as prolific as ever and was almost overwhelmed with commissions. Within a very short space of time he had picked up a faithful clientele of millionaire customers, and he and Gala were able to live in great style. His family were not forgotten—he sent money to Spain and endeavored to overcome his "William Tell complex," talking of burying the hatchet with his father.

The Return to Spain

The Dalís returned to Catalonia in 1948, nine years after Franco's victory in the Spanish Civil War. They settled into a regular rhythm of life that remained unchanged for thirty years. They spent the spring, summer, and fall in Port Lligat, where the artist went about his work in seclusion, and with the energy that always characterized him. He was at his easel at seven every morning, and worked till noon. After a brief siesta, he resumed

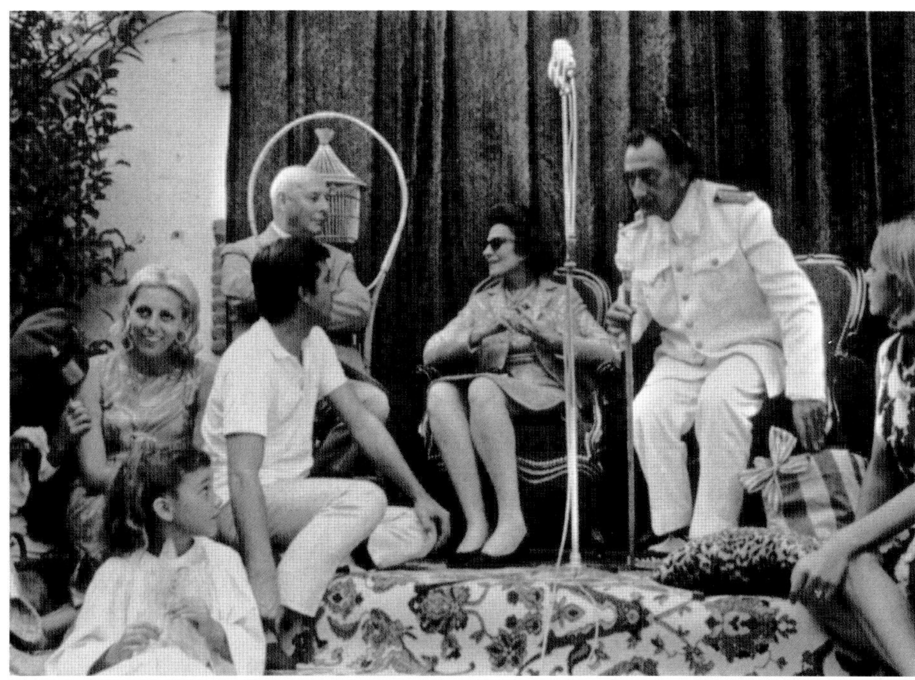

Dalí and his retinue, 1965

work until evening. From time to time, Gala and Dalí traveled to Barcelona, Madrid, or Italy. The winter months were divided between Paris and New York. In the French capital, they always stayed in the Royal Suite at the Hotel Meurice, while in New York it was Suite 1016 at the St Regis Hotel. The cities represented a life of sociability, self-promotion, and business.

By the time he returned to his homeland, Dalí's attitudes had undergone a remarkable volte-face. As a result, he lost for good the sympathies of the Communist-oriented Surrealists, for whom Dalí's lifestyle and views had long been suspect. He now not only came to terms with the right but also became an ardent supporter of Franco, who had "brought clarity, truth, and order to the country." In return, the new government promoted its artists and sought to present a new image of the country through them, in particular through Dalí, who was personally received by Franco in 1956. As when Dalí joined the Catholic Church, expediency and opportunism were to the fore: under Franco, the Church was a political power. Dalí now recommended listening to the "highest moral conscience" that the Pope represented. In 1949, and again in 1959, he sought a private audience with the Pope, and was received by both Pius VII and John XXII.

In December 1949, Anna Maria published her book *Salvador Dalí, visto por su hermana* (Salvador Dalí, As Seen by His Sister), in which she rebuts much of what was claimed in Dalí's *Secret Life*. In her version, little Salvador was a lovable child and thoroughly harmless; there was no talk of the many extravagances with which Dalí had embroidered his life. "Only when he was overcome by an abnormal desire to attract attention was he capable of doing the silliest things." She also represents him as an ungrateful son in unjustly condemning his father. Dalí's father wrote the introduction, once again making clear the difficult relationship between father and son: "I would have been spared much bitterness if I had foreseen that as an old man I should be able to read this book, which reflects the history of our family absolutely faithfully."

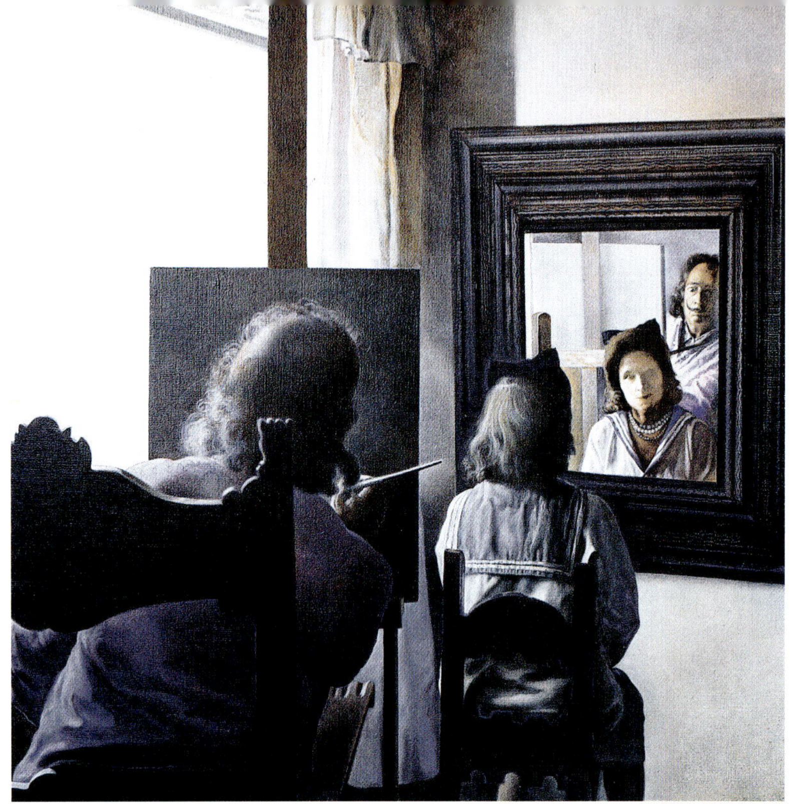

In 1973, Dalí began a portrait of Gala that also represented an exercise in stereoscopy: *Dalí from Behind Painting Gala from Behind Immortalized by Six Virtual Corneas Provisionally Reflected in Six Real Mirrors*

Dalí was much put out by his sister's account, and issued a public statement: "In 1930 my family threw me out without a penny. I owe my worldwide triumph solely to God's help, the light of Empordà, and the heroic daily self-sacrifice of an incomparable woman, my wife Gala." Shortly after Anna's book was published, their father died of prostate cancer. He bequeathed to his son only the minimum that Spanish law obliged him to.

Dalí and Co

In the 1950s and 1960s, Dalí's retinue grew substantially as his fame (and the pressure of work) increased. One key figure was John Peter Moore, who in the 1960s was taken on as Dalí's business manager—he was an Irish-born British officer who had once worked for the intelligence services, and then for London Films International in Europe. Several servants looked after the house and garden, while stage painter Isidor Bea became Dalí's right-hand man in painting, and the photographer Robert Descharnes a faithful companion in all enterprises. The days of quiet contemplation in Port Lligat were over. A whole ménage gathered around to entertain the artist as if he were a pop star. Mainly young people and constantly changing, they sometimes even accompanied him to Paris and New York. His lawyer, Michael Stout, had little time for Dalí's court, and said the artist had no real friends, and had to "make do with his transvestites, queers and strangely garbed freaks, faded models, paid companions and other hangers-on, all of them highly insignificant but hungry."

In the early 1960s, Dalí began to plan a museum of his own in Figueres. There were a number of obstacles to overcome, but construction work began in the 1970s, and in September 1974 the Teatre-Museu Dalí opened its doors in the presence of Dalí and a flock of journalists, photographers, municipal dignitaries, government representatives, and countless guests. The initial flurry of local enthusiasm for Dalí was succeeded a year later by scorn and hostility when, in the face of worldwide criticism, Franco executed five supposed Basque terrorists on 27 September 1975, his last victims before he

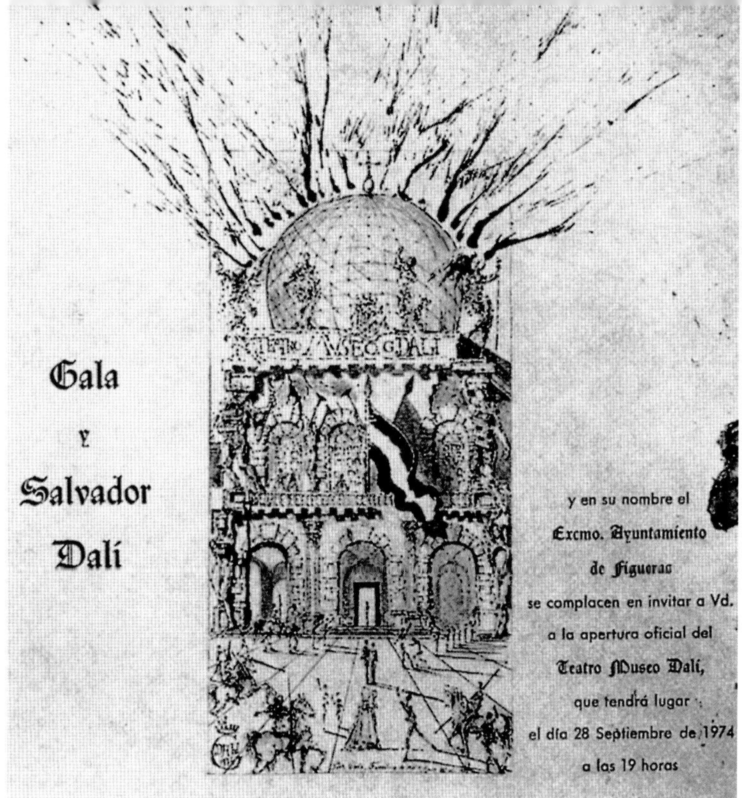

Invitation card for the opening of the Teatre-Museu Dalí on 28 September 1974.

himself died. In an interview with a French news agency, Dalí expressed strong approval of the executions with regard to Spain's future, "where there won't be any terrorism any more in a few months, because assassins will be exterminated like rats. We need three times as many executions. But for the moment these will do." After receiving threatening letters and having his house attacked, Dalí feared for his safety and fled hotfoot to America.

Dalí's Later Years

Dalí was now over seventy, and after several prostate operations he had aged greatly. The doctors treating him attributed his poor state of health less to physical than to psychological causes, in other words his "psychopathological personality structure, which has very pronounced depressive features." Years of taking unknown quantities of amphetamines had caused irreversible damage to his nervous system. His right arm had begun to shake, and painting had become a problem. Dalí and Gala spent a month at the Incasol Clinic in Marbella, a health farm for the wealthy, occupying a suite where the daily rate was a fortune.

In 1975, John Peter Moore resigned as business manager. For the text few years (until 1980), Dalí's affairs were managed by Enrique Sabater, who had been a close confidant since 1968; he took his meals with the Dalís every day, and accompanied them on their travels. Increasingly concerned, Dalí's close acquaintances were suspicious of Sabater. Collector and friend Reynold Morse wrote to Moore that Sabater had helped to "push the master through the difficult years of transition from the peak of his greatness to the beginnings of senility and nervous breakdown. ... It is very clear to us that Gala's loveless care and Sabater's terrorist methods have turned him into a shadow of his former self. We are most concerned that Sabater's income from Dalí's works is over six times his master's." Together with Robert Descharnes and several other friends, they founded a committee to support the artist in times of crisis. Meanwhile, the Spanish and international press

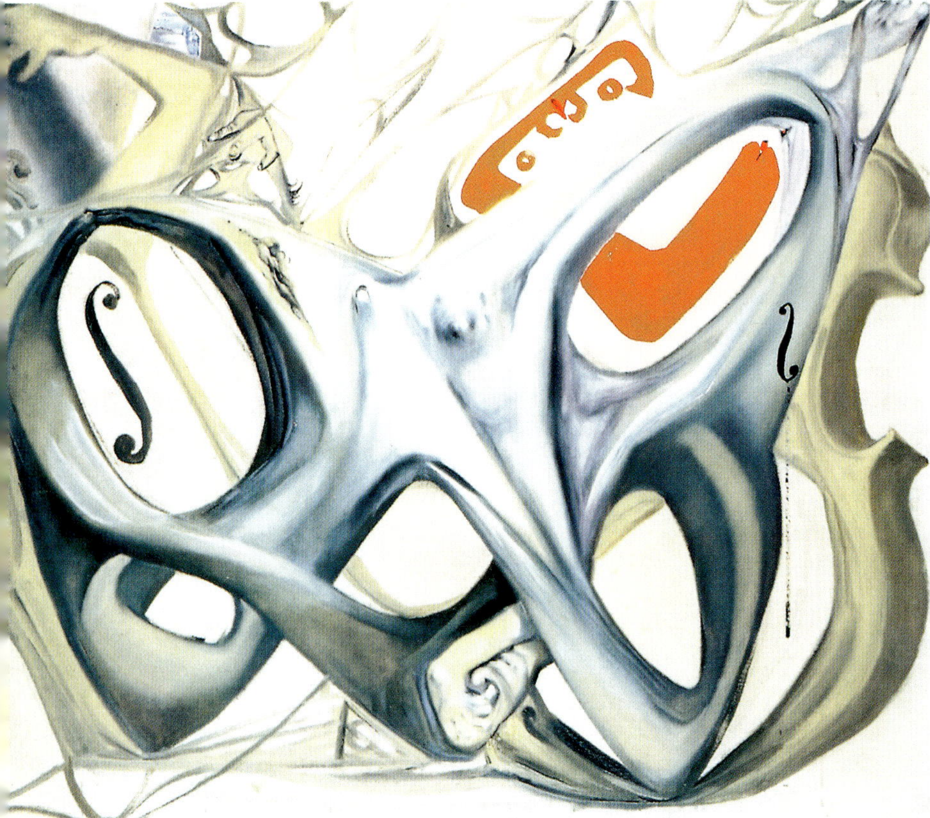

In *Topological Contortion of a Female Figure Becoming a Violoncello* from 1983, Dalí depicts the motor cramps he suffered from in his old age.

carried articles accusing Sabater of making a fortune at Dalí's expense. Sabater himself denied any wrongdoing, but was persuaded by the "Committee of the Friends of Dalí" to relinquish his post.

In 1982, Gala died. Dalí now refused to eat, and decided to retire to his castle in Púbol, where Gala was buried and where henceforth Dalí would be cared for round the clock by doctors and helpers. However, he sustained serious injuries in a fire there, and once he had recovered he returned to the tower of the Teatre-Museu Dalí, which was named the Torre Galatea in honor of his deceased muse. Dalí now had to be fed through a tube because he was unable to swallow. His voice failed, and he could communicate only in whispers. On 18 January 1989, Dalí was taken to hospital with serious cardiac weakness complicated by inflammation of the lungs. On 20 January, the parish priest performed the last rites. The international press descended on the editorial office of the local paper in Figueres to hear the mayor declare

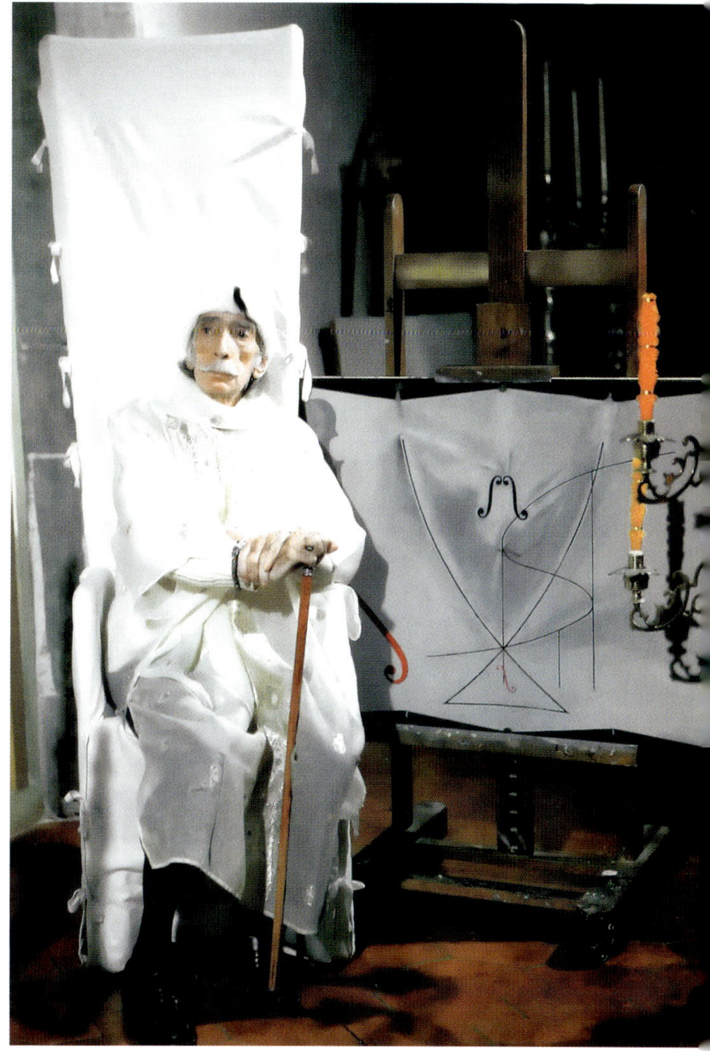
Dalí in front of his last picture, the *Swallow's Tail*.

at a press conference that Dalí's last wish was to be laid to rest in the dome of the museum. Dalí died of heart failure on 23 January. Two days later, one of the rooms of the Torre Galatea was transformed into a mortuary and opened to the public before Dalí was interred beneath the dome of the Teatre-Museu. 15,000 people came to pay their respects to the world-famous artist.

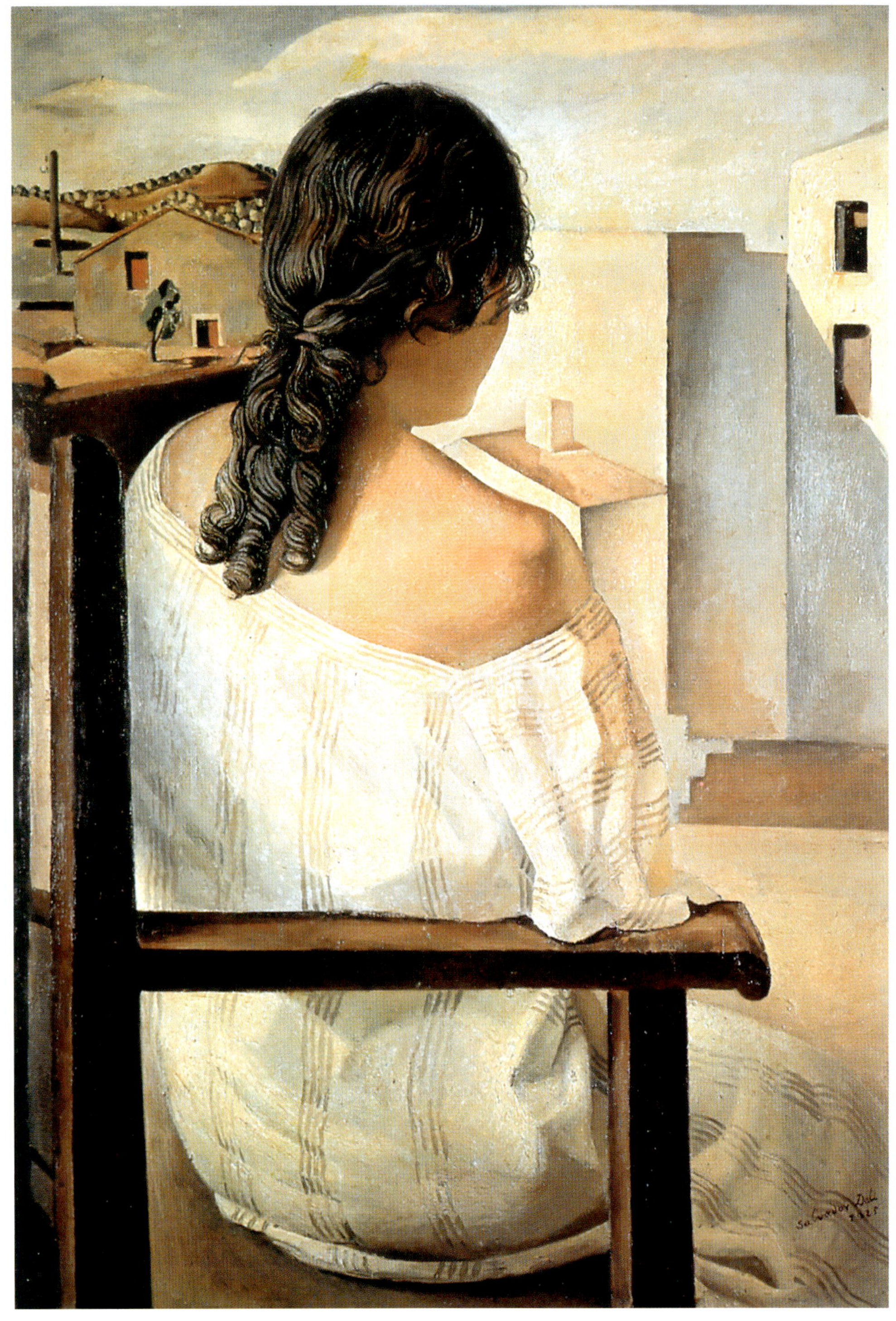

View from Behind The *Girl from Behind* is part of Dalí's first solo show at the Galerie Dalmau in Barcelona in 1925. In the catalogue for the exhibition, Dalí cites neoclassicist painter Ingres (1780-1867): "Shapes are beautiful if they are firm and full but the details don't impair the overall impression of the great mass of the body."

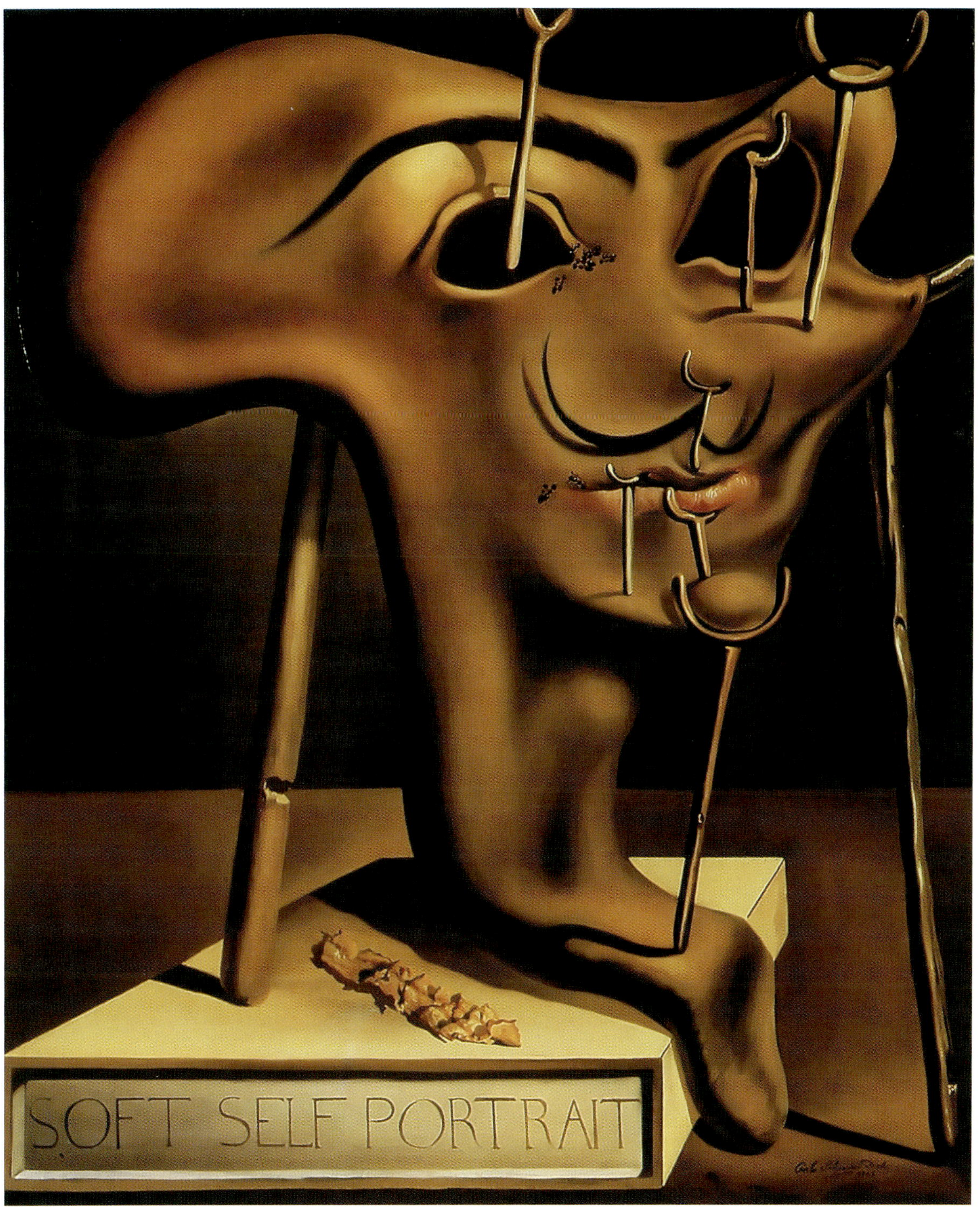

Antipsychological Self-Portrait The *Soft Self-Portrait with Fried Bacon* was on the dust jacket of the catalogue for Dalí's solo show at the Julien Levy Gallery in the spring of 1941. The catalogue said that his psychological phase was coming to an end, and "instead of the soul, i.e. the inward person, I paint the exterior, the shell, the glove of my Self."

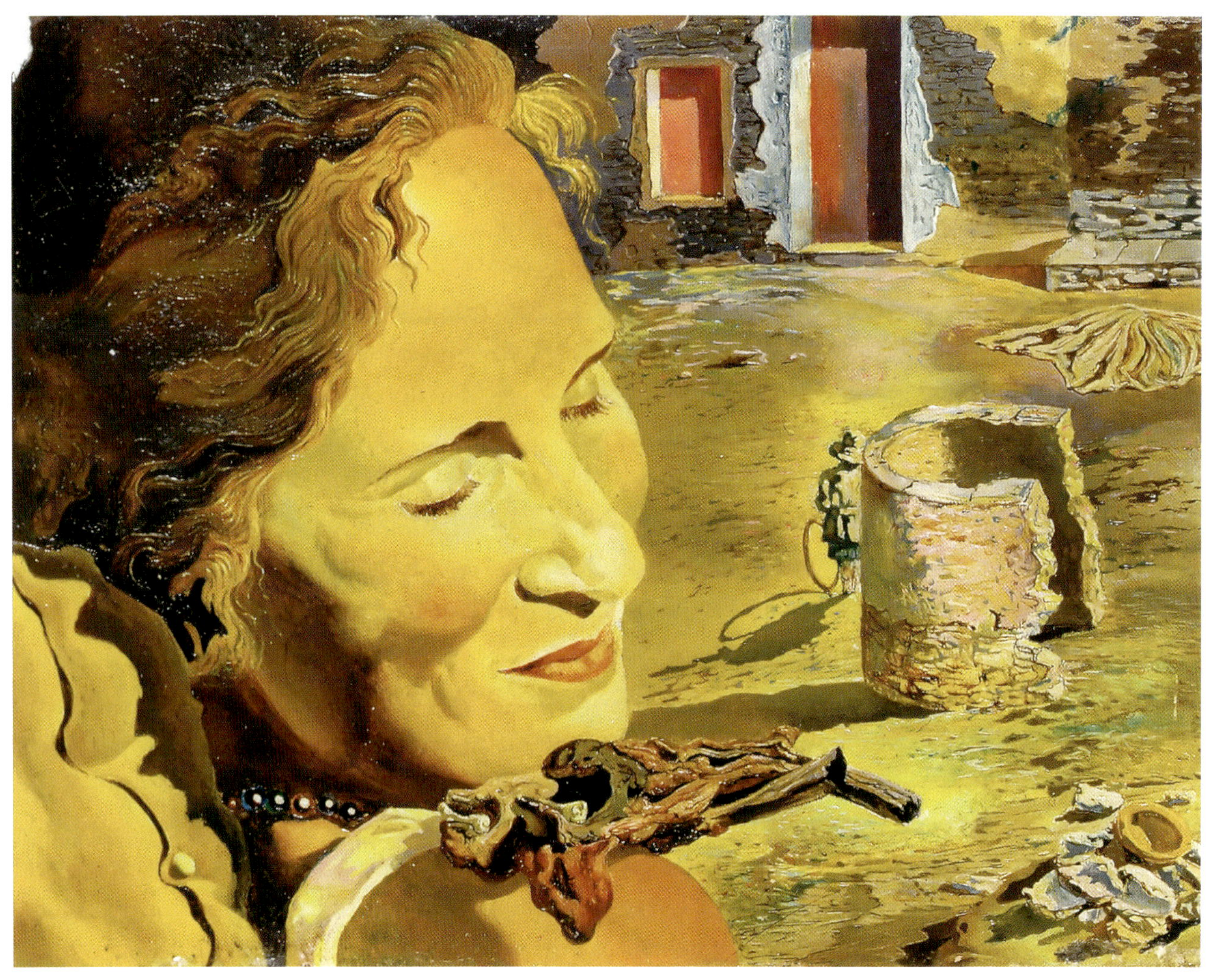

Portrait of Gala with Two Lamb Chops Balanced on Her Shoulder "On arriving in Port Lligat, I painted a portrait of Gala balancing two raw lamb chops on her shoulder. That was to say—as I later learned—that instead of eating her I decided to consume two uncooked lamb chops. The lamb chops did indeed appear to be the expiatory sacrifice of my unsuccessful sacrificial offering." Salvador Dalí.

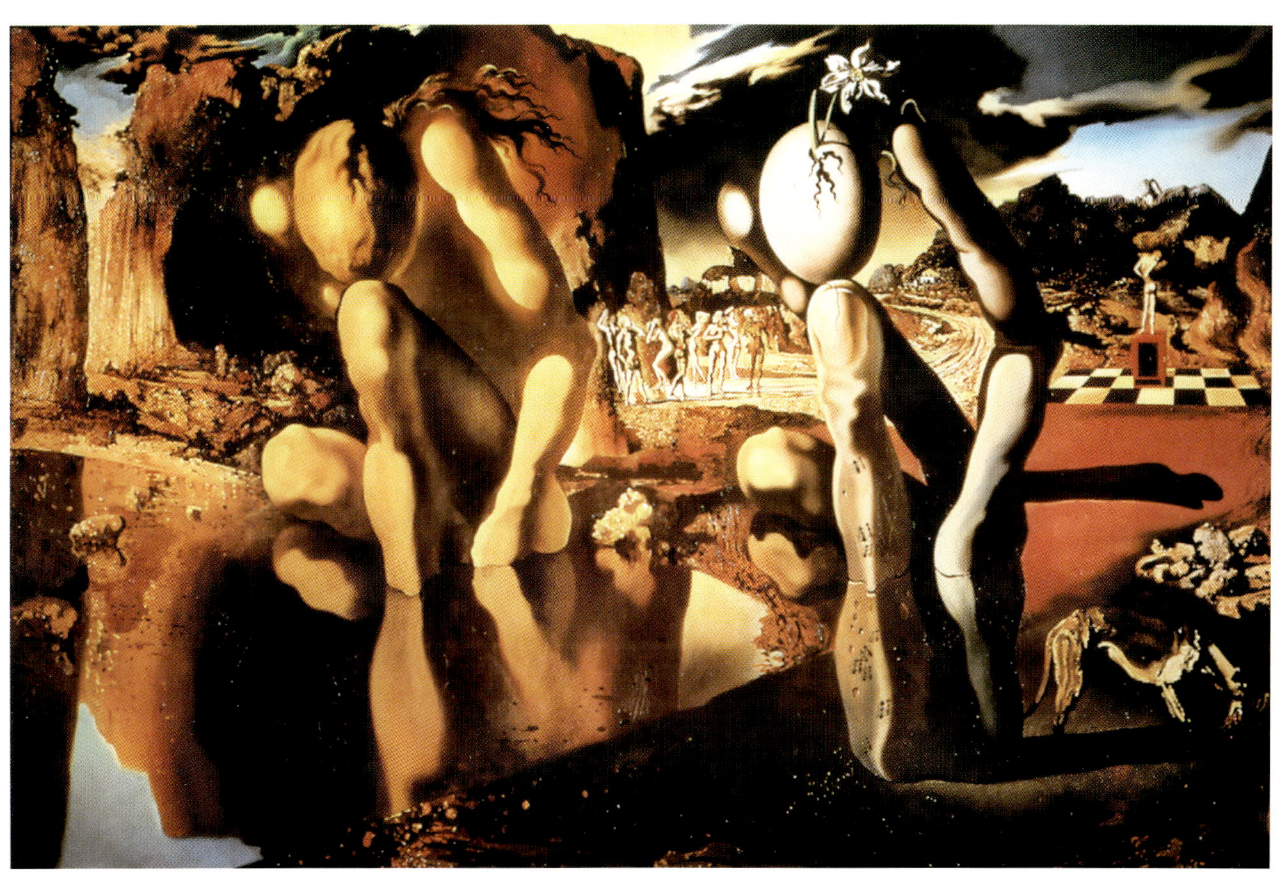

Fusion Apart from painting, writing was an important part of Dalí's creative output. In one case, the two activities were fused—Dalí wrote a long poem of the same name to go with the picture of *Metamorphosis of Narcissus*, expanding the meaning of the painting. The subject was the figure of Narcissus changing in the picture into a hand holding an egg with a narcissus sprouting from it.

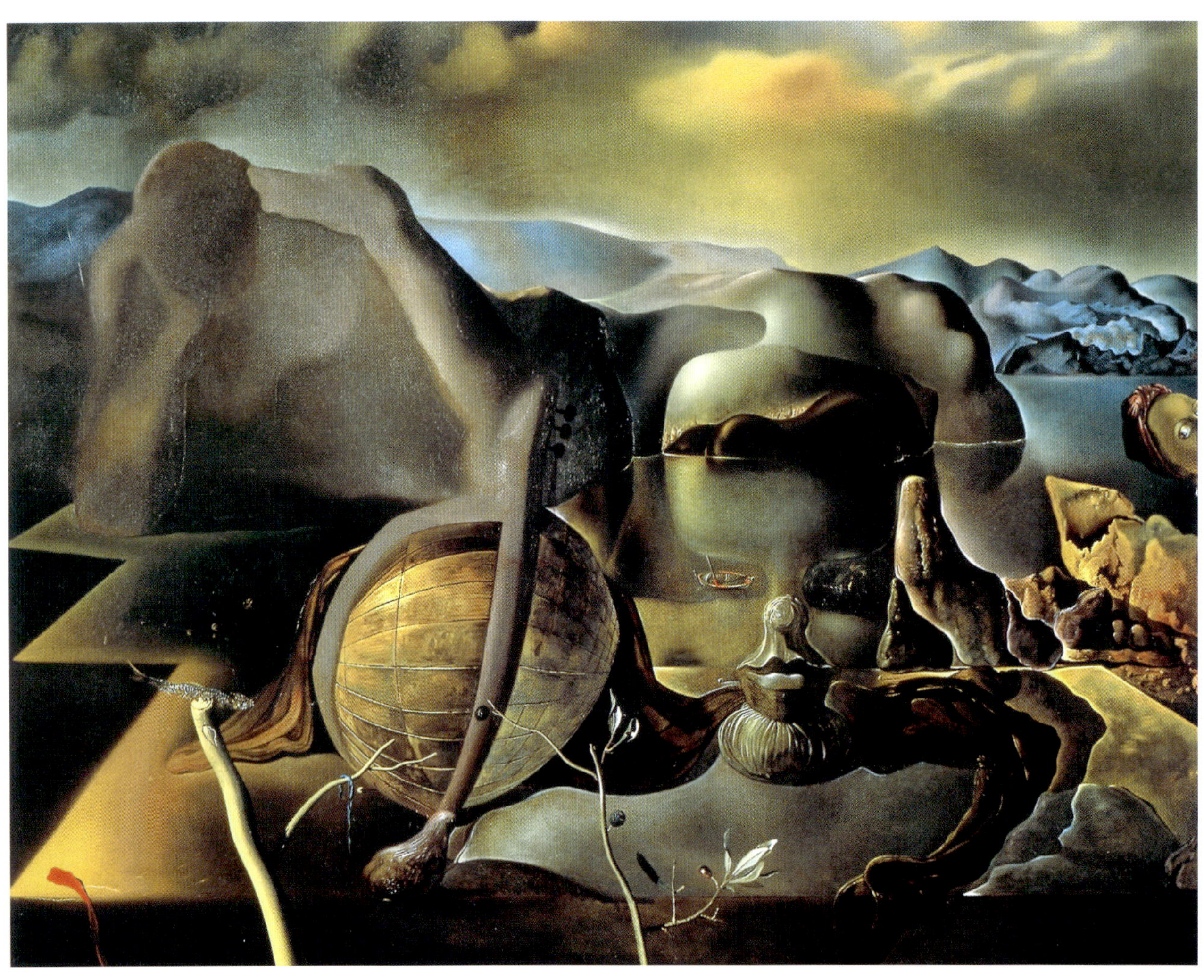

Picture puzzle As a typical example of Dalí's double and multiple pictures, the oil painting of *The Endless Enigma* (1938) reflects the intricacies of the time. It is made up of six drawn, pre-designed motifs that overlay each other. The catalogue for the exhibition at the Julien Levy Gallery in New York the same year presents the solution. It contains the drawings that have to be deciphered in the picture.

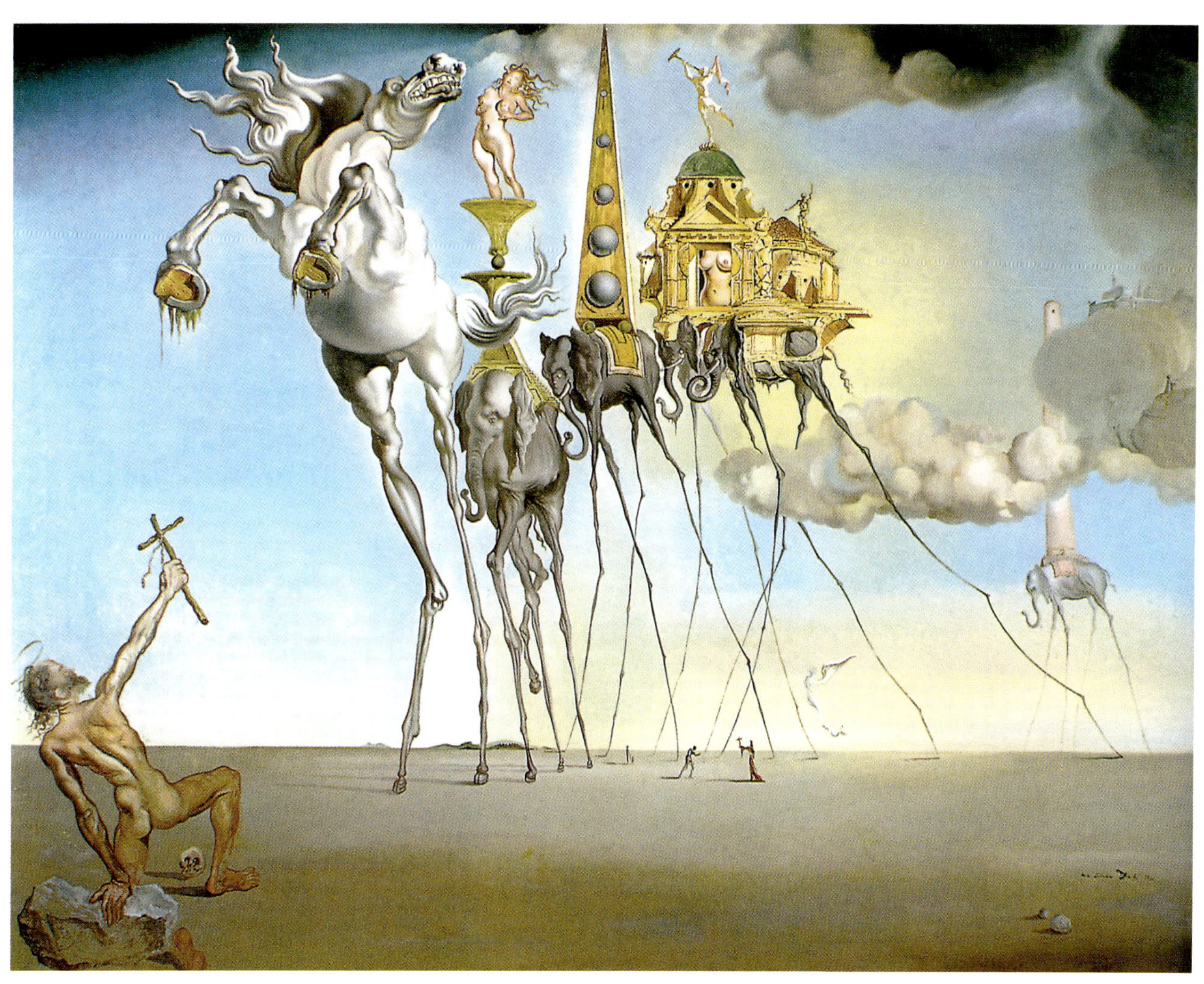

Asceticism Dalí's *Temptation of St. Anthony* was painted in New York in 1946. It tells the story of St Anthony, who had retired to the Egyptian desert to be a hermit. Temptation comes his way in the form of a parade of horses and elephants with beautiful naked women. The hermit resolutely holds up his miserable cross to ward them off.

Love

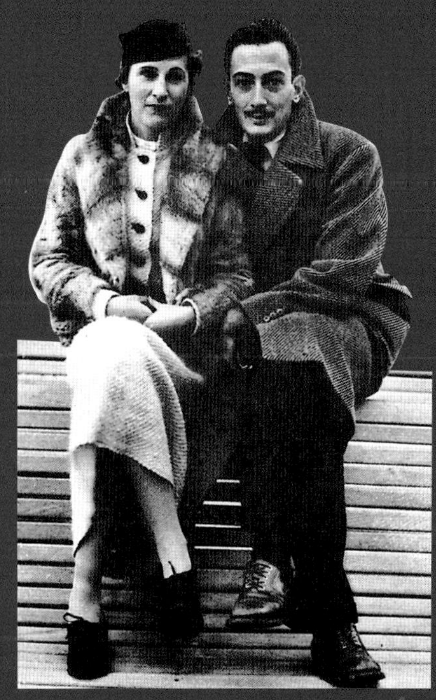

“Gala gave me the structure—in the true sense of the word—that my life lacked.”

Salvador Dalí

Gala

Probably no other artist has praised his wife as much as Dalí did Gala. He never ceased proclaiming publicly how much he owed her. In fact, he was in love with forever celebrating their love, and never missed an opportunity to sing her praises to her, apparently with real sincerity and passion. She was his wife and lover, his muse and model, the therapist of his psychoses, manager of his business affairs. "My magnificent wife, my wife Gala."

Gradiva: A Pompeian Fantasy

Shortly after his first meeting with Gala, Dalí read Wilhelm Jensen's novella *Gradiva: A Pompeian Fantasy* (1903) and Freud's analysis of the story, which sees Jensen's tale as an example of recovery from delusions. The story is about an unworldly and lonely archeologist called Norbert Hanold who one day encounters his childhood love Gradiva in Pompeii. She brings him out of his self-enclosed world and they marry. Dalí saw in Gala his very own Gradiva, the incarnation of a childhood love and healer of his delusions—the reincarnation of the enigmatic, proud heroine of the novella, whose Latin name means "the girl who steps along" (has an attractive way of walking).

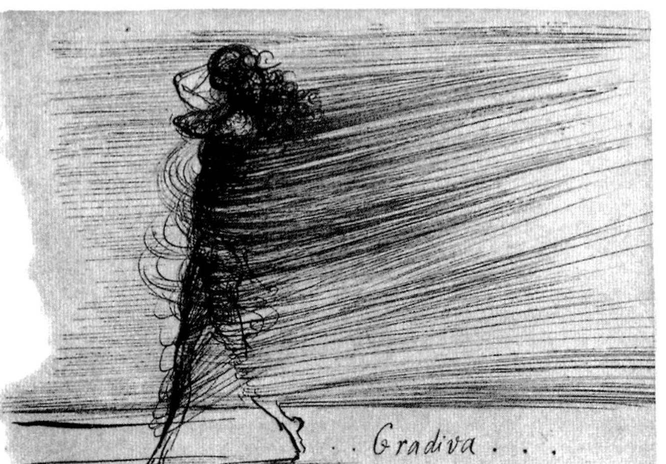

Gala as a model for Dalí's drawing *Gradiva*, from *The Secret Life of Salvador Dalí*

--> "I love Gala more than my mother, more than my father, more than Picasso, and more than money."

--> "Gala has become the basic catalyst of my life."

--> "With true passion, I let Gala dominate me."

--> "I lie prostrate at Gala's feet in a state of complete subjection and spiritualization."

--> *Gala-Salvador Dalí* is how Dalí begins to sign his pictures from the 1930s, indicating a deep attachment to his wife.

Gala
My love proves to me
that I have no memories of you
as I don't remember you
you don't change
you are outside my memory
since you are my life ...

Salvador Dalí,
from: *Love and Memory,* 1931

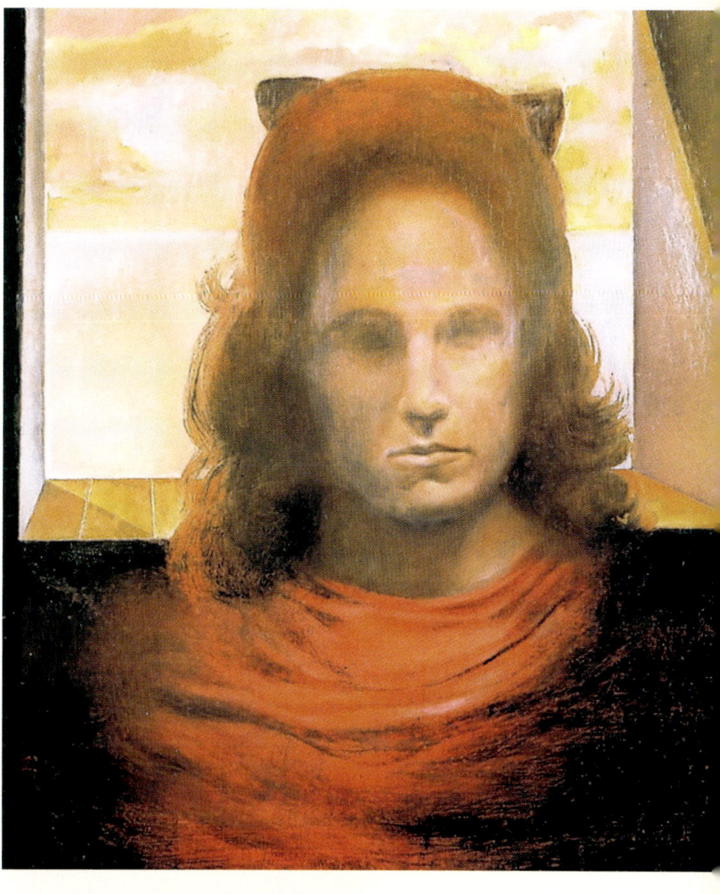

The Muse

Gala inspired Dalí to keep producing pictures. She was his favorite model, the one he painted incessantly, whether as Venus or the Madonna, nude or portrait.

The Savior

Meeting Gala meant for Dalí being cured of his neuroses, fears, and aggressive "cravings." He called her his "angel of equilibrium."

The Manager

Her shrewd head and ambition steered him to international success. She was the one who "built him up into the giant he became." (Reynolds Morse)

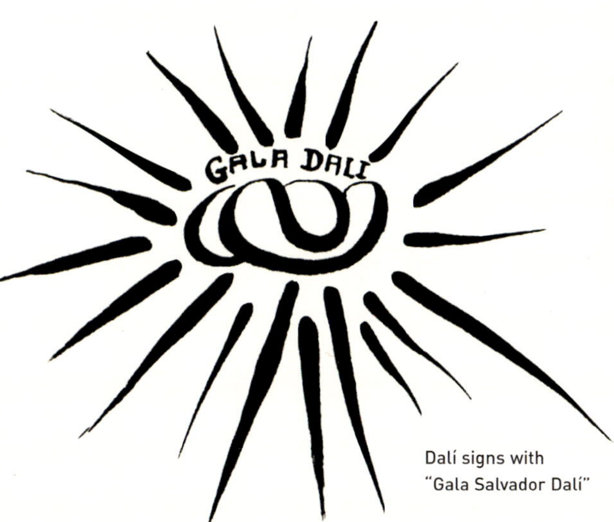

Dalí signs with
"Gala Salvador Dalí"

"Every good painter who means to produce great works of art should first marry my wife."

Salvador Dalí

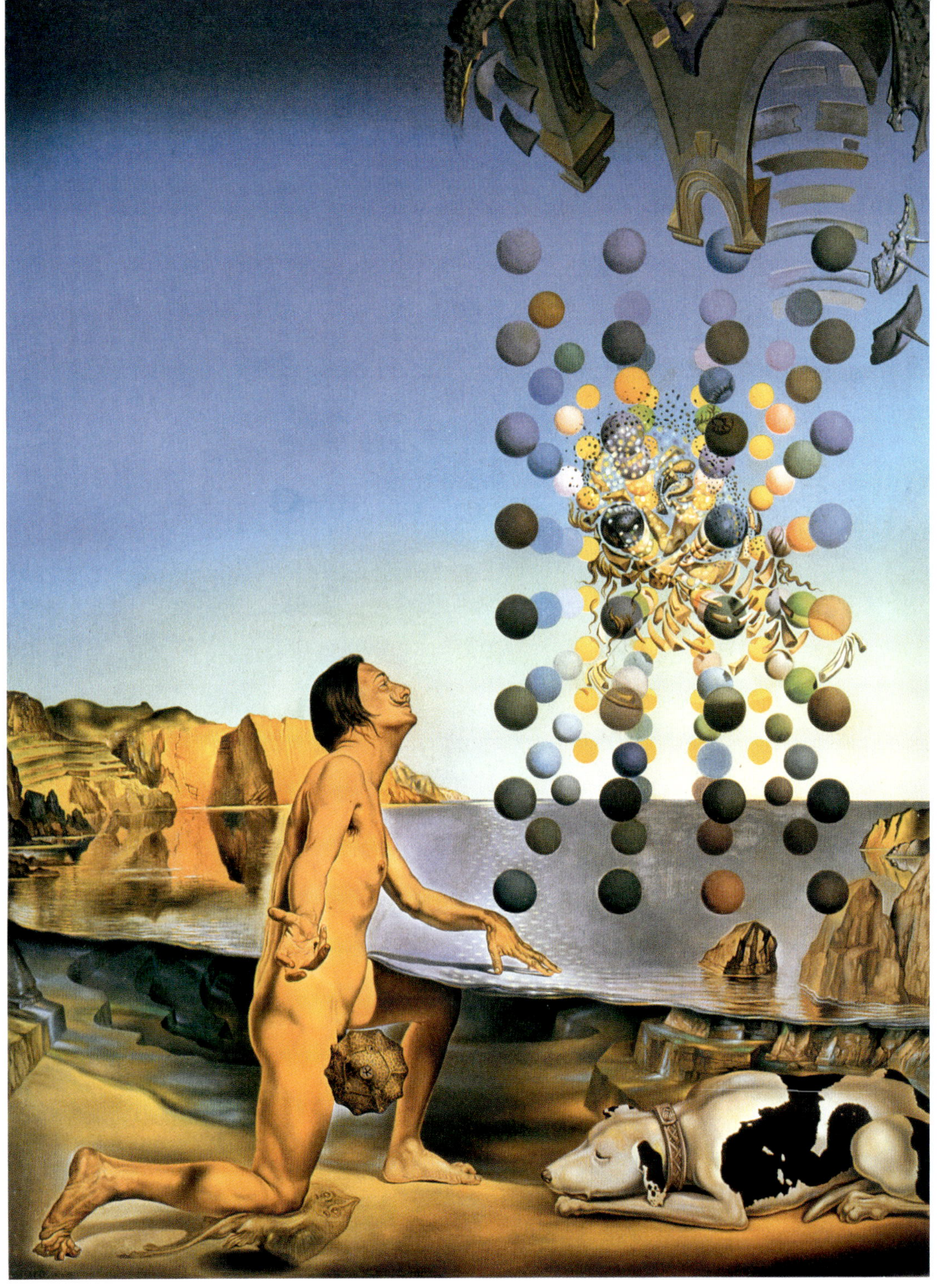

The artist kneels nude in front of a phenomenon floating over him in the shape of a woman's head broken down into elementary particles: *Dali, Nude, Contemplating Five Regular Bodies, Transformed into Corpuscles in which Suddenly Leonardo's Leda Appears, Chromosomatised by Gala's Face* (1954).

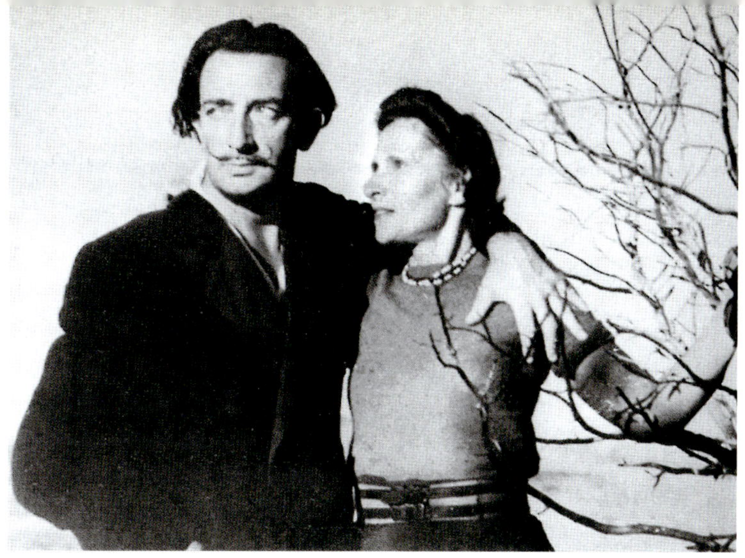

Inseparable: Gala and Salvador Dalí.

A Love for Life

Summer 1929. Dalí was twenty-five when he met a Russian woman named Elena Dimitrievna Diakonova, who called herself Gala. It was an encounter with profound long-term consequences for Dalí. For more than fifty years they lived in a happy symbiosis.

"My love for Gala is a world in itself. My wife is the missing link in the chain of my essential being."

Salvador Dalí

The Conquest

Dalí spent the summer of 1929 in Cadaqués, welcoming visitors from Paris: the "well-known" gallery owner Camille Goemans and his partner Yvonne Bernard, the "outstanding" Belgian painter René Magritte and his wife Georgette Berger, and the "great" poet Paul Eluard—as the local press reported the unusual influx of celebrities. Eluard was accompanied by his wife, Gala, and their daughter, Cécile. A little later Buñuel came along too, to work with Dalí on the screenplay for *L'Âge d'Or*.

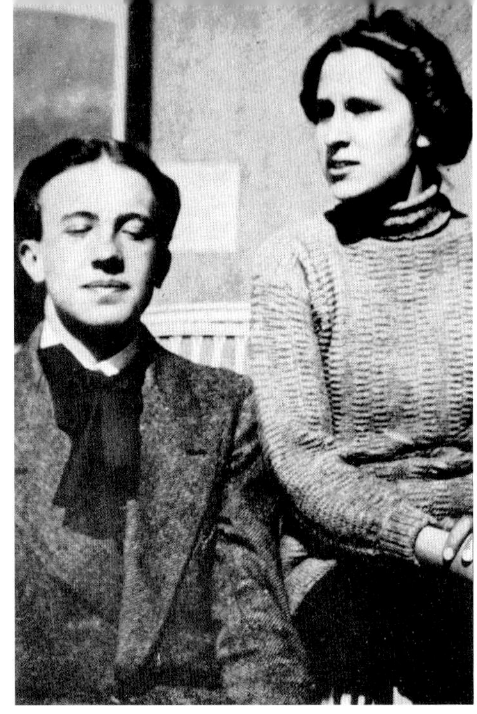

Gala in Clavadel with her first husband Paul Eluard, 1913.

Dalí has given a lengthy account of this visit in his autobiography, particularly the first encounter with Gala, the mysterious Russian woman whom he identified as the woman of his life. For Dalí, it was love at first sight. He remembered a girl from his childhood that he once loved, and thought he had found her again in Gala. "It was her! Galushka Rediviva! I recognized her at once from her naked back. Her body still looked like a child's."

Dalí now set about the process of conquest. As you might expect, it was a bizarre process, and depended on his mood at any one moment. Dalí's account tells of overtaxed nervous states that came over him, expressed in hallucinations and outbreaks of hysterical, uncontrolled laughter. Gala was put off by his behavior and his effusive, highly staged appearances: he once presented himself to her in a torn shirt, with a perfume of his own creation, and bloody armpits. She was as little impressed by his latest work, *Dismal Sport*, which reflected his obscure fantasies and delusions: "After I had devoted myself to these fantasies conjured up from childhood memories for a while, I finally decided to start a painting in which I would limit myself exclusively to reproducing each of these images as conscientiously as possible in the sequence and intensity they came up, and taking only feelings that came over me quite arbitrarily as the criterion and guideline for their arrangement."

Countless symbols and fantasy images are arrayed side by side in this painting, apparently without connection: an anus with a phallic finger penetrating it, directly beside it a chalice and host, and then a man with excrement-stained clothing. The visitors were particularly curious about the brown stains on the trousers: could Dalí be coprophagous, in other words pathologically inclined to eating feces? Gala wanted to have nothing more to do with him if what was in the painting had anything to do with his real life, but he pacified her with the explanation that those elements in the picture were of a purely artistic nature.

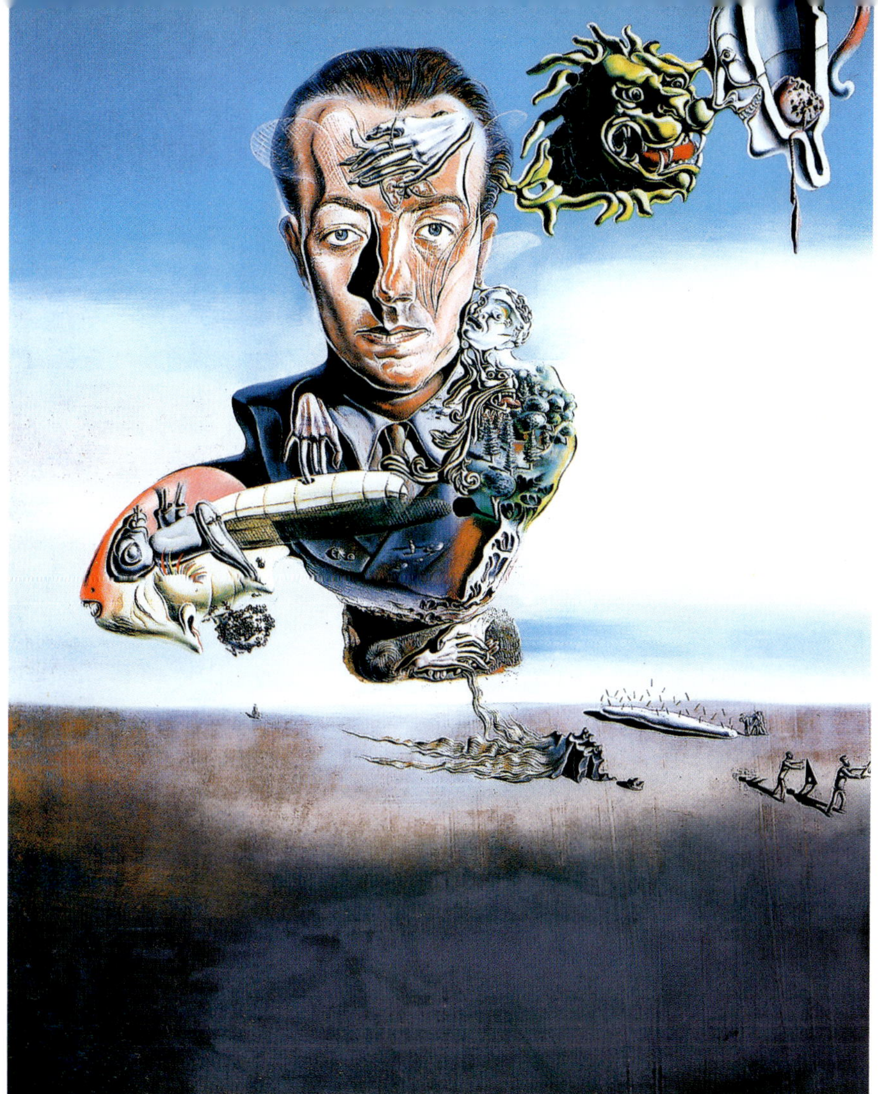

The Surrealist *Portrait of Paul Eluard* (1929) shows the great French poet and husband of Gala in the shape of a classical bust.

Dalí's efforts to make his chosen woman love him finally proved successful. The decisive love scene took place on a walk along the cliff top of Cap de Creus, "on one of the wildest, most deserted and rocky spots in Cadaqués." Dalí asked Gala: "What do you want me to do with you?" Her reply was: "I want you to kill me." A dramatic start to the love affair, but we only have Dalí's version. Whatever Gala meant by it, Dalí took it literally, and they became embroiled in a conversation about death. He did not kill her, as it turned out. After all, he got a promise from Gala that "they would never leave each other again." This pact was taken seriously by both of them.

Family and Marriage

Salvador's liaison with Gala caused distinct unease in Dalí's family. A relationship with a Frenchwoman (as was supposed in the village) was in itself occasion enough for gossip in conservative Empordà, and then it turned out that she was still married and had a daughter! Dalí senior vented his indignation in a letter to his son's friend, Lorca: "His vileness has gone so far as to accept money and board from a married woman, who feeds him with the consent and approval of the husband so as to make the break easier at a suitable moment. I'm sure you can imagine how painful so much dirty business is to us."

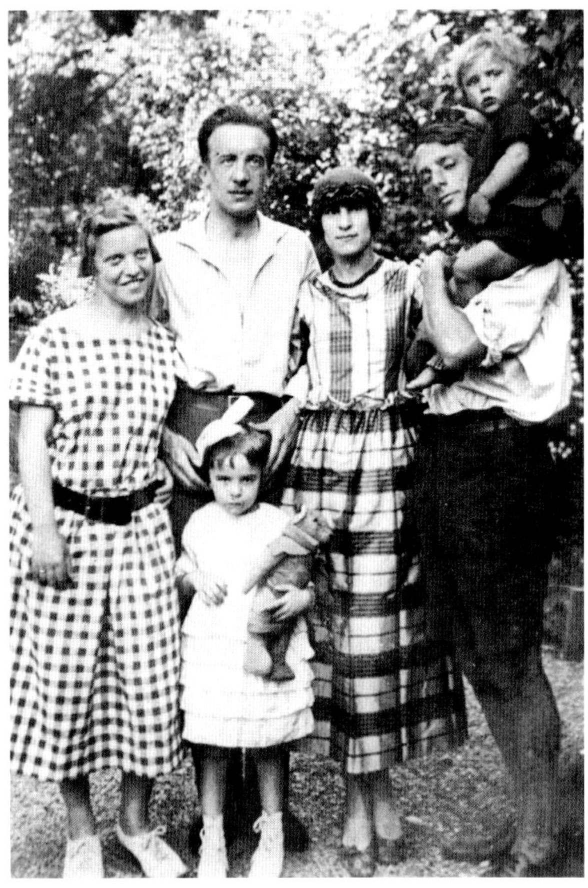

An apparently happy large family: in the middle Gala and Paul Eluard with their daughter Cécile, left and right Lou and Max Ernst with Jimmy on his shoulders. Saint-Brice, 1924.

Dalí's sister, Anna Maria, was also convinced, as she later noted in her book about Dalí, that her easily influenced brother had lost his peace of mind through Gala. His works, which up to that date had reflected his inner harmony, had given way to terrible hallucinations that, after he made the acquaintance of Gala and the Surrealists, manifested themselves in obscene images. "His compulsion to draw attention to himself under the prompting of an unscrupulous influence was the only explanation we could find."

Gala and Paul Eluard

Gala, or Elena Dimitrievna Diakonova, was not French but Russian. Born in Kazan in 1894, she grew up with her mother, who after the death of Gala's father moved in with a prosperous lawyer. Antonina Diakovna was a cultivated woman who mixed with painters and writers. Elena (Gala) spent her childhood in Moscow, where she went to a private school and had a broad education, though in Tsarist Russia university was out of the question for women. When she was eighteen, she was sent to the Clavadel sanatorium in Davos (Switzerland) to cure her tuberculosis. There she made the acquaintance of French poet Eugène-Émile Grindel, who later adopted the pen name Paul Eluard.

Gala fell in love and in 1916 followed Eluard to Paris, where they married. Their daughter Cécile was born shortly after, but she grew up with Eluard's mother; Gala kept her daughter at arm's length all her life. Eluard was involved in the vibrant literary and artistic world of avant-garde Paris, associating with the Dadaists and

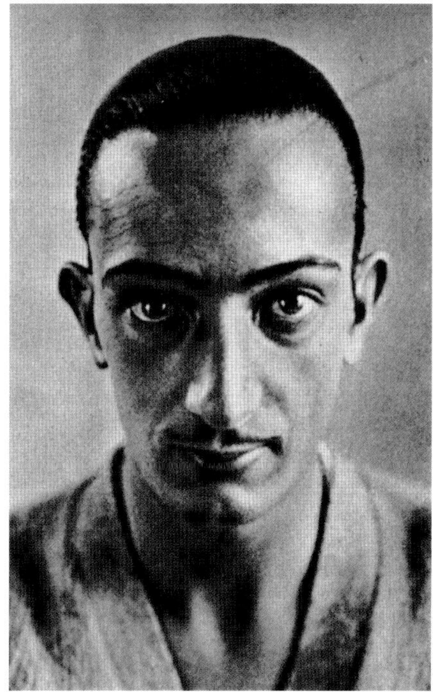

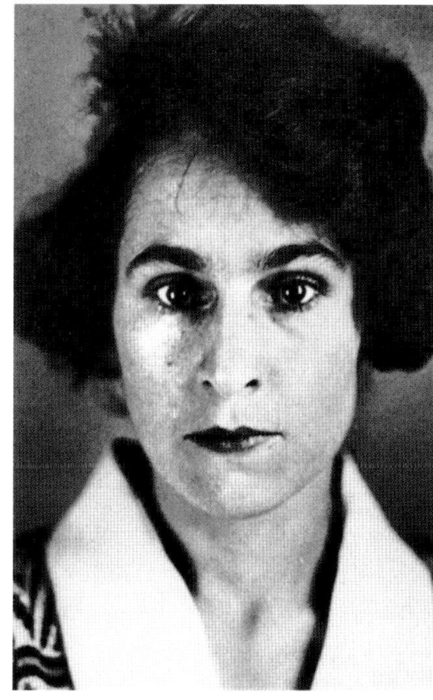

Photo of Dalí in 1929, when he got to known Gala.

Portrait of Gala shortly before her first meeting with Dalí.

later the Surrealists. Gala was admitted to the circle round Breton, Aragon, and Soupault as a muse. As Eluard's own fame as a poet grew, the couple made the acquaintance of the up-and-coming painter Max Ernst, with whom Gala had an affair. Just as she had already inspired many of her husband's poems, she now inspired Ernst's paintings, appearing as the naked *Belle Jardinière* and in the group picture *Au Rendez-Vous des Amis*. This was not the only relationship that Gala and Eluard entertained in a mutual agreement for an open marriage.

When Gala separated from Eluard after the summer in Cadaqués, he initially thought the liaison with Dalí would likewise be a transient affair, but three years later, in 1932, Gala terminated the fifteen-year marriage for good by getting a divorce. Custody of Cécile was awarded to the father. Gala and Eluard remained friends, which did not exclude occasional sexual encounters as well. Without pressurizing Gala, and while remaining on good terms with Dalí, Eluard continued to love Gala; a hundred yearning letters to Gala written up to 1948 document his passion.

On the morning of 30 January 1934, Dalí and Gala had a civil wedding at the *mairie* of Paris's 14th arrondissement. The church wedding followed on 8 August 1958 in the Santuari dels Angels, in the mountains near Girona, six years after the death of Eluard.

Together

Despite threats from Dalí's father, who did not want to have the couple anywhere near him, Dalí and Gala bought a small fisherman's cottage not far from Cadaqués. Port Lligat was a tiny fishing village on the Cap de Creus promontory. The small bay was surrounded by hills and accessible only via a goat track or by boat, and could unhesitatingly be described as the world's end. Port Lligat now became Dalí and Gala's joint home. The cottage could hardly be described as luxurious, not having electricity, running water or any amenities. This was where the couple spent a large part

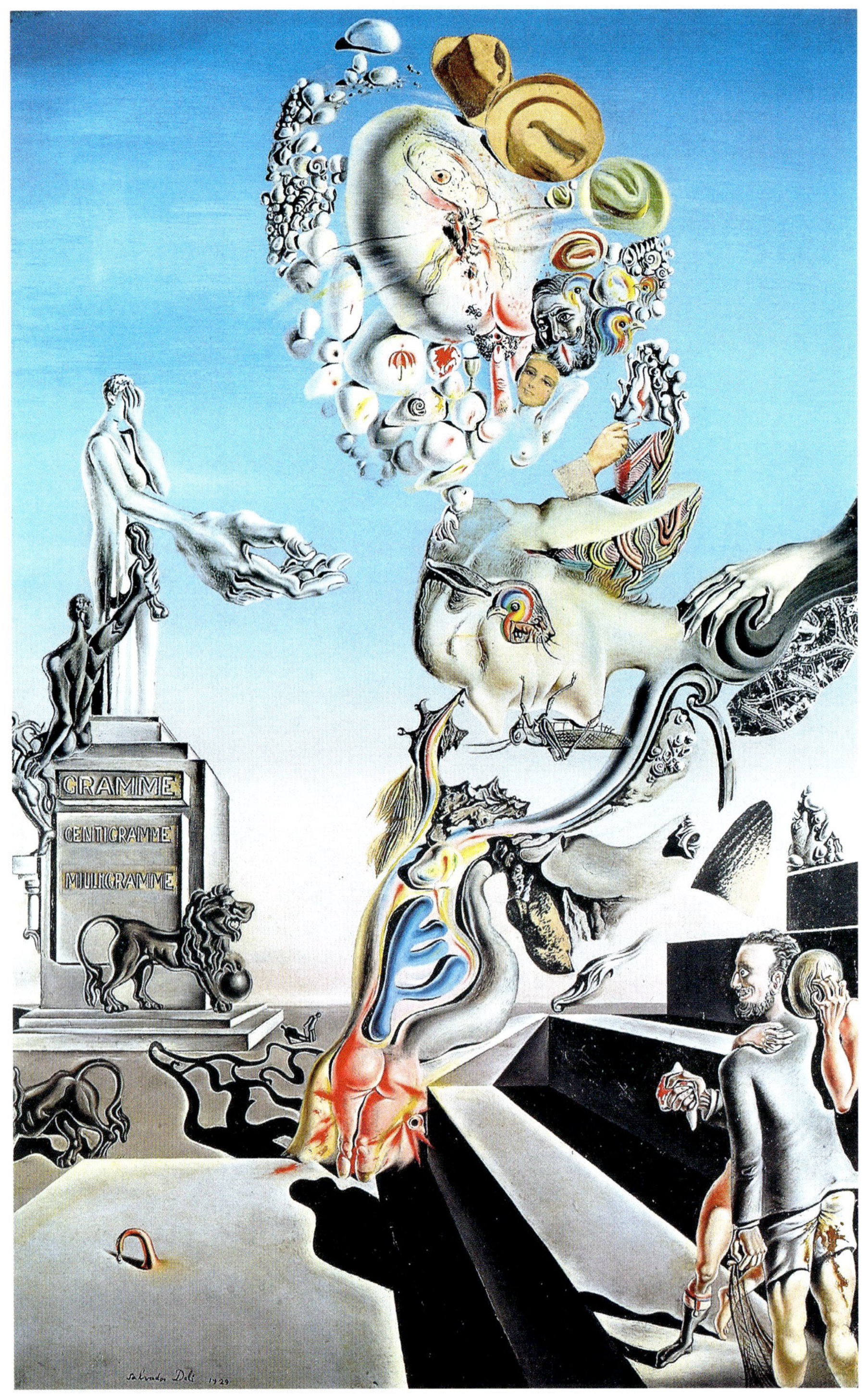

Illustrious company *Dismal Sport* was painted before the encounter with Gala, and caused a stir in the ranks of the Surrealists. The purchase of the work by the Vicomte de Noailles and its incorporation in his collection of art soon silenced the wagging tongues—the painting would in future hang between a Cranach and a Watteau.

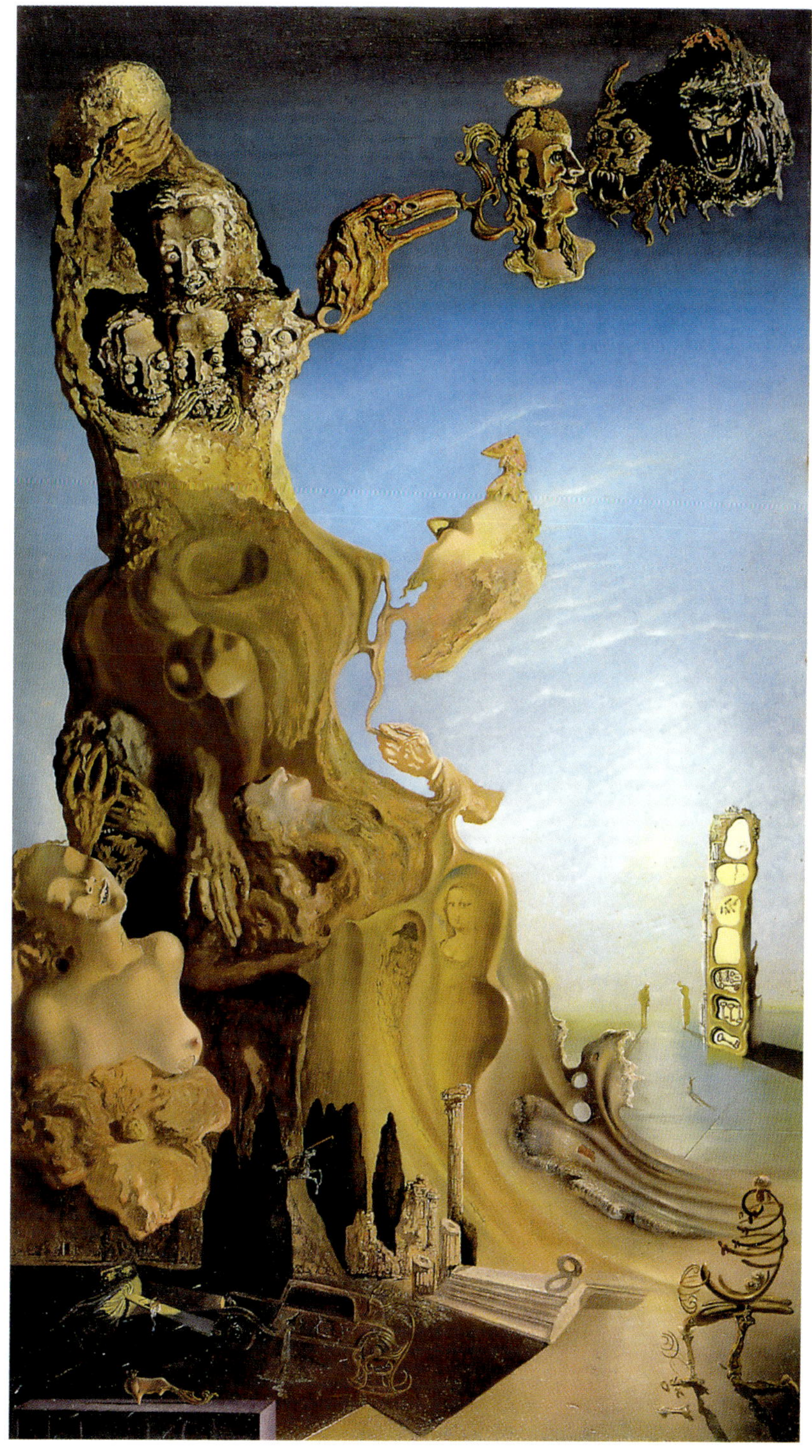

Tribute to Gala *Imperial Monument to the Child Woman* was painted in 1929, and was the first major work to allude to his relationship with Gala. Dalí interpreted the picture both as an exorcism of the fears of childhood and youth. The rocky dream structure suggests scenes of desire and shame.

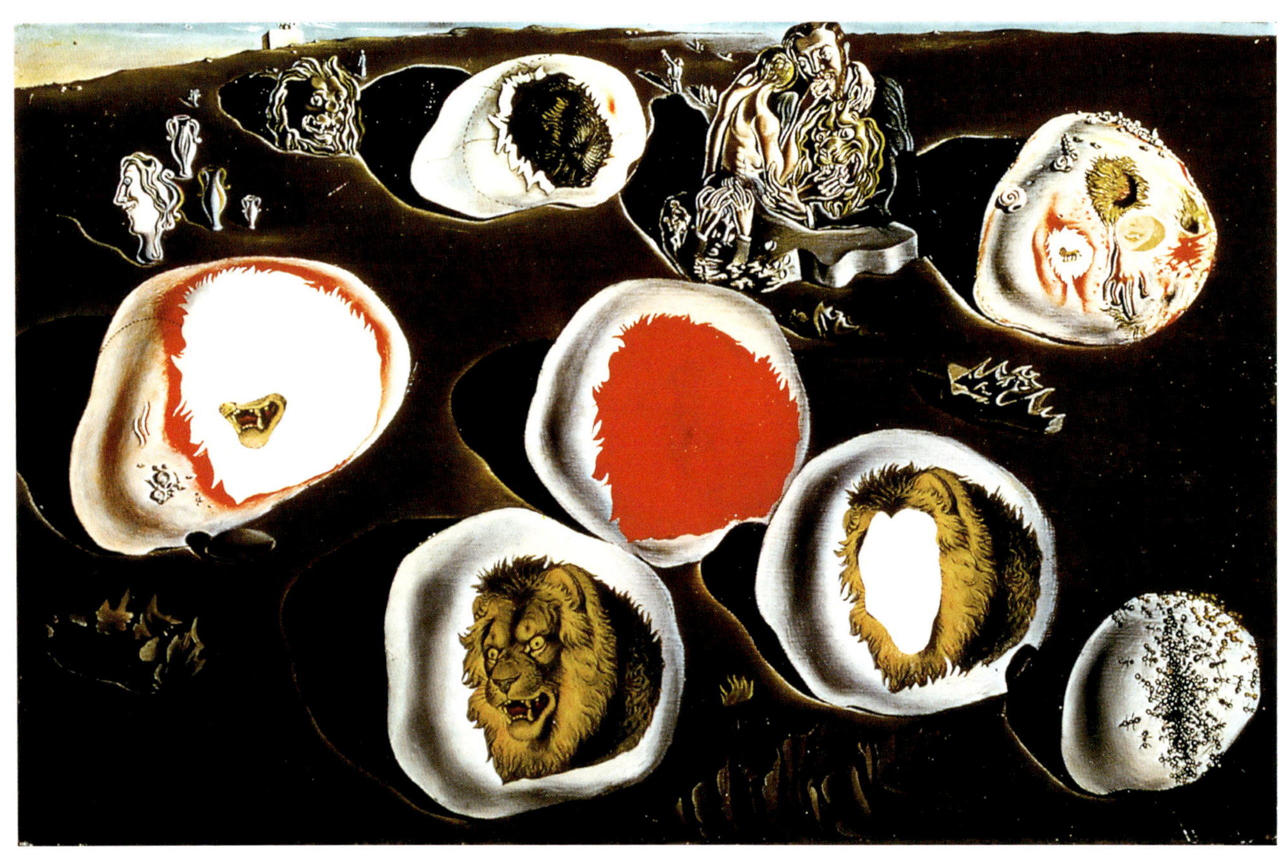

Desire Dalí showed *Accommodations of Desire* at his first exhibition in Paris at Camille Goemans in 1929. The picture was painted around the time he met Gala, and shows Dalí's idea of desire, represented by the two fear-inspiring lion heads. The first owner of the picture was André Breton.

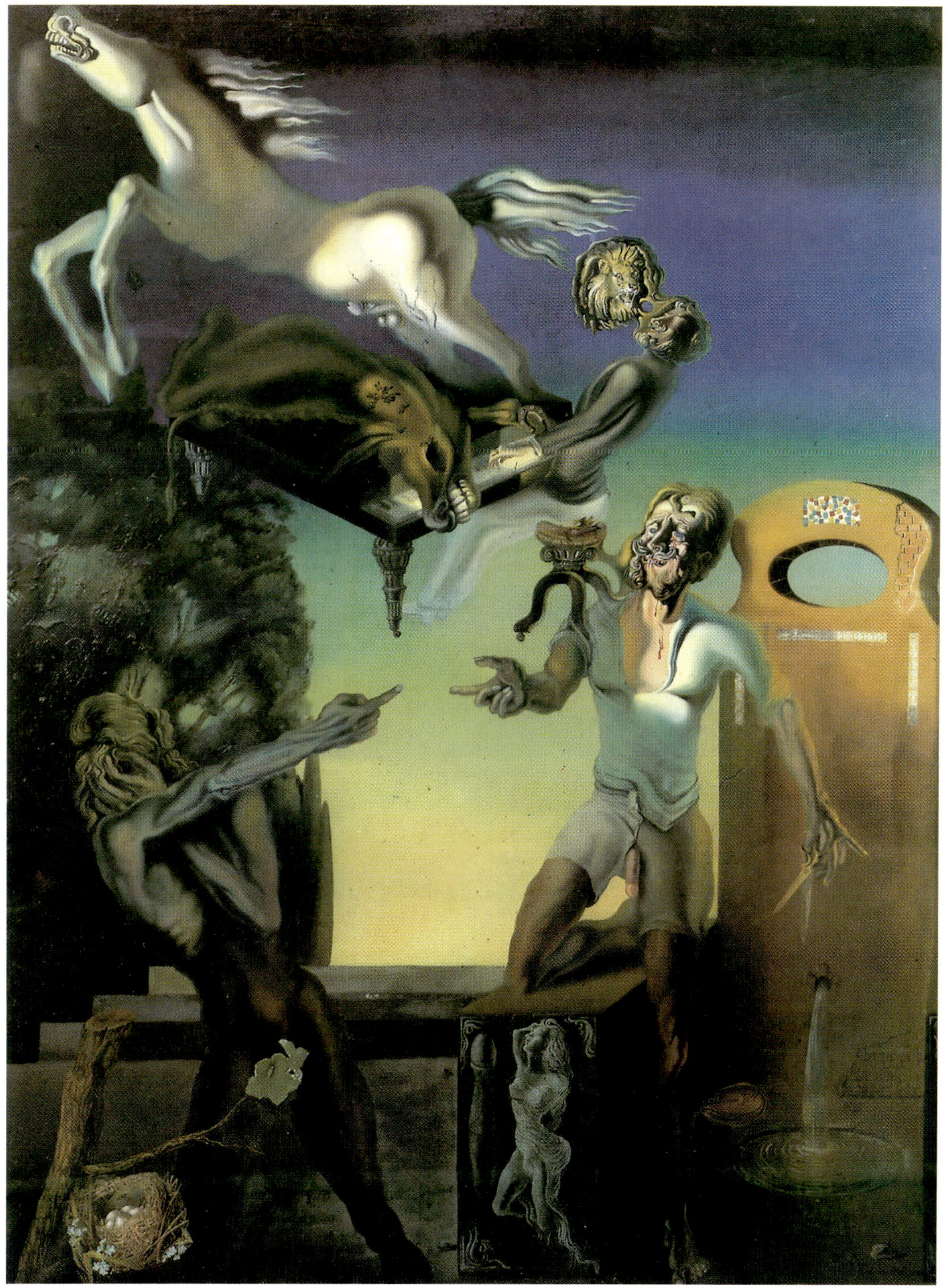

Family ties *William Tell*, painted in 1930, was the first in a series of paintings with Tell as a symbolic figure for the father. The subject alludes to the uneasy relationship with his father, which was in large part due to Dali's affair with Gala. Dalí mocks his father with the beard and breasts, and the genetalia projecting from the flies in his underpants. The lion's head stands for unleashed sexual desire, while the rearing horse and the donkey's corpse represent the fatal dangers of sexuality.

View of Dalí and Gala's house in Port Lligat.

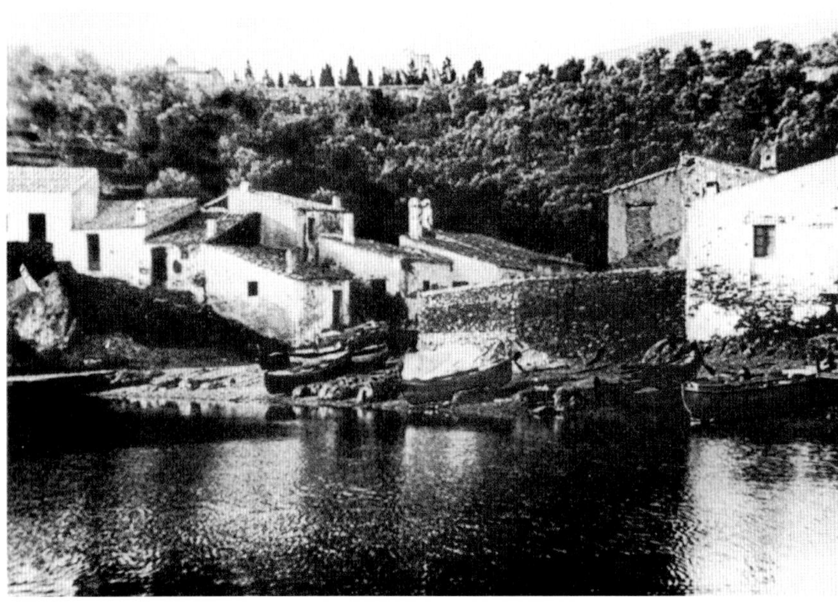

of their lives in cozy togetherness, cut off from the bustling hinterland. In the early days, they invested great energy in enlarging and improving the house year after year, so that eventually the simple cottage was transformed into a small palace. "We got a builder's carpenter in, and Gala and I together designed all the details, from the number of steps to the size of the small window. Ludwig II of Bavaria did not put half as much thought into any of his palaces as we did into our little hovel. It was to consist of a room around thirteen feet square, which served as a dining room, bedroom, studio and entrance hall."

Dalí and Gala lived a quiet life there, rarely interrupted by visitors. "We live there in solitude and in the rhythm of the cosmic pulse. We fish for sardines by the new moon and know that lettuce shoots up at that time instead of forming heads. We ponder the brilliant inspirations of Paracelsus rather than listen to the radio; we prefer to dream of the world of the invisible with our eyes open rather than be led astray by television; we fly on to the peaks of the absolute instead of fighting for the development of a utopian socialism. I look after my field and my boat—i.e. the picture I happen to be painting—and like a good worker I take pleasure in simple things."

Dalí painted every day except Sunday, from dawn to dusk, while Gala looked after the household, spent time in the open air and on the beach, swam, and read close at hand. And she acted as his model, Dalí having begun to paint her incessantly.

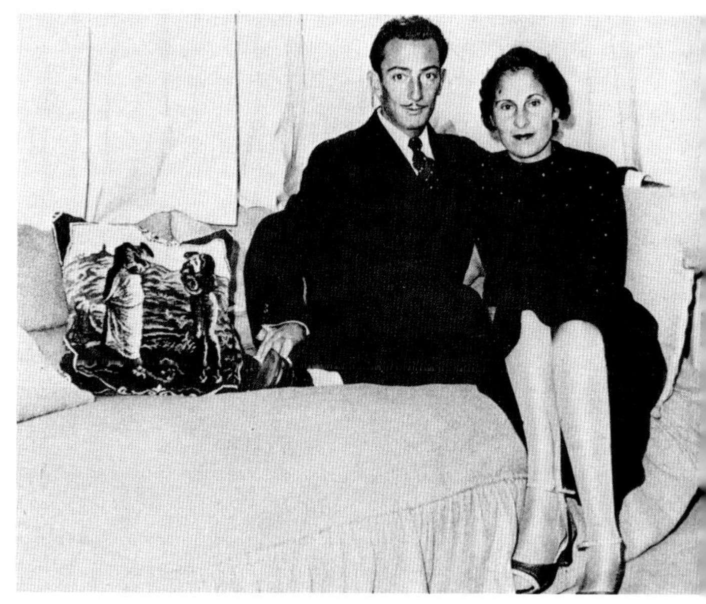

Gala and Salvador Dalí in their Paris apartment.

Gala the Muse

The first major work to contain a reference to Gala was *Imperial Monument to the Child-Woman*, painted in 1929. It features Gala as the Child-Woman, a bust of graceful beauty in the middle of the Cap de Creus landscape, where their affair began. Front right in the picture a skeleton (Dalí calls it a "Javanese marionette") acts as a kneeling lover paying homage to its muse.

The *Accommodations of Desire* was also painted shortly after their first meeting. According to Dalí, it expressed his fear of sexual relations with Gala: "I'd never 'slept with anyone' in my life, and I imagined this act as fearfully violent and that my physical strength would not be up to it—'that's not for me.'" Later he became even clearer, explaining that the lion jaws hinted at his "terrible fear of being unmasked when possessing a vagina, that would lead to the revelation of my impotence."

William Tell is one of his coarsest paintings sexually, and relates to his troubled relationship with his father, to being thrown out of his home, and to his father's hostility to the relationship with Gala. Dalí wrote: "William Tell is my father, and I am the small child he holds in his arms. ... He wants to eat me. At his feet is a very small nut that contains a whole child, which is an image of my wife Gala. She is constantly threatened by this foot ..."

William Tell and Gradiva (1931) also has a direct autobiographical reference. Two naked figures stand in front of a rock, with the man prodding the woman's armpit with his penis. The Gradiva of the title is Gala, and William

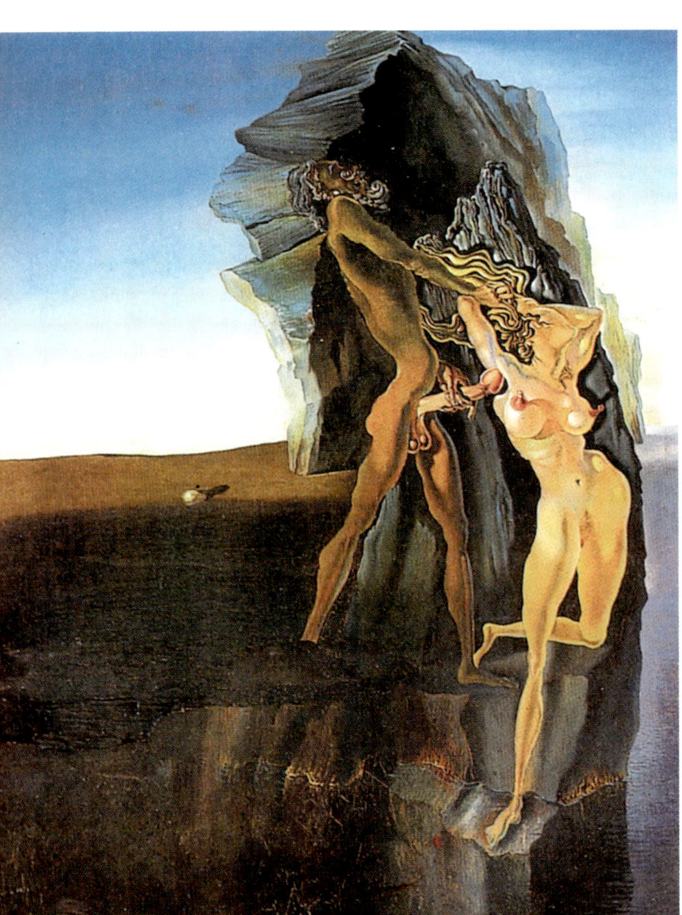

Secret desire? *William Tell and Gradiva*, 1931.

Tell is, as before, Dalí's father. The title suggests that, in this picture, Dalí is secretly attributing his father's rejection of Gala to desire. As this remains unfulfilled, it is not the sexual organs that come together. The sexual act is replaced by a simulation effected by a hand and armpit.

Dalí painted his muse again and again: as *Galatea of the Spheres* or *Leda Atomica* or *The Madonna of Port Lligat*, as Venus, an angel, or St Helen. Or simply as *Galarina* in a classically beautiful portrait testifying to Dalí's devotion and admiration. Contrasting with the many immaculate pictures of Gala are the accounts of contemporaries, who show her in a less flattering light. In the writings of Anaïs Nin, who lived with the Dalís in Hampton Manor in Virginia, she appears as a cool, arrogant woman who treated everyone else as servants: "Mrs. Dalí never raised her voice, never enticed, never charmed. She simply assumed we were there to serve the great unchallenged genius Dalí." In the estimation of a biographer, Gala was "such an uncompromising, self-willed, egotistical person totally uninterested in the feelings of others that everyone shuddered who had to deal with her."

Lucrative Business

But Gala was not only a source of inspiration for Dalí. She removed all obstacles from his path; even as a child, he had been clumsy in anything practical. She carried out all the everyday necessities so that he could get on with his art in peace. This meant above all dealing with the business side. As soon as they met, in Cadaqués in 1929, she bore off some his pictures with

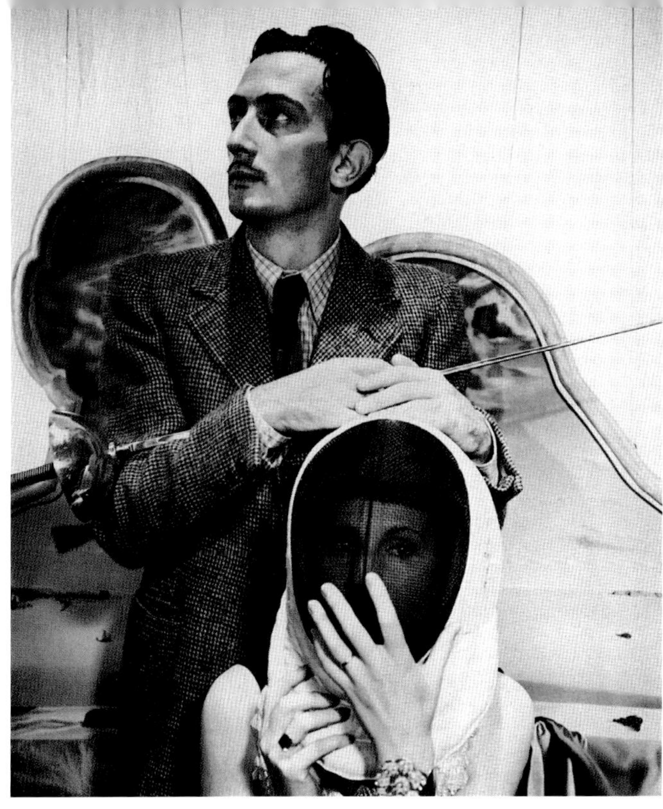

Ironic quote: Dalí and Gala in the battle of the sexes in front of the silhouette work *Couple with Their Heads Full of Clouds*.

her back to Paris and immediately set about her role as muse—a very practical muse. It included everything to do with Dalí's artistic development, visiting galleries and potential clients in her function as his agent, organizing and running exhibitions, negotiating sales and concluding contracts: in fact, the tireless management of the whole financial side of their life. Like the artist, she was in this respect openly ambitious. All her efforts were directed at boosting Dalí's fame and securing their joint income. It was a task she pursued obstinately and very successfully. Dalí never tired of thanking her. Because of her encouragement and constant support, he became one of the richest and most famous men in the world.

Machine Guns and Water Melons

That Dalí had sexual problems is evident from various comments in his diaries and memoirs. He talked of a panicky fear of sexual diseases that his father had dinned into him as a child. His father had placed on the piano, in a position where it could not be ignored, a medical volume illustrating the "terrible consequences" of sexual diseases.

"But above all, I long suffered the wretchedness of thinking I was impotent. Naked, when I compared myself with school friends, I discovered that my penis was small, pitiful and soft. I can remember a pornographic novel whose Don Juan peppered female genitals as it were with a machine gun and said with cruel delight that he enjoyed hearing women squish like watermelons. I persuaded myself that I would never be capable of making women squish like watermelons." At the time he met Gala, Dalí assures us, he had never had contact with any other woman, and that's how it remained to the end of his life. He found satisfaction only from masturbation, and in his youth it made him feel guilty. "At that time, my libido had degenerated into really erotic lunacies as a result of this kind of impotence complex. ... I disguised myself as a king and masturbated, and if I had not found Gala, with whom I discovered normal love, so to speak, all my delusions would quite certainly have exceeded the dimension of paranoia two years later and become psycho-pathological."

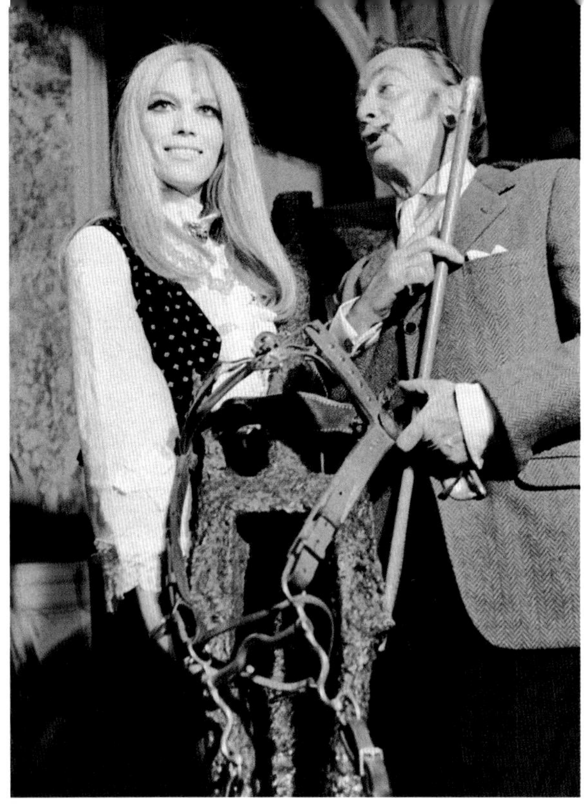

Dalí with Amanda Lear

Later Years

In the 1960s, Dalí and Gala drifted apart as, by mutual agreement, both of them pursued their own separate interests. Dalí collected around him a whole ménage of good-looking young people whom he generally "ordered" from Jean-Claude Du Barry, owner of a model agency in Barcelona. His preference was for androgynous, angelic-looking types, particularly young men, who had to look as girlish as possible. His needs were artistic and voyeuristic rather than sexual: no physical relationships were ever involved. His swarm of admirers enlivened the evenings in Port Lligat and accompanied him on his journeys to Paris and New York. From 1965, Amanda Lear was always at his side, and on social occasions took on Gala's role, which provided lots of material for the gossip columns. Lear was a transsexual of sensational beauty, previously known as Alan Tap. After changing sex, she changed career from a top model for Mary Quant to singer and European disco queen. On the way there, she had numerous affairs, with (among others) David Bowie and Bryan Ferry.

In 1969, Dalí took twenty-year-old Columbian Carlos Lozana into his retinue as a particular favorite. Lozana afterwards described the erotic ceremonies that Dalí organized in various places and rented palaces for his voyeuristic amusement. Dalí's role was that of master of ceremonies in these, giving directorial instructions and openly masturbating.

Gala was by then an old woman who longed for peace and quiet. In 1969, Dalí bought her a dilapidated medieval *castell* in the village of Púbol in the Lower Empordà region, fifty miles (eighty kilometers) from Port Lligat. Despite his other amusements, she remained the most important person in his life. After costly restoration, Gala moved in the following year, and

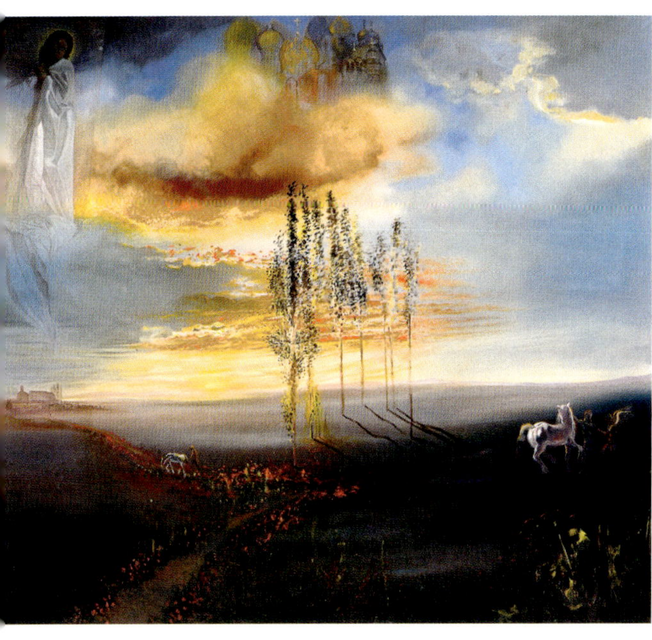

Gala's Castle in Púbol, painted 1973.

even Dalí was only admitted on written invitation.

Gala had meantime become known for her promiscuity. Her numerous affairs involved very young men with whom she went on trips, and on whom she spent the wealth that she had accumulated for Dalí during the years of exile in America, despite their extravagant lifestyle. For a while her lover was William Rotlein, a homeless heroin addict she had picked up in Brooklyn and who was forty years her junior. With him, she traveled to Rome, Florence, Turin, and Verona. The Italian press carried accounts of an "unusual love affair between the grandmother and the boy." Her last great love was young actor Jeff Fenholt. For seven years he spent the summers with Gala behind high walls at her mystery-shrouded residence in Púbol. The affair with Fenholt cost her a fortune: among her gifts was $1.5m for a house in Long Island. Fenholt later denied that sex had any part in their relationship.

Love had in the interim long gone out of the window in the relationship between Dalí and Gala. Ill and old, the two of them often quarreled. In public, however, Dalí continued to proclaim his entire love and admiration for Gala. After an operation on her gall bladder, and breaking her thigh bone in a fall, Gala's condition steadily worsened. She no longer ate, and her conversation wandered. Shortly before she died, she asked Amanda Lear to look after Dalí. Death came at 6 am on 10 June 1982 in Port Lligat. At her own request, she was interred in the crypt of the *castell* in Púbol, laid out in a red Dior dress.

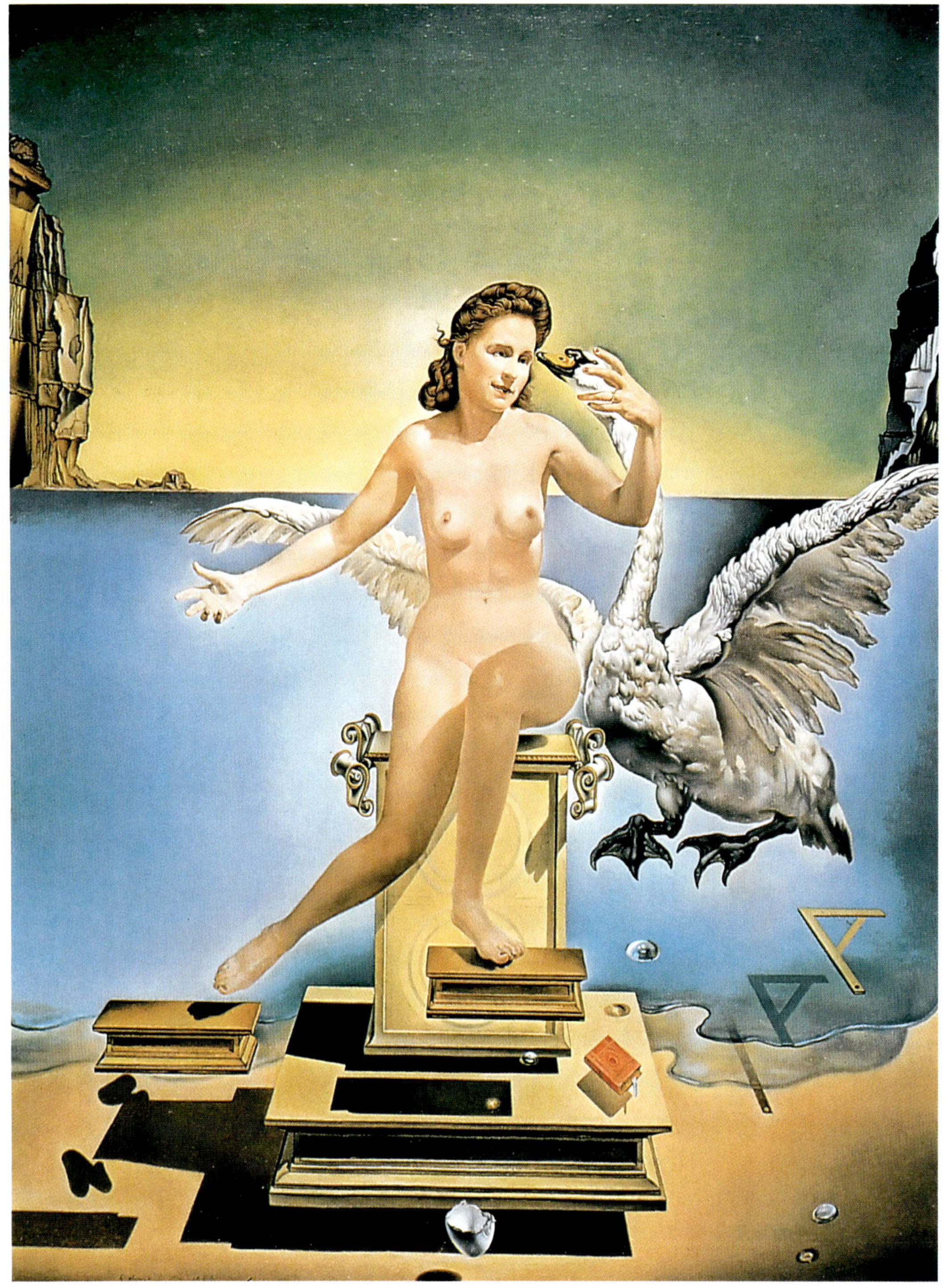

Weightless *Leda Atomica* is an impressive rendering of the Greek myth of Leda (represented by Gala), wife of the King of Sparta who is importuned by Zeus in the form of a swan. The painting was done in 1949 as one of the principal works of Dalí's "atomic" phase, following detailed sketches and collaboration with Roman mathematician Matila Ghika. The laws of gravity don't apply to this image—even water hovers above the surface of the earth.

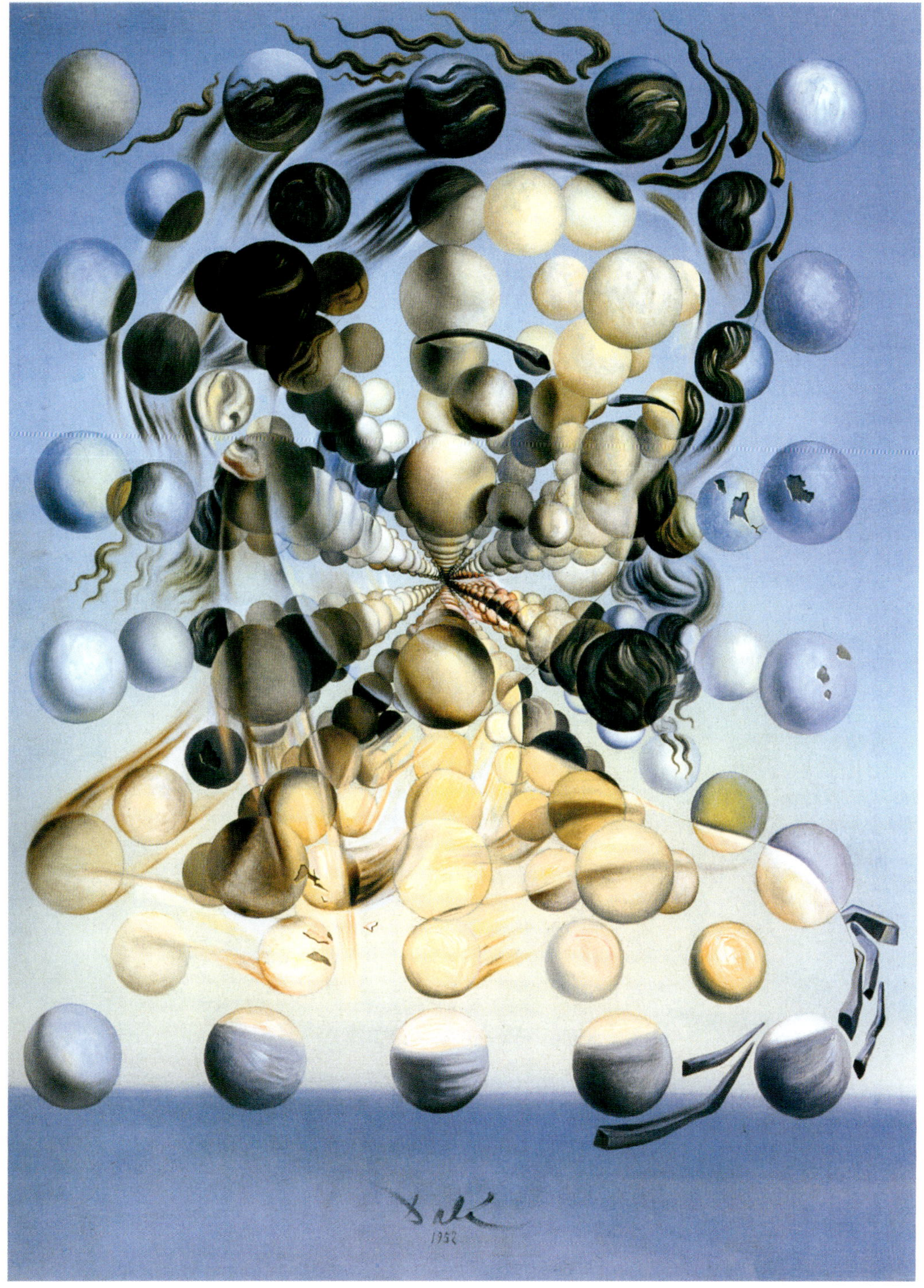

Nuclear mysticism After World War II, Dalí's interest turned chiefly to science. *Galatea of the Spheres*, a piece of technical virtuosity by Dalí, demonstrates his fascination for the DNA model in its molecular structure.

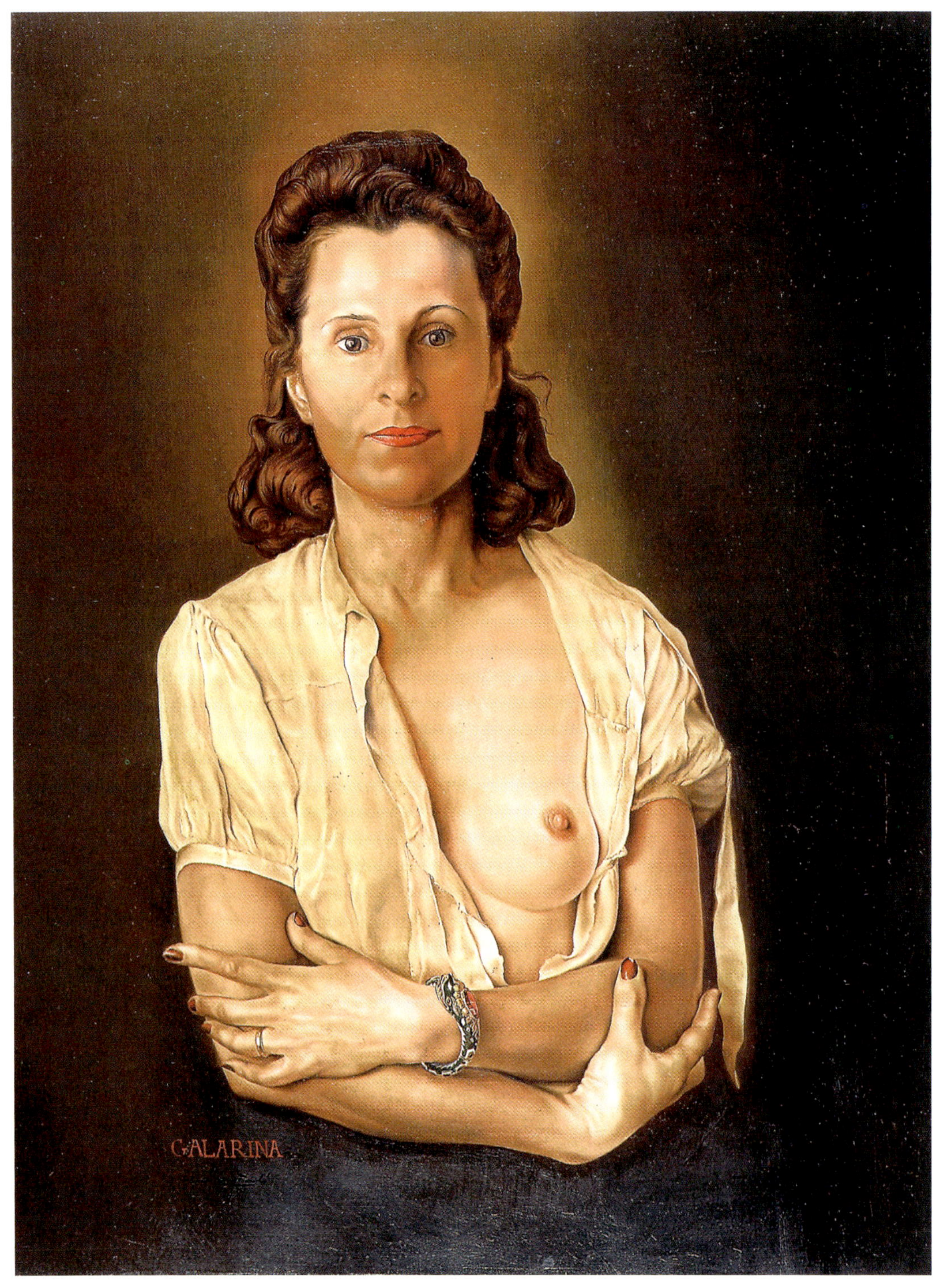

Untouchable Gala appears immaculate in *Galarina*, painted 1944-45. This remarkable work—according to Dalí, "like Vermeer", was the result of 540 hours of work. It is now in the Teatre-Museu Dalí in Figueres.

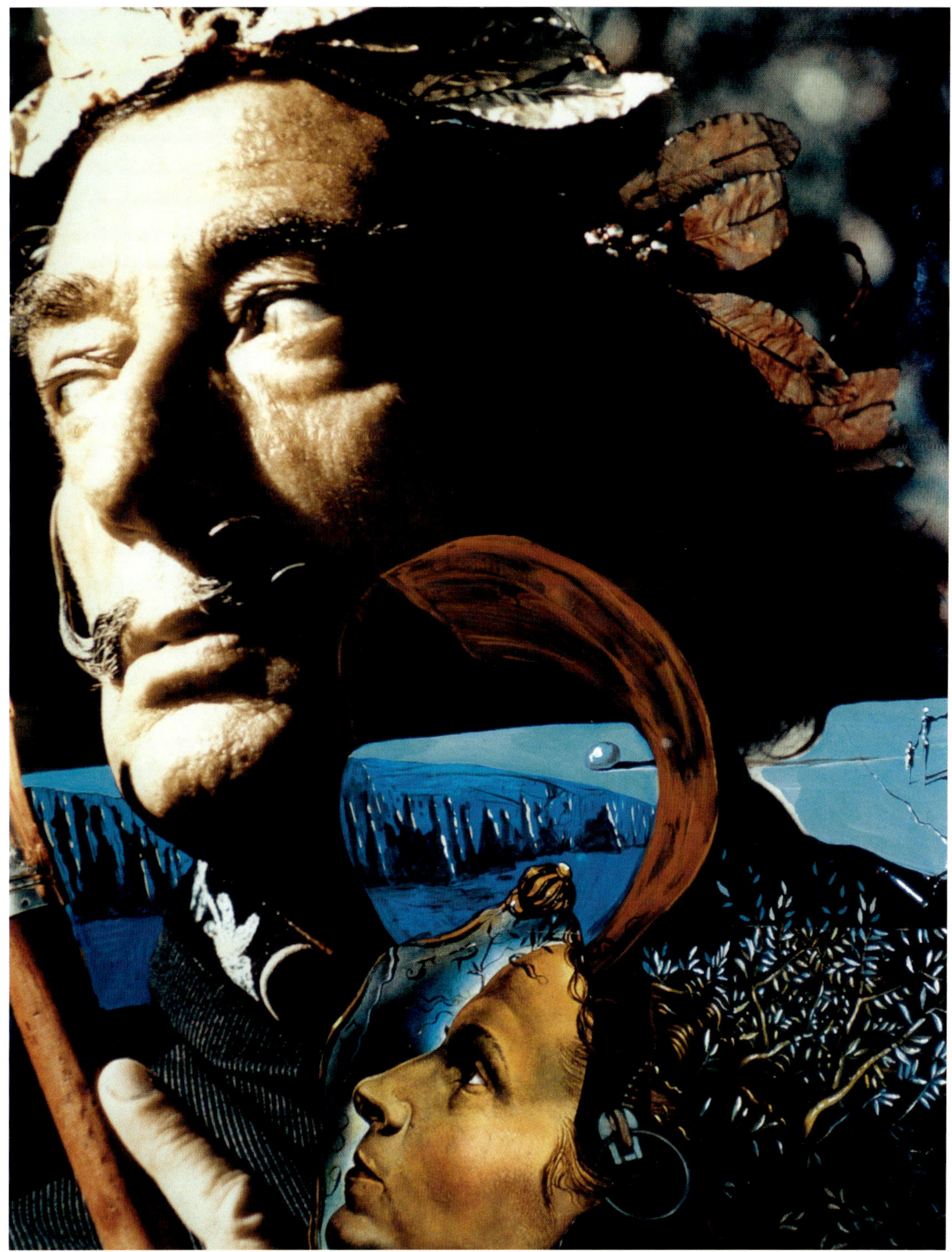

Collage As a multi-media artist, Dalí made extensive use of photographs, in his paintings, collages, montages, and his stagy public appearances. *Self-Portrait with Gala* dates from 1970 and lauds their love and union.

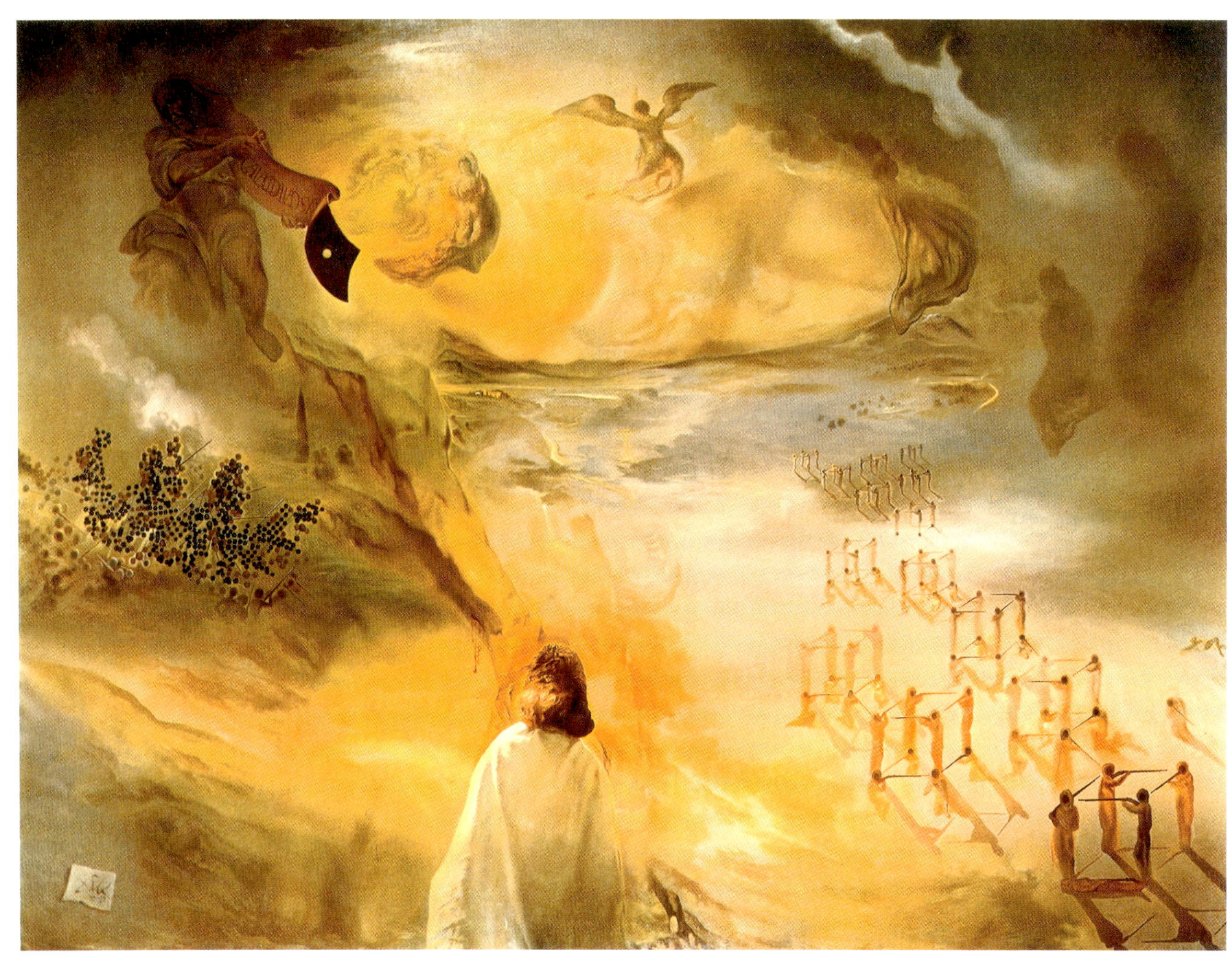

"My longest title in one word" Another picture with the unpronounceable title *Galacidalacidesoxyribonucleicacid* (1962) focuses on Gala. The huge painting (305 x 345 cm) is subtitled *Tribute to Crick and Watson*, who had just received a Nobel Prize. The spiral-shaped DNA molecule in the middle represented according to Dalí "Christ's ascension into the arms of God."

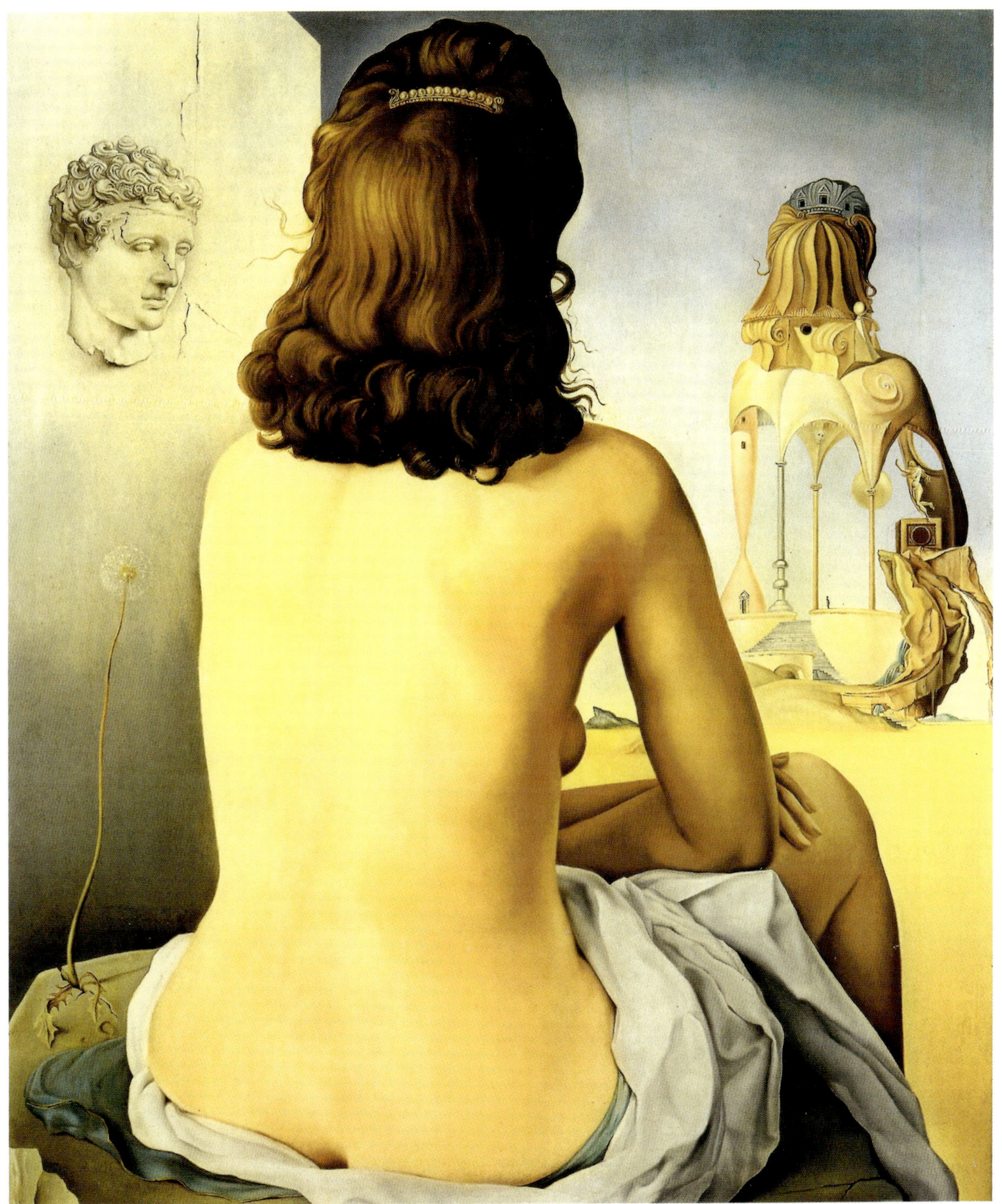

Memory "At the age of five, I saw an insect eaten by ants, leaving only the carapace. You could see the sky through the holes in the shell. Whenever I want to get closer to purity, I always look at the sky through flesh." said Dalí of his picture *My Wife, Nude, Contemplating Her Own Flesh Becoming Stairs, Three Vertebrae of a Column, Sky and Architecture*.

Dalí Today

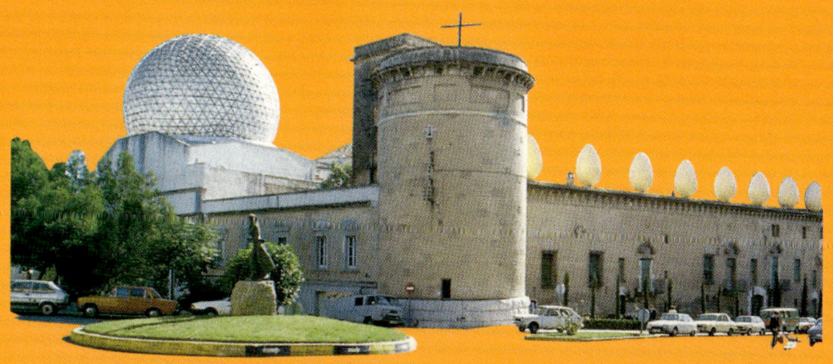

“I would like it to become the spiritual center of Europe.”

Salvador Dalí about the
Teatre-Museu Dalí

Dali's legacy ...

... is to be found largely in Spain. Dalí made sure of that by bequeathing over 250 paintings and 2,000 drawings to the Spanish state in his will. It was his express wish to leave as many works as possible in his homeland and to transform his birthplace Figueres into a "cultural and museum Mecca of Spain and the world." So the town in northern Catalonia owes its popularity to its native son and his Teatre-Museu Dalí, which is the second most visited museum in Spain after the Prado.

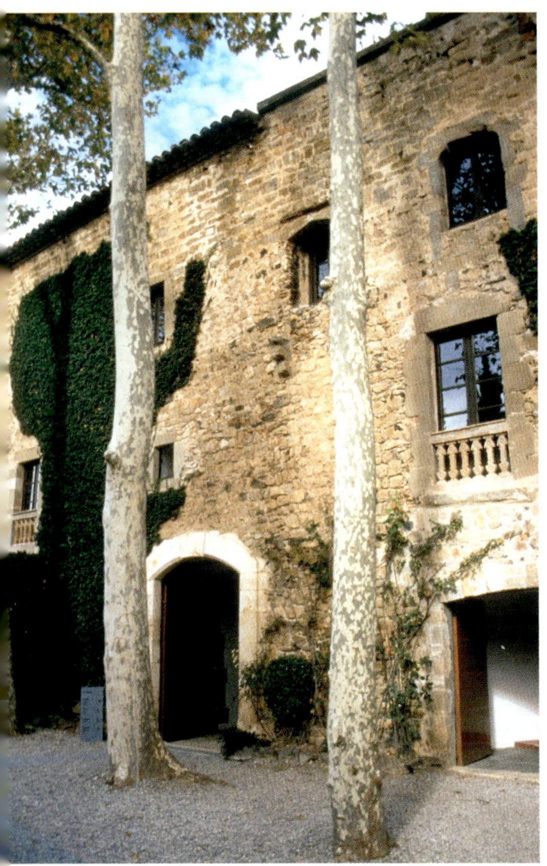

Castell Gala Dalí, Púbol, Dalí's gift to his muse.

The Dalí Triangle

There are three Dalí attractions in the locality: the Teatre-Museu Dalí in Figueres, which was opened in the artist's lifetime; the house in Port Lligat, where Dalí and Gala spent a large part of their life together; and the castle in Púbol, Gala's last residence, where her vault can be visited. Catalonia promotes this "Dalí triangle" very successfully—they attract well over a million visitors a year.

Dalí Centenary

--> Spain honored one of its most famous sons on 11 May 2004, the centenary of Dalí's birth. King Juan Carlos I and Queen Sofia officially launched "Dalí Year" in Figueres. Celebrations were particularly notable in Catalonia, with numerous exhibitions, conferences, theater and opera performances, and concerts. There were major retrospectives in Barcelona and Madrid, and other cities in Europe, America, and Asia put on exhibitions, notably Venice, Philadelphia, and Rotterdam.

Dalí the Film

Well-known artist personalities can be good material for box office successes, as films about Picasso, Frida Kahlo, and Klimt have shown. It is no surprise therefore that New Zealand director Andrew Niccol intends to make a film about the extraordinary life and work of Salvador Dalí called *Dalí and I: The Surreal Story*, based on the biography of that name by art dealer Stan Lauryssen, who was a friend of Dalí and his wife. The film is expected to be in the cinemas in 2008. It will be interesting to see how Oscar winner Al Pacino comes across as the extravagant artist Dalí.

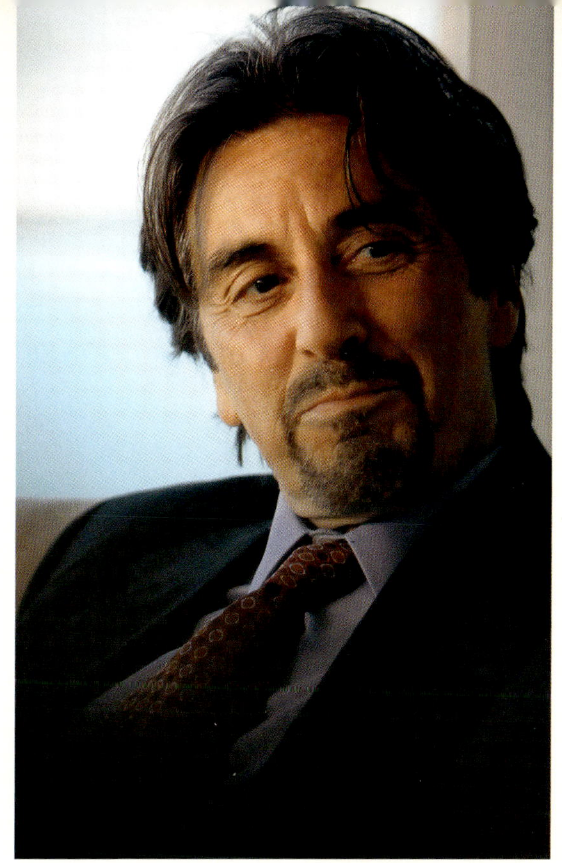

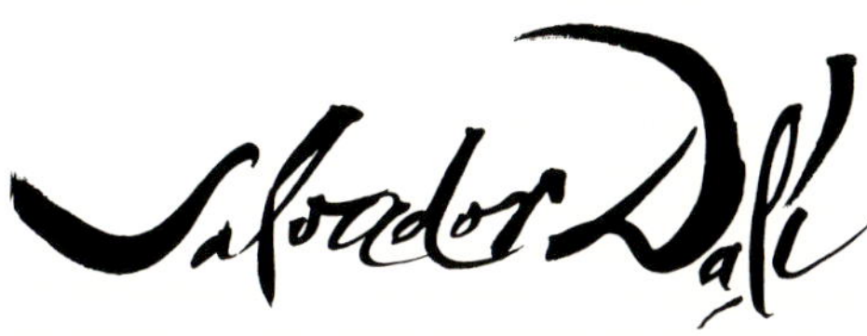

Chaos in the Art Market

Dalí leaves posterity a wealth of paintings, watercolors, drawings, graphics, sculptures, jewelry, and objects of all kind. But watch out: not everything that carries the artist's name is the real thing. A flood of forgeries inundated the market around 1965 after Dalí began signing tens of thousands of blank sheets that would then be printed with lithographs. In 1981 the scandal went international when the suspicion was voiced that he had actually had a hand in the forgeries, or at least done nothing to stop them. The supposed originals were in fact an excellent deal for Dalí, as he was paid an additional $40 per sheet. The extent of the fraud caused chaos, and the situation is still unresolved. An astonishing 40,000 forged printed graphics have so far been discovered, but how many more are still in circulation remains unclear.

"My guardian spirits are Catalan, my own genius comes from Catalonia, the country of gold and asceticism."

Salvador Dalí

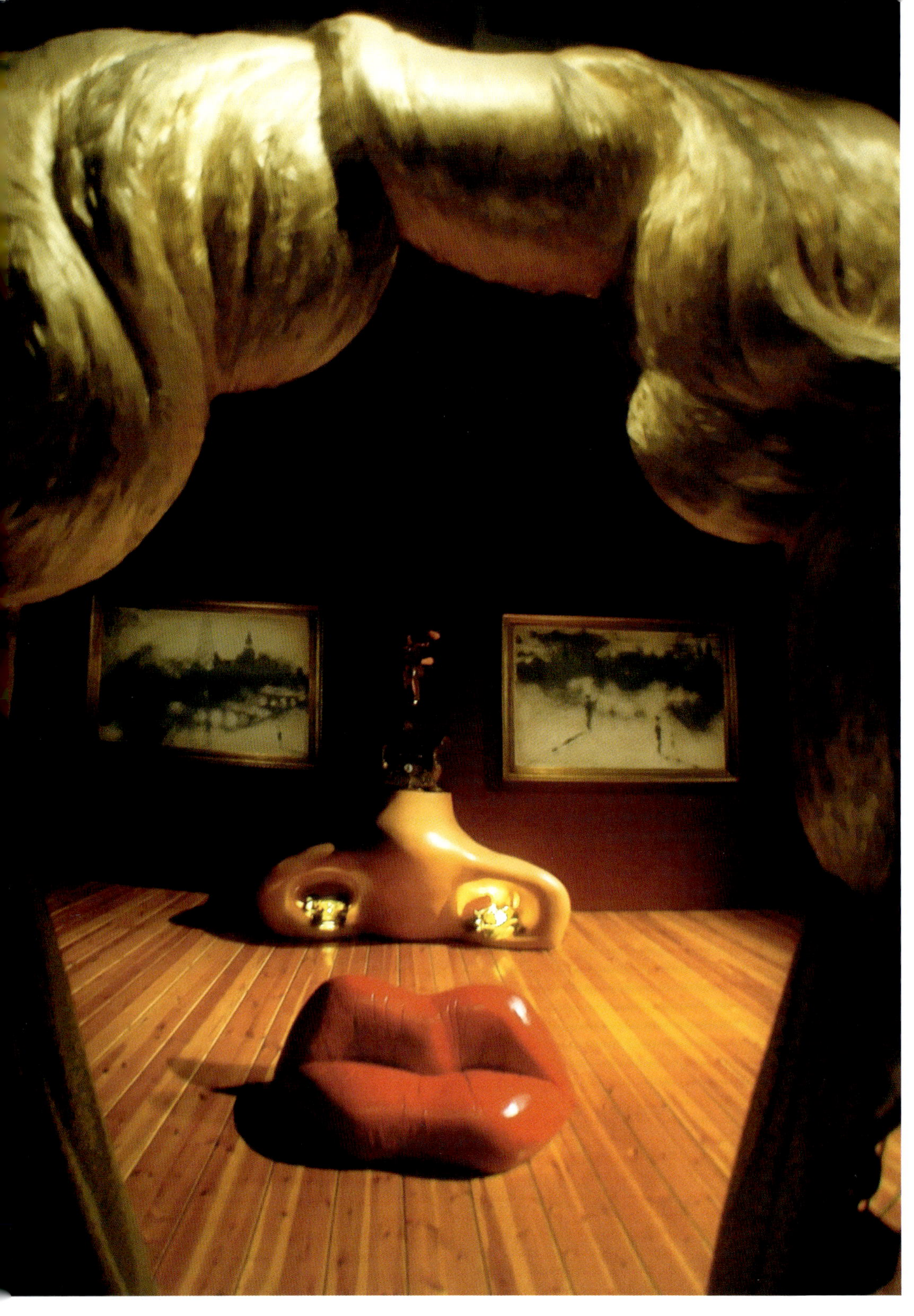

Mae West (1892–1980) was an icon of 1930s Hollywood. In his Teatre-Museu, Dalí had the idea of turning his collage of 1934–35 (right) into a "real" walk-in room. The sofa, a bright red sofa made of plastic and shaped like lips, subsequently went into serial production.

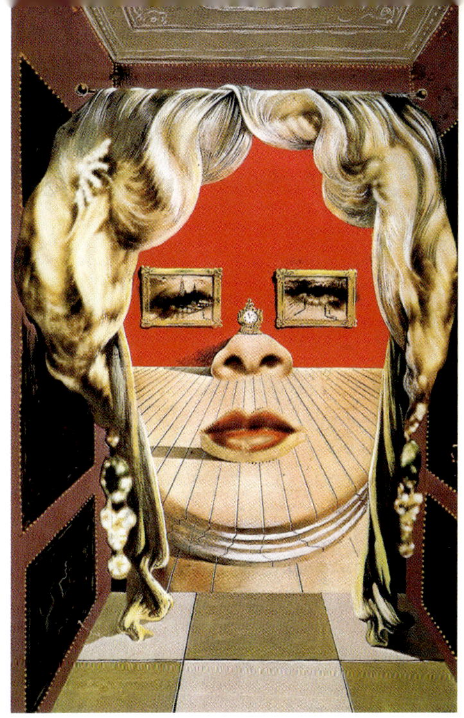

Face of Mae West (Usable as a Surrealist Apartment), 1934–1935

A Catalan Celebrity

Dalí's life was, like his work, closely linked with his native region, specifically the landscape of Empordà in the north-east of Catalonia. Empordà is a plain that extends to the sea, and is sheltered in the north by the eastern foothills of the Pyrenees. Dalí's links with the region were umbilical: it inspired him, and was present in his entire work.

Tribute to Dalí

Nowadays Catalonia promotes itself with trips to "Salvador Dalí's paradise," the bare landscapes of Empordà, which is an ever-recurrent setting in his pictures. For a closer look at the artist's life and work, the best places to start are the towns of Figueres, Portlligat, and Púbol.

"I need the link with my home in Port Lligat, just as Raphael needed Urbino in the transition from the particular to the universal."

Salvador Dalí

Opened in 1974, the Teatre-Museu Dalí in Figueres is opposite the church where Dalí was baptized. It is housed in the former town theater, and it was here that the fourteen-year-old Dalí first exhibited his work in 1918: an apt venue for someone who would later consider himself an eminently theatrical artist. The theater was largely destroyed in 1939 during the Spanish Civil War, but at

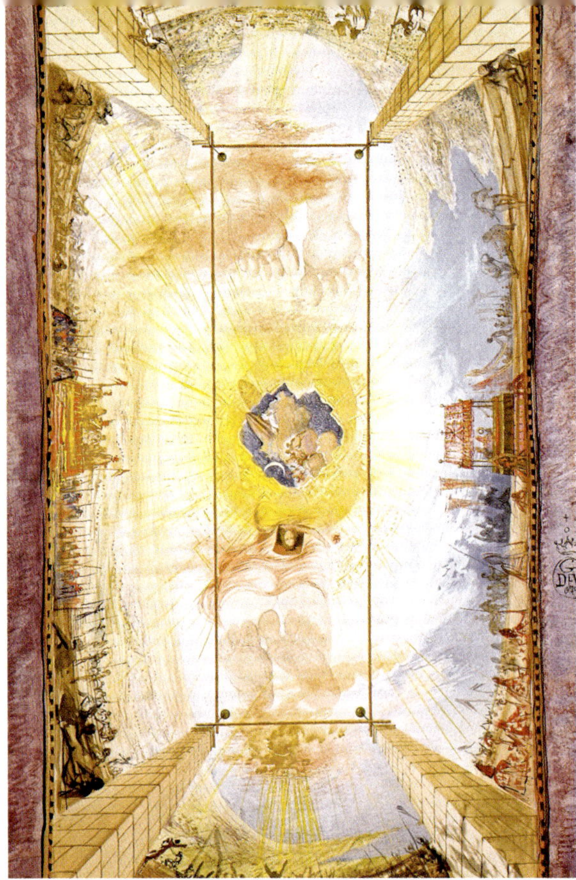

Sketch for one of the ceiling paintings done by the artist at the Teatre-Museu Dalí.

Dalí's initiative a museum was built within the ruins of the old theater, the glass dome of which is now an emblem of Figueres visible from afar.

The museum collection contains around 4,000 works of art, including important paintings such as *The Girl from Figueres*, *Galarina*, and *Leda Atomica;* works such as the *Mae West Room* (a walk-in room with the face of Mae West) and *Rainy Taxi* installations were done specially for the museum. At the artist's request, the works are distributed around the entire building without chronological or thematic order, and without titles. An adjacent building contains the Dalí Jewel Gallery, with Dalí's designs and pieces of jewelry, which the Gala-Salvador Dalí Foundation acquired from Japan in 1999 for 5.5m Euros ($7.5m). The importance of the museum lies not however in the works in the museum collection. The Teatre-Museu itself is the largest walk-in Dalí art work of them all, and was designed by him down to the last detail, from the monumental eggs on the roof through the pseudo-classical wall and ceiling paintings down to the poster for the state lottery inside. The artist's tomb is also there, beneath the dome.

Dalí's home in Port Lligat has been open to the public since 1997, and is interesting because it played such a special part in the artist's life and work. This was where he did what he considered his most significant works. The building itself is impressive as the result of a forty-year reconstruction process that turned a humble fisherman's cottage into the present labyrinthine Dalí palace. The house with its furniture and personal objects can be visited by prior appointment. The castle in Púbol, which is about fifty miles (eighty kilometers) from Port Lligat, has not only an art collection but also Gala's private rooms as well, with a collection of *haute couture* clothes and the couple's opulent Cadillac. It also contains the vault where Gala was interred.

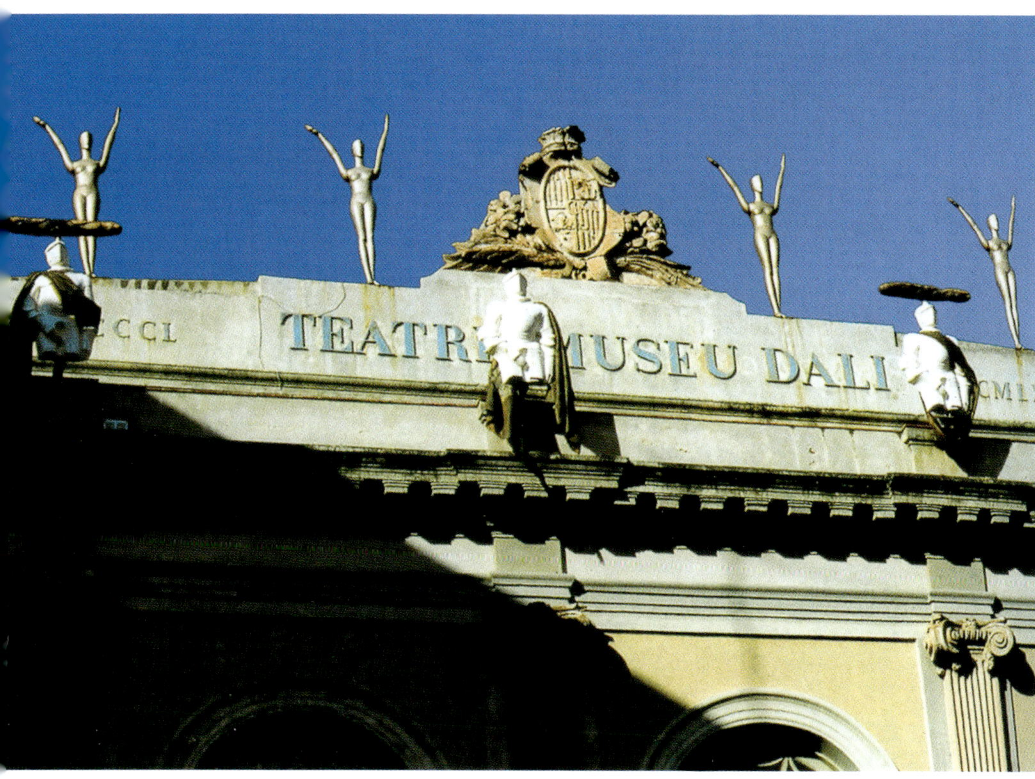

Following an idea of Dalí's, the façade has the Teatre-Museu has a mock acroterion in the form of gilt Art Deco mannequins on pedestals.

Another Dalí museum that opened its doors during the artist's lifetime began in Ohio in 1971 but moved to its present location in St Petersburg, Florida, in 1982. The basic collection is the largest private collection of Dalí works anywhere, and was amassed by married couple Reynold and Eleanor Morse, who were long-standing acquaintances of Dalí. It comprises 95 oil paintings, 100 watercolors and drawings, and 1,300 other items (graphic works, sculptures, photos, and documents).

Critical Reaction

Despite all the praise heaped on him, Dalí is not only among the best-known but also the most controversial of Surrealist painters. His place in the history of 20th-century art is still not established.

He is seen as the precursor of 1960s Pop culture, and his imagination and extraordinary draughtsmanship are incontestable, but the figure of the artist himself is always getting in the way of an appreciation of his works.

His political closeness to the Franco regime, his fascination with the Hitler phenomenon, his sudden very ostentatious conversion to Catholicism, his self-serving delusions of grandeur combined with his eccentric form of self-projection all add up to reasons for many art historians and critics to hold him in contempt. Even his pandering to the mass market from the late 1930s, the stereotype repetitions of his motifs, his seeming association with fraudulent dealings, and his unerring instinct for the opportunities the mass media and mass culture provided—and with which he was so successful on the American market—have weakened his position in the art market.

But, art or commerce, the Dalí legend persists, one way or another, and one thing is certain—Dalí would have been delighted.

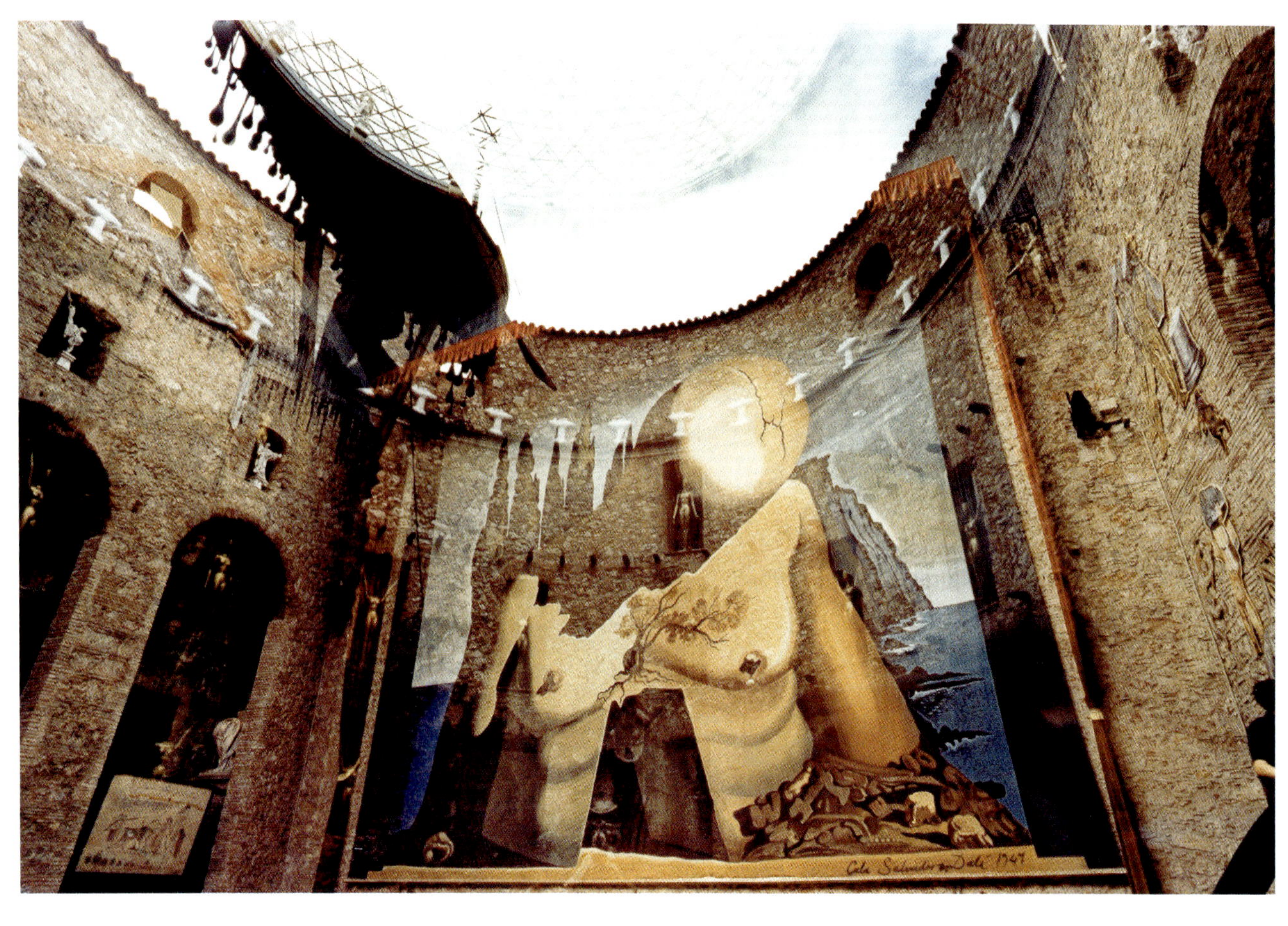

A glimpse of Dalí's world Dalí's dream of a museum of his own came true. With a budget of 12m pesetas (ca. 73,000 euros), the former municipal theater was turned into a *gesamtkunstwerk*—the Teatre-Museu Dalí.

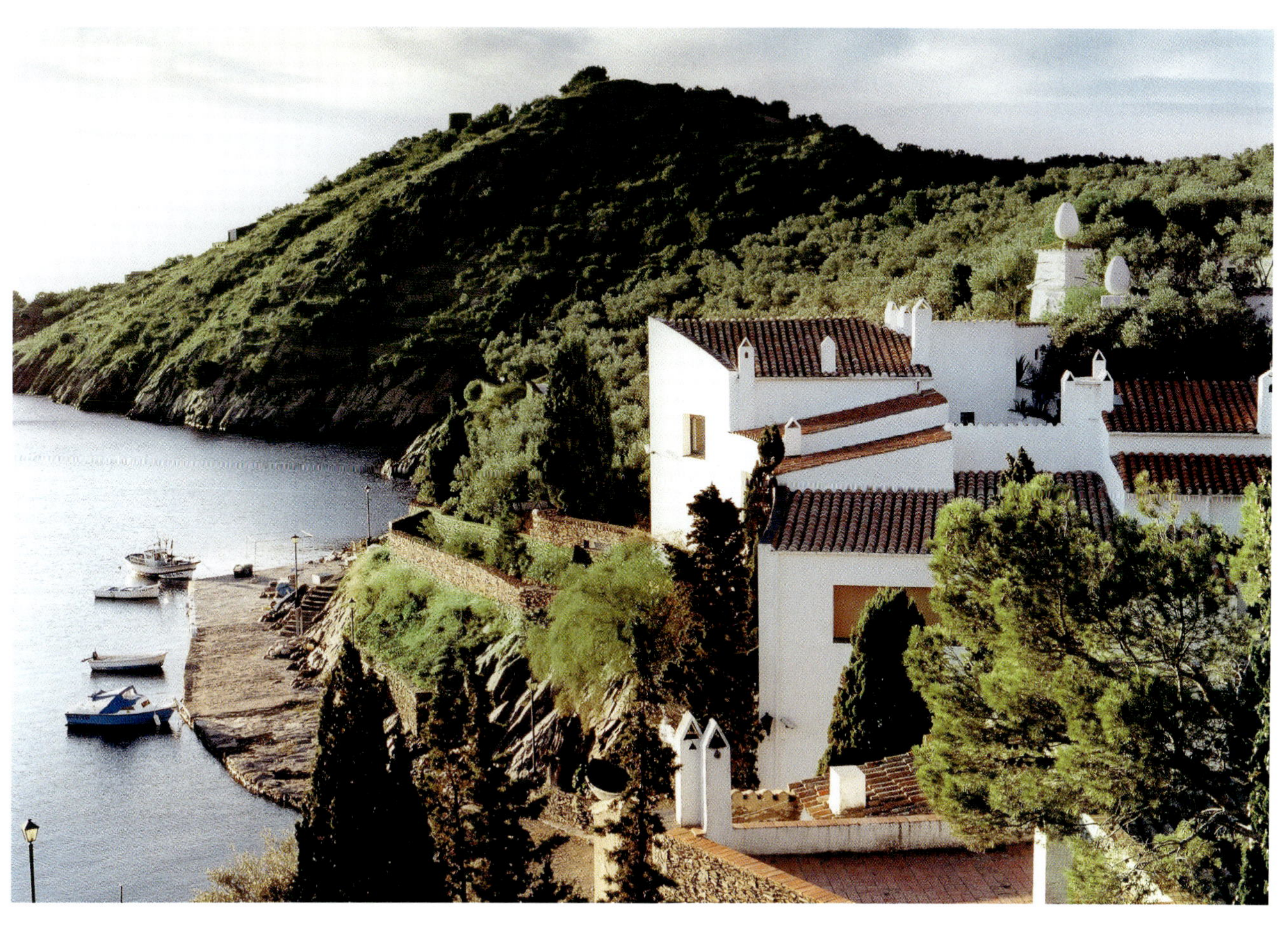

Habitat The Dalís' home in the small fishing village of Port Lligat on the Costa Brava, has been open to the public since 1997. Originally a modest cabin, more and more rooms were added over the years as the Dalís used it as a refuge even during periods of great success in Paris and New York.

Picture list

p. 5: Dalí in his studio in Paris
p. 6: Cover of *Destino* Magazine, 1948
p. 7 left: Salvador Dalí, *Soft Construction with Boiled Beans (Premonition of Civil War)*, 1936, oil on canvas, 51 x 78 cm, The Philadelphia Museum of Art
p. 7 right: Sigmund Freud, 1909
p. 8: Max Ernst, *Rendezvous of Friends*, 1922, oil on canvas, 130 x 193 cm, Museum Ludwig, Köln
p. 9: Invitation to the Surrealism exhibition at Pierre Colle, 7–18 June 1933
p. 10: Salvador Dalí, poster design—regular meeting of the Surrealist conferences, 1935, gouache on packing paper, 78 x 50 cm, private collection
p. 11: Sigmund Freud, *The Interpretation of Dreams*, 1900
p. 12: René Magritte, *The Rape*, 1934, oil on canvas, 73,2 x 54,3 cm, Menil Foundation, Houston
p. 13: Pablo Picasso, *Guernica*, 1937, oil on canvas, 100 x 80 cm, Prado, Madrid
p. 15: Salvador Dalí, *Aphrodisiac Jacket*, 1936, smoking jacket with liqueur glasses, shirt, and ascot on a clothes hanger, 88 x 79 x 6 cm, private collection
p. 16: Salvador Dalí upon his arrival in New York, December 1936
p. 17 top: Dalí holding the edition of *Life Magazine*, in which his article *Dalí's Dollars* was printed, 1970
p. 17 bottom: Philippe Halsman, *Dalí's Mustache*, 1954
p. 18: Salvador Dalí, *Persistence of Memory*, 1931, oil on canvas, 24 x 33 cm, The Museum of Modern Art, New York
p. 19: Cover of *Time Magazine*, 14 December 1936, photography by Man Ray
p. 20: Catalog cover for the Dalí exhibition from 2 November-10 December 1934 at the Julien Levy Gallery in New York
p. 21: Page from the *New York Evening Journal*, edition from 14 November 1934
p. 22: Salvador Dalí, *Don Quixote and Sancho Panza*, 1968, etching, 49 x 39 cm
p. 23: Salvador Dalí with his secretary Enrique Sabater
p. 24: Film sequence from *Un Chien Andalou (An Andalusian Dog)*, 1929
p. 25: Film sequence from *Un Chien Andalou (An Andalusian Dog)*, 1929
p. 26: Salvador Dalí, *Portrait of Luis Bunuel*, 1925, oil on canvas, 70 x 60 cm, Luis Bunuel Collection, Mexico
p. 27: Salvador Dalí, *Portrait of Mrs. Isabel Styler-Tas*, 1945, oil on canvas, 65,5 x 86 cm, Nationalgalerie, Berlin
p. 29: Salvador Dalí, *Lobster Telephone*, 1936, telephone with a painted plaster lobster, 18 x 12,5 x 30,5 cm, Deutsches Post-museum, Frankfurt am Main
p. 30: Salvador Dalí as a magician, November 1963
p. 31 top: Salvador Dalí, *The Railway Station at Perpignan*, 1956, oil on canvas, 295 x 406 cm, Museum Ludwig, Cologne
p. 31 bottom: Salvador Dalí, *Young Virgin Auto-Sodomized by the Horns of her own Chastity*, 1954, oil on canvas, 40,5 x 30,5 cm, Playboy Collection, Los Angeles
p. 32: Salvador Dalí, *Dream Caused by the Flight of a Bee Around a Pomegranate One Second Before Awakening*, 1944, oil on canvas, 51 x 40,5 cm, Fondazione Thyssen-Bornemisza, Lugano-Castagnola
p. 33: Salvador Dalí, *Self-Portrait*, *c.* 1921, oil on canvas, 52 x 45 cm, Private collection
p. 34: Salvador Dalí with his uncle Anselm Domènech, a bookseller from Barcelona. In the background, the painting *Harlequin and Small Bottle of Rum*, 1925
p. 35: Salvador Dalí, *The Girl of Figueras*, 1926, oil on panel, 32 x 27 cm, The Salvador Dalí Museum, St. Petersburg, FL
p. 36: the Surrealists in Paris (left to right): Tristan Tzara, Paul Eluard, André Breton, Hans Arp, Salvador Dalí, Yves Tanguy, Max Ernst, René Crevel and Man Ray, *c.* 1930
p. 37: Salvador Dalí, *Cubist Gestalt*, 1926/27, oil on canvas, 152 x 90 cm, Fundación Gala-Salvador Dalí, Figueres, Gift of Dalí to the country of Spain
p. 38: Salvador Dalí, *Swans Reflecting Elephants*, 1937, oil on canvas, 51 x 77 cm, private collection
p. 39: Salvador Dalí, *Paranoiac Visage*, 1931, from: Le Surréalisme au service de la révolution, Paris, Nr. 3, December 1931
p. 40: Salvador Dalí, *The Bathers of Es Llanér*, 1923, oil on board, 72 x 103 cm, private collection
p. 41: Salvador Dalí, *Cubist Self-Portrait*, 1923, gouache and collage on board, 104,9 x 74,2 cm, Museo Nacional Centro de Arte Reina Sofía, Madrid
p. 42: Salvador Dalí, *Girl Standing at the Window*, 1925, oil on canvas, 103 x 75 cm, Museo Nacional Centro de Arte Reina Sofía, Madrid
p. 43: Salvador Dalí, *Unsatisfied Desires*, 1928, oil, mussels, and sand on board, 76 x 62 cm, private collection
p. 44: Salvador Dalí, *The Great Masturbator*, 1929, oil on canvas, 110 x 150 cm, Museo Nacional Centro de Arte Reina Sofía, Madrid
p. 45: Salvador Dalí, *The Enigma of William Tell*, 1933, oil on canvas, 201,4 x 346 cm, Moderna Museet, Stockholm
p. 46 left: Salvador Dalí, *Atavism of Twilight*, 1933/34, oil on panel, 14 x 18 cm, Kunstmuseum Bern
p. 46 right: Jean-François Millet, *The Angelus*, 1859, oil on canvas, 55 x 66 cm, Musée d'Orsay, Paris
p. 47: Gala, wearing the shoe-shaped hat, *c.* 1936
p. 48: Salvador Dalí, *The Three Sphinxes of Bikini*, 1947, oil on canvas, 30 x 50 cm, private collection
p. 49: Cover of *Mystic Manifesto*, 1951
p. 50: Salvador Dalí, illustration for Lautréamont's *The Songs of Maldoror*, 1933/34, whereabouts unknown
p. 51: Salvador Dalí, *The Apotheosis of the Dollar (Salvador Dalí in the Act of Painting Gala in the Apotheosis of the Dollar, in which One may also Perceive to the Left Marcel Duchamp*

Disguised as Louis XIV, behind a Curtain in the Style of Vermeer, which is but the Invisible Monument Face of the Hermes of Praxiteles), 1965, oil on canvas, 400 x 498 cm, formerly with the Museo Perrot-Moore, Cadaqués; Fundación Gala-Salvador Dalí, Figueres
p. 52: Salvador Dalí, *The Enigma of Hitler*, *c.* 1939, oil on canvas, 51,2 x 79,3 cm, Museo Nacional Centro de Arte Reina Sofía, Madrid, gift of Dalí to the country of Spain
p. 53: Salvador Dalí, *Melancholy, Atomic, Uranic Idyll*, 1945, oil on canvas, 65 x 85 cm, Museo Nacional Centro de Arte Reina Sofía, Madrid
p. 54: Salvador Dalí, *Madonna of Port Lligat*, 1950, oil on canvas, 144 x 96 cm, Minami Group Collection, Tokyo
p. 55: Salvador Dalí, *Assumpta Corpuscularia Lapislazulina*, 1952, oil on canvas, 230 x 144 cm, private collection
p. 56: Salvador Dalí, *Fifty Abstract Paintings Which as Seen from Two Yards Change into Three Lenins Masquerading as Chinese and as Seen from Six Yards Appear as the Head of a Royal Bengal Tiger*, 1963, oil on canvas, 200 x 229 cm, Minami Art Museum, Tokyo
p. 57: Salvador Dalí, *Tuna Fishing*, 1966/67, oil on canvas, 300 x 400 cm, Paul Richard Trust
p. 59: Salvador Dalí, 1967
p. 60: Salvador Dalí y Cusí with his first born son Salvador, *c.* 1903
p. 61 top: Dalí with "My Secret Life" on his forehead
p. 61 bottom: Salvador Dalí, *The Sacred Heart*, 1929, indian ink on canvas, 68,5 x 50,1 cm, Musée National d'Art Moderne, Centre Georges Pompidou, Paris
p. 62: Salvador Dalí, *Self-Portrait with Raphaelesque Neck*, 1920/21, oil on canvas, 41,4 x 53 cm. Fundación Gala-Salvador Dalí, Figueres, gift of Dalí to the country of Spain
p. 63: Dalí's parents
p. 64: Salvador Dalí, *Portrait of My Dead Brother*, 1963, oil on canvas, 190 x 190 cm, private collection
p. 65 left: Salvador Dalí und Ana María
p. 65 right: the Dalí family on the beach of Es Llanér (from left to right): aunt María Teresa; mother and father of the artist; Salvador Dalí; Tieta, the mother's sister; Dalí's sister, Anna María; grandmother Anna, *c.* 1911
p. 66 left: Dalí with his classmates at the Art Academy San Fernando (kneeling in the middle, head propped up on head),1922/23
p. 66 right: Dalí with a shaved head after being rejected by his family, 1930
p. 67: Dalí at the time of his military service with his friend the poet Federico García Lorca, 1928
p. 68: Salvador Dalí, *Cadaqués*, 1923, oil on canvas.95 x 125 cm, The Salvador Dalí Museum, St. Petersburg, FL
p. 69: Salvador Dalí, *Fair of the Holy Cross-The Circus*, 1921, gouache on board, 52 x 75 cm, Fundación Gala-Salvador Dalí, Figueres
p. 70: Salvador Dalí, *Penya-Segats (Woman by the Cliffs)*, 1926, oil on olive panel, 26 x 40 cm, private collection
p. 71: Salvador Dalí, *The Girl from Ampurdán*, 1926, oil on plywood, 51 x 40 cm, The Salvador Dalí Museum, St. Petersburg, FL
p. 72: Salvador Dalí, *Portrait of my Father*, 1925, oil on canvas, 104,5 x 104,5 cm, Museo de Arte Moderno, Barcelona
p. 73: Salvador Dalí, *Portrait of the Artist's Sister*, 1925, oil on canvas, 99 x 99 cm, Museo Nacional Centro de Arte Reina Sofía, Madrid, gift of Dalí to the country of Spain
p. 74: Salvador Dalí, *Portrait of Sigmund Freud*, 1937, indian ink and gouache on a gray background, 35 x 25 cm, private collection
p. 75: Dalí reading to Gala and Caresse Crosby from *The Secret Life of Salvador Dalí*
p. 76: Dalí presents General Franco with a painting of his granddaughter on horseback
p. 77: Dalí and his retinue, 1965
p. 78: Salvador Dalí, *Dalí from Behind Painting Gala from Behind Immortalized by Six Virtual Corneas Provisionally Reflected in Six Real Mirrors*, 1972/73, oil on canvas, each 60 x 60 cm, Fundación Gala-Salvador Dalí, Figueres
p. 79: invitation to the opening of the Teatro-Museo Dalí on 28 September 1974
p. 80: Salvador Dalí, *Topological Contortion of a Female Figure Becoming a Violoncello*, 1983, oil on canvas, 60 x 73 cm, Museo Nacional Centro de Arte Reina Sofía, Madrid, gift of Dalí to the country of Spain
p. 81: Dalí at the age of 79 in front of his last painting, the *Swallow's Tail*, in the Púbol Castle, 1983
p. 82: Salvador Dalí, *Girl from Behind*, 1925, oil on canvas, 103 x 75 cm, Museo Espanol de Art Contemporáneo, Madrid
p. 83: Salvador Dalí, *Soft Self-Portrait with Fried Bacon*, 1941, oil on canvas, 61 x 50,8 cm, private collection
p. 84: Salvador Dalí, *Portrait of Gala with Two Lamb Chops Balanced on Her Shoulder*, 1933, oil on panel, 6 x 8 cm, Fundación Gala-Salvador Dalí, Figueres
p. 85: Salvador Dalí, *Metamorphosis of Narcissus*, 1937, oil on canvas, 50,8 x 78,3 cm, Tate Gallery, London
p. 86: Salvador Dalí, *The Endless Enigma*, 1938, oil on canvas, 114,3 x 144 cm, Museo Nacional Centro de Arte Reina Sofía, Madrid
p. 87: Salvador Dalí, *The Temptation of St. Anthony*, 1946, oil on canvas, 89,7 x 119,5 cm, Musées Royeaux des Beaux Arts de Belgique, Brussels
p. 89: Gala and Salvador Dalí during their first trip to America, November 1934
p. 90: Salvador Dalí, drawing from *The Secret Life of Salvador Dalí*
p. 91 top: Salvador Dalí, *Portrait of Gala*, 1965, oil on panel, 37,9 x 34,8 cm, Museo Nacional Centro de Arte Reina Sofía, Madrid, gift of Dalí to the country of Spain
p. 91 bottom: Gala Dalí's signature

p. 92: Salvador Dalí, *Dalí, Nude, Contemplating Five Regular Bodies, Transformed into Corpuscles in which Suddenly Leonardo's Leda Appears, Chromosomatised by Gala's Face*, 1954, oil on canvas, 61 x 46 cm, private collection
p. 93: Salvador Dalí and Gala
p. 94: Paul Eluard and Gala in Clavadel, 1913
p. 95: Salvador Dalí, *Portrait of Paul Eluard*, 1929, oil on board, 33 x 25 cm, private collection
p. 96: Lou Ernst, Paul Eduard, Gala, Max Ernst with Jimmy, standing in front: Cécile Eluard, 1924
p. 97 left: Self-Portrait of Dalí, 1929
p. 97 right: Self-Portrait of Gala, 1927
p. 98: Salvador Dalí, *Dismal Sport*, 1929, oil and collage on board, 44,4 x 30,3 cm, private collection
p. 99: Salvador Dalí, *Imperial Monument to the Child Woman*, 1929, oil on canvas, 140 x 80 cm, Museo Nacional Centro de Arte Reina Sofía, Madrid, gift of Dalí to the country of Spain
p. 100: Salvador Dalí, *Accommodations of Desire*, 1929, oil on panel, 22 x 35 cm, The Metropolitan Museum of Art, New York
p. 101: Salvador Dalí, *William Tell*, 1930, oil and collage on canvas, 113 x 87 cm, private collection
p. 102: Port Lligat, 1930
p. 103: Salvador Dalí with Gala in Paris
p. 104: Salvador Dalí, *William Tell and Gradiva*, 1931, enamel on panel, 30 x 24 cm, private collection
p. 105: Salvador Dalí and Gala in front of *A Couple with Their Heads Full of Clouds*, 1936
p. 106: Salvador Dalí with Amanda Lear, 1965
p. 107: Salvador Dalí, *Gala's Castle in Púbol*, c. 1937, oil on canvas, 1560 x 189,7 cm, private collection
p. 108: Salvador Dalí, *Leda Atomica*, 1949, oil on canvas, 61,1 x 45,3 cm, Fundación Gala-Salvador Dalí, Figueres
p. 109: Salvador Dalí, *Galatea of the Spheres*, 1952, oil on canvas, Fundación Gala-Salvador Dalí, Figueres
p. 110: Salvador Dalí, *Galarina*, 1944/45, oil on canvas, 64,1 x 50,2, Fundación Gala-Salvador Dalí, Figueres, gift of Dalí to the country of Spain
p. 111: Salvador Dalí, *Self-Portrait with Gala*, 1970, photo-collage, Museo Perrot-Moore, Cadaqués
p. 112: Salvador Dalí, *Galacidalacidesoxyribonucleicacid*, 1963, oil on canvas, 305 x 403 cm, The Salvador Dalí Museum, St. Petersburg, FL
p. 113: Salvador Dalí, *My Wife, Nude, Contemplating Her Own Flesh Becoming Stairs, Three Vertebrae of a Column, Sky and Architecture*, 1945, oil on panel, 61 x 52 cm, José Mugrabi Collection, New York
p. 115: Teatre-Museu Dalí, Figueres, exterior view
p. 116: Gala Dalí Castle in Púbol, exterior view
p. 117: Al Pacino
p. 118: Teatre-Museu Dalí, Figueres, *Mae West Room*, 2003
p. 119: Salvador Dalí, *Face of Mae West (Usable as a Surrealist Apartment)*, 1934/35, gouache on newspaper, 31 x 17 cm, The Art Institute, Chicago
p. 120: Salvador Dalí, sketches for a ceiling painting in the Teatre-Museu Dalí, 1970, pencil, watercolor and gouache on board, 104,4 x 75 cm, Fundación Gala-Salvador Dalí, Figueres
p. 121: Façade of the Teatro-Museo Dalí
p. 122: View into the Teatre-Museu Dalí, Figueres, 2003
p. 123: Port Lligat, Salvador Dalí's residence, 2003

If you want to know more

Selct biblioggraphy

A must for Dalí fans is Dalí's autobiography *The Secret Life of Salvador Dalí*, first published in 1942. In his own inimitable colorful style he looks back at his career up to that date.

Ralf Schiebler's book *The Reality of Dreams* (Prestel 2005) is about Dalí's obsessions, examining the subconscious motivation of his work.

In their book on Dalí *(Dalí 1904–1989)*, Robert Descharnes and Pierre Gilles provide an opulent overview of the artist's huge oeuvre (Taschen 2000).

Linde Salber's well-informed monograph on Dalí closely links pictures and text in an exposition of the artist's life and work (Rowohlt 2004, in German).

Meredith Etherington Smith has also written an extensive and very readable biography of Dalí *The Persistence of Memory* (Da Capo 2001).

Ian Gibson's approach in *The Shameful Life of Salvador Dalí* is likewise biographical. The book is particularly strong on Dalí's relationships with Garcia Lorca and with his wife Gala (W W Norton 1998).

Dalí's wife is also the focus of *Gala. Mein Leben mit Eluard und Dalí*. Author Dominique Bona brings the artist's enigmatic muse and manager to life (Fischer Verlag 1996, in German). The French edition was published by Flammarion, Paris 1995.

One of the Adventures in Art series, Angela Wenzel's book *The Mad Mad Mad World of Salvador Dalí*, is an introduction for children (Prestel 2003).

Imprint

The pictures in this book were graciously made available by the museums and collections mentioned, or have been taken from the Publisher's archive with exception of:
Artothek, Weilheim: Pages 13, 18
akg-images, Berlin: Page 111
akg-images / Elizabeth Disney: Page 116
akg-images / Erich Lessing: Cover, page 32
LAIF / Zuder: Page 123
LAIF / Moleres: Page 118
LAIF: Page 122
Menil Foundation, Houston: Page 12
The Metropolitan Museum of Art, New York: Page 100
Musée de Sainte-Denis, Foto Atelier René Jacques: Page 94
The Philadelphia Museum of Art: Page 7 left
UNIVERSAL PICTURES/ ALBUM/ AKG: Page 117 top

The Library of Congress Control Number: 2007928998
British Library Cataloguing-in-Publication Data: a catalogue record for this book is available from the British Library.
The Deutsche Bibliothek holds a record of this publication in the Deutsche Nationalbibliografie; detailed bibliographical data can be found under: http://dnb.ddb.de

Prestel Verlag
Königinstrasse 9
80539 Munich
Tel. +49 (89) 38 17 09-0
Fax +49 (89) 38 17 09-35

Prestel Publishing Ltd.
4 Bloomsbury Place
London WC1A 2QA
Tel. +44 (0) 20 7323-5004
Fax +44 (0) 20 7636-8004

Prestel Publishing
900 Broadway. Suite 603
New York, N.Y. 10003
Tel. +1 (212) 995-2720
Fax +1 (212) 995-2733

www.prestel.com

Translated from the German by Paul Aston
Editorial direction by Claudia Stäuble
Copy-edited by Chris Murray
Series editorial and design concept by Sybille Engels, engels zahm + partner
Cover, layout, and production by Wolfram Söll
Lithography by kaltnermedia, Bobingen
Printed and bound by Druckerei Uhl GmbH & Co.KG, Radolfzell

Printed in Germany on acid-free paper

ISBN 978-3-7913-3813-2